THE

METIS

MEMORABLE EVENTS

and

MEMORABLE PERSONALITIES

GEORGE & TERRY GOULET

FabJob Inc.

19 Horizon View Court Calgary,

Alberta, T3Z 3M5

The Western Metis Historical and Cultural Society received contributions for the research and writing of this book by the authors from the Government of Canada through the auspices of the Office of the Federal Interlocutor for Metis and Non-Status Indians.

The Manitoba Museum has granted permission to the authors to use an image on the cover of this book. Image of "Bison Diorama" © The Manitoba Museum.

The Diorama artist was Clarence Tillenius.

Cover photographer - Terry Goulet.

Library and Archives Canada Cataloguing in Publication Data

Goulet, George R. D. (George Richard Donald), 1933

The Metis: memorable events and memorable personalities/

George & Terry Goulet.

Includes bibliographical references and index.

ISBN-13: 978-1-894638-98-2

ISBN-10: 1-894638-98-0

1. Métis-History. 2 Métis-Biography. I. Goulet, Terry II. Title.

FC109.G69 2006 971.004'97 C2006-901984-3

Printed in Canada

.... the new nation under their leaders are coming forward to clear their native soil of intruders.

Alexander Greenfield Macdonell
1816 letter to Duncan Cameron.

... gratitude and filial love require us to make a point of saying "We are Metis".

Louis Riel, Circa 1880

We know who we are .... we don't need anybody to tell us who we are. .... We self-identify, just like everybody else in this country.

Reply to: "Who is Metis?'
Harry Daniels, c. 1981

In this Act "aboriginal peoples of Canada" includes the Indian, Inuit and Metis peoples of Canada.

Canadian Constitution, 1982

ACKNOWLEDGEMENTS

We wish to express our appreciation to various people and institutions that in one way or another have assisted us with this book.

In this respect there are many people with whom we had interviews, discussions and meetings. We would like to give special thanks to Senator Thelma Chalifoux, Robert Coulter, Sharon Morin, Laurena Daniels, Cheryl Storkson, Tantoo Cardinal, Dale Gibson, Albert Peeling, Audrey Poitras, George de la Giroday Goulet, Mike and Laura de Jonge, Keith Henry, Henry Hall, Wilfred Goulet and Anson Ng.

Our appreciation is also extended to FabJob Inc., its staff and in particular to Tag, Catherine and John.

Among the numerous archives, libraries, museums, forts, and institutions whose staff provided us with their services we would like to thank the staff of the:

> Office of the Federal Interlocutor for Metis and Non-Status Indians, National Archives of Canada, Archives of Manitoba and British Columbia, Hudson's Bay Company Archives, Manitoba Museum, St. Boniface Museum, RCMP Centennial Museum, American Indian Film Institute, National Library of Canada, Law Library and McKimmie Library of the University of Calgary, Manitoba Legislative Library, Calgary Public Library, Batoche Museum, Fort Carlton Museum, Fort Vancouver Museum, Fort Langley Museum, and Fort Clatsop Museum.

Any errors herein are the responsibility of the authors.

This book is dedicated to our remarkable Metis children and grandchildren and to the Metis Nation.

Calgary, Alberta, 2006

TABLE OF CONTENTS

ACRONYMS AND ABBREVIATIONS

Acronyms and abbreviations used in the text include the following:

ch.	chapter
CAP	Congress of Aboriginal Peoples
CPR	Canadian Pacific Railway
CSP	Canada Sessional Papers
ed.	edition and/or editor
HBC	Hudson's Bay Company
Man.	Manitoba
MNC	Metis National Council
NAC	National Archives of Canada
NCC	Native Council of Canada
no.	number
NWC	North West Company
NWMP	North West Mounted Police
p.	page
RCAP	Royal Commission on Aboriginal Peoples
s.	section
Sask.	Saskatchewan
SCR	Supreme Court Reports
v.	versus
vol.	volume

EXPLANATORY NOTE

Chapter Reference Sources

At the end of an applicable Chapter, resource materials are listed under the heading "Chapter Reference Sources". Further information on these sources is provided in the "Bibliography". In the "Bibliography" the sources are arranged alphabetically under the last name of the applicable author or editor referred to in the "Chapter Reference Source".

Chapter I

A UNIQUE INDIGENOUS PEOPLE

From the screeching wheels of the Red River carts to the thundering hoofs of stampeding buffalo, to the foot stomping jigging to a fiddler's refrain, to the cry of a new born babe, the saga of the Metis people unfolds into a panorama of colorful events and personalities.

In addition to their fur-trading activities, many Metis acted as guides and interpreters, thereby contributing to the exploration and settlement of many areas of North America. They also played a very significant role in a large part of Rupert's Land being brought into the Confederation of Canada as the Provinces of Manitoba, Saskatchewan and Alberta. To adequately appreciate them and their unique qualities, it is only fitting that this indigenous nation should be viewed from a factual account of their history, heritage, culture and way of life.

At the outset some of the misconceptions concerning the Metis that have developed over the years need to be addressed. A not uncommon misunderstanding by some is that the Metis only played a role in the history of Canada at the time of Louis Riel and the Red River Resistance of 1869-70, or at the time of Gabriel Dumont and the North-West Uprising of 1885.

Another erroneous belief is that to be Metis one's European ancestors had to be of French descent, or been employed by the Hudson's Bay Company, or resided in the Red River area, or in Rupert's Land. All of these limiting opinions fail to take into consideration many facets of the Metis people including their early history, their nomadic lifestyle, and the integral role that the fur trade played in their livelihood.

In the very early days of colonization, furs were the main export from North America to Europe. In time the financial benefits of the fur trade fueled the exploration and the initial development that occurred in many areas of North America. At its height the fur trade extended from the Atlantic Ocean in the east to the Pacific Ocean in the west, and from Hudson Bay in the north to the Gulf of Mexico in the south.

Upon leaving the confines of the colonies, the early explorers and traders entered the hinterland where there were no European women. Consequently, they formed unions with the Indian women that produced a generation of mixed-blood children then called half-breeds.

There were peoples of mixed-blood in Canada since shortly after the Europeans first came into contact with the natives a number of centuries ago. However, mixed blood in itself does not constitute Metis identity. This identity required the development of a common culture, history and way of life.

It was these factors that were responsible for the evolution of the historic native-born Aboriginal peoples of the Metis Nation whose roots are found primarily in Western Canada and the North West United States.

The focus of this book is on these Metis of the Metis Nation and their fascinating role in the history of Canada. Accordingly special emphasis has been placed on the fur trade that occurred in the area of land from Hudson Bay and northern Canada in the north to the Great Lakes in the south and westward to the Pacific Coast where it extended from the border of Alaska in the north to the San Francisco area in the south.

The nurturing of this distinct indigenous people, of mixed European and Indian blood, in this geographical area occurred during the latter part of the 1700s and into the early part of the 1800s. Consequently the Metis were identifiable and were readily recognized by a non-Metis, Alexander Greenfield Macdonell, as being a "new nation" as early as 1816. The descendants of the offspring of this indigenous nation are members of the Metis Nation of today.

Over the years the Metis had to fight military, legal, political, social, cultural, and constitutional battles to survive as a distinctive people. Successful on some occasions, crushed on others, they did not flag nor fail in their determination to persevere as a distinct culture and society in their traditional homeland of western North America.

The early Metis, a historical indigenous people, created a unique culture for themselves and for future generations. Their collective consciousness empowered them in their struggle for their collective causes.

The undaunted spirit of the Metis involved them in many notable episodes and produced many fascinating personalities. This book chronicles some of the remarkable events and profiles only a few of the outstanding individuals from this group. A common thread in the lives of the personalities of the Metis portrayed herein was pride in their Metis heritage.

SECTION A

THE METIS

Hall and Lowe photo Provincial Archives of Manitoba No. N5730

Louis Riel

A Metis Icon

Provincial Archives of Manitoba No. N12762; Kerr, John 5

Cuthbert Grant

Premier Metis Leader

Chapter II
THE TERM "METIS"

In Canada the term "Metis" indicates a person of mixed American Aboriginal and European descent. Its ultimate derivation is from the Latin words *miscere* and *misticius* meaning "to mix" and "mixed race" respectively.

The word itself is French and one of its literal translations is "half-breed". When English was spoken in the 19th century and earlier "half-breed" was normally used to denote all Metis, whether of Scottish, English, or French ancestry. On the other hand when French was spoken the term "Metis" was used. It wasn't until the 1930s that Metis started to be used instead of the term half-breed when English was being spoken.

A similar term with the same roots used for Latin Americans of mixed Spanish/Portuguese men and Amerindian women is "mestizo".

Today some consider the term "half-breed" to be offensive. However, not to be more offensive, it is used in this book in its appropriate historical context in the interest of integrity.

A number of other words were used in past days to refer to the Metis. They include "bois-brûlé" (burnt wood, because of their dark complexion), "michif" (also a Metis language), "country born", and others.

Historical figures, correspondence, and government legislation used the term half-breed. For example two renowned Metis leaders Cuthbert Grant and Louis Riel used that term when speaking in English. The English version of the federal statute, *The Manitoba Act, 1870* (pursuant to which Manitoba became a Province), used "half-breed". The French version of that Statute used "Metis" in place of "half-breed".

Louis Riel had this to say about the Metis and the word itself:

> The Metis have as paternal ancestors the former employees of

> the Hudson's Bay and Northwest Fur Companies and as their maternal ancestors Indian women of various tribes The French word, "Metis", is derived from the Latin participle mixtus, which means "mixed"; in French "mele"; it expresses well the idea that is sought to be conveyed. However appropriate the corresponding English expression "Halfbreed" might have been for the first generation of the mixture of blood, now that European blood and Indian blood are mixed in every degree, it is no longer generally applicable.
>
> The French word 'Metis' expresses the idea of this mixture in the most satisfactory manner possible, and thus becomes a suitable name for our race. Why should we care to what degree exactly of mixture we possess European blood and Indian blood? No matter how little we have one or the other, do not both gratitude and filial love require us to make a point of saying: 'We are Metis!"

In stating that the Metis should not care about their degree of blood mixture, Riel was prescient and anticipated by more than a century a provision in the Powley decision. In that 2003 judgment the Supreme Court of Canada unanimously ruled, among other matters, that to be a Metis a "minimum" blood quantum was not required. However, as indicated therein, mixed ancestry by itself is not sufficient to constitute a Metis for the constitutional purposes outlined in the Powley Case discussed in a later chapter of this book.

Chapter Reference Sources

- "Metis, Louis Riel's Last Memoir, The" by Louis Riel *Hold High Your Heads (History of the Metis Nation in Western Canada)*, by A.-H. de Tremaudan, p. 200.
- "Metis: The People and the Term" by John Foster in *Louis Riel and the Metis*, ed. A. S. Lussier, ch. 5.
- "Metis" by Jennifer S. H. Brown, *Canadian Encyclopedia*, p. 1477-79.

Chapter III

GENESIS OF THE METIS NATION

The historical Metis were a unique, native-born people of Western Canada, the Great Lakes region on both sides of the border, and some northwestern areas of the United States. They and their descendants were the offspring of the European men (who came to these parts of the New World primarily to engage in the fur trade) and of the North American Indian women with whom they mated.

In their earliest days, the traditional homeland of the Metis was the northern part of western North America extending from the Great Lakes to the Rocky Mountains and to Northern Canada. It was a seemingly boundless territory with stunning contrasts. Here and there were great lakes (both in size and grandeur); picturesque verdant valleys; babbling brooks; the great northern plains abounding with buffalo; virgin forests teeming with wildlife; resplendent rivers swarming with fish; and vast prairies, later to become the "bread basket of the world".

This fabulous area was the home and native land of the Metis, a land where their destiny as a unique people, born of many trials, was to be fulfilled. The traditional Metis homeland had no provincial boundaries or international borders.

Historically, these Metis of mixed Euro-Canadian and Indian ancestry developed their own shared culture, customs, traditions, way of life, and collective identity separate from those of their Indian foremothers (many of them Cree, Ojibway, Chipewayan, and Saulteaux) and their European forefathers, primarily French and Scottish.

While they had inherited some cultural and other traits from each of their parental ancestors, the Metis had their own distinctiveness as a people - they were not Indians and they were not Europeans but rather a special blend of white and native. In time they coalesced into an independent "New Nation".

A number of circumstances contributed to Metis "ethnogenesis" - that is to say their development and recognizability as and self-awareness of having become a distinct social, cultural and political people. These factors included their common Euro-aboriginal ancestry, their remoteness from a populous civilization, their way of life including their roles in the fur trade and the buffalo hunt, lack of elaborate structural controls, their shared kinship and communal experiences, and the sluggish pace of settlement in the fur trade hinterland.

The cultural creativity of the Metis and their heritage embraced their own language and their own symbols, clothing, flags, means of transportation, dance, music, poetry, and song. Folklore and folk heroes emerged from their experiences, as did political and paramilitary leaders. They pursued their own way of life in their traditional Metis homeland. They had a collective consciousness of being a distinct people separate from that of their forebears with a new sense of national identity and nationhood.

There were no other peoples in the entire world that combined the defining characteristics, culture, and customs of these classic Metis people. They constituted a nation - the Metis Nation - a unique people whose common history was culturally distinct, socially allied and politically effective.

The historical Metis of Western Canada have been called the "children of the fur trade". The fur trade is uniquely involved in the history of Canada from the earliest days of exploration of North America.

It is believed that the first explorers to make a settlement in North America were the Vikings in the 10th century. Several centuries after the Vikings discontinued their travel to the New World, the first explorers of the Americas were searching for a route to the riches of the Orient.

They noted an abundance of fish in the Americas. This led to fishermen from a number of European countries coming to the eastern coast of North America to fish. In time the fishermen started trading European goods with the Indians for furs. In due course they found that the fur trade was more lucrative than fishing.

The fur trade eventually resulted in European settlement in Canada by the French. Over the years the traders traveled further and further inland in order to find new sources of furs. For a number of these traders, the search for furs was combined with an attempt to find the elusive Northwest Passage to the Orient.

Early fur traders in New France were unlicensed "coureurs de bois" (runners of the woods) from the Montreal area who, without permission from the colonial authorities, traveled inland to the Lake Superior country in order to engage in illicit fur-trading with the natives. The most prominent coureurs de bois in New France were Pierre Esprit Radisson and his brother-in-law Medard Chouart des Groseilliers.

In due course, New France initiated a licensing system in an attempt to control the coureurs de bois. However Radisson and Groseilliers were arrested and fined in 1660 for their unlicensed fur-trading expedition to Lakes Superior and Michigan.

This precipitated their defection to the English and their meeting with King Charles II that resulted in the formation on May 2, 1670 of the Hudson's Bay Company (HBC), under the governorship of the King's cousin Prince Rupert. The HBC was granted extensive powers over, and a monopoly on trading rights in, a huge area of land in what is now primarily Western Canada. This Royal grant consisted of all the land whose waterways drained into Hudson Bay and was called Rupert's Land.

The HBC was formed as a fur trading company with a view to reaching the interior of the continent via Hudson Bay. In 1684 York Factory was the first permanent trading post established on Hudson Bay by the HBC. Due to continued disputes between England and France, ownership of York Factory shifted between these two countries from 1684 until 1713. The Treaty of Utrecht awarded ownership of York Factory to England in 1713.

With respect to fur trading into the interior of the continent, the licensing of fur traders in New France led to Montreal merchants hiring coureurs de bois to travel inland to establish more sustained relations with the natives. These respected licensed traders became known as voyageurs. Subsequently this term was also applied to the other employees of the fur trading companies who transported goods by canoe to and from trading posts in the interior.

A prominent Quebec fur trader in the 18th century was Pierre La Verendrye who explored westward where he set up fur trading posts between Lake Superior and Lake Winnipeg in the 1730s. He and his sons were responsible for opening up the west to the mainly French fur traders from Quebec.

His son Louis Joseph participated in the Seven Years War between England, France and other countries. The North American phase of this War was known as the French and Indian War. After the War ended in 1763, participation of the French in the fur trade and exploration of the West was greatly decreased.

After the Battle of the Plains of Abraham in 1759, New France had fallen into the hands of Great Britain. As a result, many Scottish entrepreneurs settled in Montreal. They effectively took over the French fur trade and became resolute rivals of the Hudson's Bay Company (HBC). These Scottish entrepreneurs were the precursors of the North West Company (NWC).

The NWC was a syndicate of partners formed in Montreal with a significantly different governing structure than that of the HBC, a royally chartered joint stock company owned and governed by an absentee committee in London, England. As well, the mixed-blood descendants of the voyageurs and staff of the NWC came from different backgrounds than those of the Hudson's Bay Company.

The NWC was organized in the 1770s largely by

Scottish Highlanders such as Simon McTavish, and another Scot James McGill, whose surname today adorns a prestigious Montreal university. These Scottish leaders hired employees mainly from Quebec to engage in the fur trade and to travel to, and frequently winter at, the various posts that were established by the NWC throughout western North America, where fur-bearing animals were plentiful.

The NWC Metis emerged from the mostly Quebec voyageurs, coureurs-de-bois, fur traders, engagés, winterers (the wintering partners were also called "hivernants") and, latterly, buffalo hunters and provisioning freighters and traders. The voyageurs, engagés, and others traveled to the Indian country to barter European and other goods for fur pelts and frequently remained there over the winter. This led to the use of the word "hivernant" to also describe others who wintered in the Indian country.

These Nor'Westers and the voyageurs married Indian women 'a la façon du pays' that is in accordance with the custom of the country and without benefit of the clergy, of whom there were very few in the fur-trading country. These men married not only for companionship and conjugal relations, but also to establish kinship with Indian tribes. They did so in order to form alliances and to advance fur-trading with them, especially since the natives favored this arrangement in their dealings. The Indian women became their "country wives".

Their relationships with the native women resulted in the birth of many mixed-blood offspring and the embryonic beginnings of the historic Metis people. The native women and the fur traders were the progenitors of the Metis people. The Metis children of these unions frequently also became voyageurs and employees of the fur companies as did their children. These progeny normally lived and remained in the Indian country.

Many of the partners of the NWC also wintered at the various posts and eventually it became a matter of privilege to have been a "winterer" for the Company. Some of these English-speaking partners of the NWC married native women 'a la façon du pays' and fathered mixed-blood children.

In 1785 the Beaver Club was formed in Montreal by some of the partners of the NWC. Membership was limited to gentlemen who had actually wintered in the Indian country. Ironically, this requirement excluded from membership in the Club one of the principal founders of the NWC, Simon McTavish.

Each year the NWC held an annual general meeting of the Montreal and wintering partners at their major supply depot Fort William (now part of Thunder Bay, Ontario). The structure of the NWC partnership changed from time to time as some partners retired or died and new members were admitted into the partnerships. In many cases new partnerships were created for employees for successfully managing forts, or for their exploration abilities.

The NWC united with its Montreal competitor the XY Company in 1804. This created an even stronger opponent to their fur trading rival, the HBC.

The other main group of Metis that developed was originally called half-breeds or "country born", and was largely English-speaking Protestants in the employ of the HBC. These "English Metis" were primarily of Scottish, not English descent. Their fathers came from the isles and glens of the Orkney Islands, the Scottish Highlands and Ireland.

After York Factory was granted to the English by the Treaty of Utrecht in 1713, the fur trading of the HBC was centered there. From York Factory the furs were shipped to England and the ships would bring back European goods to the HBC forts on the Bay. The last stop of the HBC ships traveling to the Bay was to the Orkney Islands where they picked up their last supplies and many young Orcadians before heading across the Ocean.

Officials of the HBC preferred a Scots lad to an English bloke because they viewed the Scots as hardier and more capable of coping with the harsh climactic conditions of Canada. These young men were on the whole honest and industrious with cautious dour natures, ideal for fur-trading with the Indians.

As the prominent Red River resident Alexander Ross stated of the Orkneymen in his book *The Red River Settlement*:

> In whatever sphere of life they are placed, either high or low, in prosperity or adversity, their well-known habits of industry and frugality follow them.

For a number of decades the HBC employees did not have to journey from the HBC forts constructed on or near Hudson Bay. The HBC had the Indians travel long distances to these forts, rather than sending their employees from the forts to where the natives gathered the furs. This procedure was gradually changed due to the opposite, more successful, methods of the fiercely competitive NWC, which established trading posts and forts in the Indian country.

When some forts were established by the NWC and the HBC they were called a House rather than a Fort. For example Rocky Mountain House was a major trading post for furs in the West.

The Metis, emanating from the HBC tradition, were initially viewed as English if they and their mothers stayed at the trading fort, and as Indians if they and their mothers lived with her native family. Ethnogenesis did not develop early in this tradition.

In the early days the London Committee of the HBC was reluctant to assume the expenses and troubles of supporting "country wives" and their children. The HBC discouraged its lower rank employees from such relationships, although the Company turned a blind eye to their officers taking Indian wives. This restriction could not be effectively enforced.

This hindered for many decades the "half-breed" offspring of these unions (unlike those in the NWC tradition) from viewing themselves as a distinct ethnic and cultural group since mixed ancestry by itself is insufficient to constitute ethnogenesis. These descendants were not viewed as a unique people.

In the early stages the French Metis were more active than their English counterparts: they viewed themselves as free and easy entrepreneurs with the right to roam the prairies. In pursuing the buffalo they were semi-nomads. They were hardy and hearty and loved to sing and socialize. They were Great Plains buffalo hunters, voyageurs, coureurs-de-bois, traders, freighters and York boat men.

They were also fabulous guides. They helped great Canadian and United Stated explorers like Alexander Mackenzie, Simon Fraser, David Thompson, and Meriwether Lewis and William Clark on their expeditions. They physically lugged canoes and supplies around rapids, blazed trails, and performed an invaluable service as interpreters. With the help of the Metis, as with that of the Indian, the white men's expeditions were immensely assisted in these guided tours.

The Metis were transporters and provisioners of pemmican and other items, primarily for the NWC which had much less constraint on them than the HBC had over its servants. In 1778 Peter Pond, a fur trader with the NWC, was introduced to pemmican by the Chipewyan Indians in the Athabaska Region. Through Pond the fur trade was introduced to pemmican in 1779 and it became a vital food to the fur trade.

Pemmican was pounded dried buffalo meat mixed with melted fat and, often, saskatoon berries. It could be stored and easily transported to the fur traders. In his book *When Fur Was King*, Henry John Moberly mentioned that in 1854 HBC Governor George Simpson offered him a dish of food. The food's appearance to this very young apprentice clerk looked like "bear's drippings", and he thought Simpson was playing a joke on him until Simpson first ate some himself. Moberly then tried it and wrote that it was "berry pemmican of the best quality, made of dried pounded buffalo tongues, marrow fat, sugar and dried saskatoon berries". To his surprise he "found it extremely good".

In discussing pemmican in his *Narratives* David Thompson stated in part:

> .... it is made of the lean and fleshy parts of the Bison dried, smoked, and pounded fine; .... Pimmecan [sic] is made up in bags of ninety pounds weight, made of the parchment hide of the Bison with the hair on; .... it [is] the staple food of all persons, and affords the most nourishment in the least space and weight, ... it would be admirable provision for the Army and Navy.

Both the HBC and the NWC had forts near the junction of the Red and Assiniboine Rivers (in what is now the city of Winnipeg). The HBC fort at the forks was built in 1812. It was initially called Fort Douglas, and later became Fort Garry. The NWC fort was on the opposite side of the Red River (in what is now St. Boniface) and was known as Fort Gibraltar.

The English Metis in the HBC tradition were much less nomadic and entrepreneurial then their French Metis counterparts emanating from the NWC tradition; this became further evident in relation to the Red River Colony or Settlement (also known as the Selkirk Settlement). The origins of this Settlement arose from the humanitarian efforts and the ambitious mercantile nature of Thomas Douglas, Fifth Earl of Selkirk, as well as the corporate designs of the HBC to expand their trade into the Athabaska Country in opposition to the NWC that had been there for decades.

Lord Selkirk had previously attempted a settlement of dispossessed Scottish Highlanders in 1803 in Prince Edward Island. The following year he also established an unsuccessful colony in Baldoon, Upper Canada.

Since Lord Selkirk was a major shareholder of the HBC, in 1811 the HBC granted him a huge tract of land of 116,000 square miles in what is now southern Manitoba and Saskatchewan, and northern parts of North Dakota and Minnesota.

It was called Assiniboia and within it Selkirk established the Red River Colony in 1812. He peopled it with poor immigrants and their families from Scotland and

Ireland. In addition to furthering the aims of the HBC, Selkirk wanted the Selkirk settlers to become self-sufficient by means of agriculture.

The Selkirk settlers were not Metis, but in due course the Red River Settlement (whose center became the forks of the Red and Assiniboine Rivers) became the place to which retired HBC employees and their families retired.

In 1823 George Simpson (sometimes referred to as "the Little Emperor") who was not yet Governor of the entire HBC, but was the head of its Northern Department in Rupert's Land, wrote the following to Andrew Colvile (his HBC mentor in London):

> A great number of discharged servants with their Families have this season gone to the Settlement which will relieve Establishments greatly ....

Simpson himself had a Metis country wife, Margaret Taylor, and a number of English Metis children by her. However, he returned to his Scottish homeland and while there he married his cousin, Frances Ramsay Simpson in 1830. On bringing his bride Frances to the West, he rid his Metis wife and their children from his life and had them exiled from the fort.

The Red River Settlement was to become the heart of the Metis Homeland - their home and native land. No further immigrants arrived from Scotland, but many Metis clerks and engagés who retired from or were let go by the fur trading companies, as well as other Metis, made the Red River Colony their home. They brought their wives and Metis children, and over time the Metis married among themselves rather than with the Indians.

When the HBC and NWC merged in 1821, the custom of the fur traders had been to have native "country wives" because there were no white women in the West. Since the NWC fathers were mostly from Quebec, their Metis progeny were mainly French-speaking Roman Catholics.

In due course intermarriage occurred between Metis men and Metis women of both French and Scottish-English derivation. Widespread inter-family relationships developed as did common traditions and historical Metis communities in their homeland.

These Metis had become an essential economic and provisioning presence for the NWC prior to the merger. After the merger of the HBC and NWC, many of the Metis as "freemen" later traded furs in contravention of the HBC's monopoly.

Metis ethnogenesis in what is now Western Canada was in its incipient stages in the latter part of the 18th century. It came to fruition early in the 19th century through not only the factors mentioned above, but through a series of events that significantly impacted on the Metis. It was further solidified by memorable events that occurred in later decades.

Ensuing chapters of this book discuss a number of these momentous events in which the history and heritage of the Metis people was formed, commencing with the Battle of Seven Oaks.

Chapter Reference Sources

- *Birth of Western Canada, a History of the Riel Rebellions, The,* by George F. G. Stanley, ch. I; .
- *Canadian Prairies, A History, The,* by Gerald Friesen, p. 66-69.
- *David Thompson's Narrative of his explorations in Western America,* ed. J. B Tyrell, p 312-313.
- *Fur Trade Wars, The Founding of Western Canada,* by J. M. Bumsted, p. 48-50.
- *Hold High Your Heads (History of the Metis Nation in Western Canada),* by A.-H. de Tremaudan, Part One; and p. 19-33.
- *Home From the Hill, A History of the Metis in Western Canada,* by Don McLean, ch. 2 and 3.
- *Homeland to Hinterland, The Changing Worlds of the Red River Metis in the Nineteenth Century,* by Gerhard J. Ens, ch. One.
- *Life of Louis Riel, The,* by Peter Charlebois, p. 12-16.
- *Louis Riel and the Metis,* editor A. S. Lussier, ch. 5.
- "Metis" by Jennifer S. H. Brown, *Canadian Encyclopedia,* p. 1477-79.
- *Metis, Canada's Forgotten People, The,* by D. Bruce Sealey and Antoine S. Lussier, ch 1; 2.
- *Metis Legacy,* editors Lawrence J. Barkwell et al, p. 71-73.
- *New Peoples - Being and Becoming Metis in North America, The,* editors Jacqueline Peterson and Jennifer S. H. Brown, *passim.*
- "Origins of the Mixed Bloods in the Canadian West" by John E. Foster in *The Prairie West, Historical Readings,* editors R. Douglas

Francis and Howard Palmer, p. 86-99.

- *Red River Settlement: Its Rise, Progress, and Present State, The,* by Alexander Ross, p. 110.
- *Strange Empire, Louis Riel and the Metis People,* by Joseph Howard, p. 39-45.
- *When Fur was King,* by Henry J. Moberley and W. B. Cameron.
- "Women and the Fur Trade" by Sylvia Van Kirk, *The Beaver Outfit,* Winter, 1972, p. 4-21.

Chapter IV

METIS SYMBOLS and THEIR ORIGINS

The development of the historic Metis of the Red River and the west as a "New Nation", a unique people, in the early part of the 19th century was due mainly to their distinctive culture, their customs, their common ancestry and kinship, their shared history, heritage, way of life and homeland.

These factors contributed to the growth of a culture and symbols that distinguished the Metis from their European and Indian forebears and, for that matter, from all other peoples.

Their unique cultural evolution extended to their own flags, sashes, vehicles, language, food, clothing, folklore, folk heroes, poetry, songs, music and dance. The following provides a sketch of some of the symbols and customs that formed the fabric of the Metis nation.

1. Metis Flags

There have been a number of Metis flags in the past. A book on the evolution of the Metis flags with illustrations titled *Flags of the Metis* by Calvin Racette shows a number of designs over the years. Included among them were the figure eight, fleur de lis, shamrocks, a buffalo, a crucifix, and combinations of these elements as well as others. It has been said that the fleur de lis represented the Blessed Virgin Mary, while the shamrock represented the Holy Trinity.

The original flag had a horizontal white figure eight placed in the middle of it and was first seen in 1815, the year in which the North West Company (NWC) gave it to the Metis. It had a red field with a white figure eight within it. In the "Selkirk Papers" a contemporary observer, James Sutherland of the Hudson's Bay Company (HBC), is quoted as writing at that time of the Metis flag:

> It is red with a figure of 8 placed horizontally in the middle of it and it is said to be a present from the N.W. Co. to ... the Half Breeds as a recompense for their exertions against the

> [Red River] colony, Spring 1815....

In his journal, Peter Fidler wrote of this flag that it was about 4½ feet square, red and the figure eight was of a different color.

The Metis soon embraced this figure eight flag as a symbol of their own identity. A variation of this flag had a blue, rather than a red, field. The use of blue in the flag was representative of the French influence.

Some people believe that on approaching a fur-trading post Metis voyageurs could tell whether French or English was spoken at it - a blue NWC flag indicated French, a red HBC flag English.

During the 1869-70 Red River Resistance a different Metis flag appeared. An on-site observer James Hargrave wrote of a "Raising of the National Flag" ceremony at Fort Garry on December 10, 1869. He described the hoisting of a flag bearing three fleur de lis positioned above a single shamrock. Another contemporary referred to the same flag as having a fleur de lis and a shamrock on a white ground.

The author Peter Charlebois stated that initially this flag's fleur de lis was blue on a white background with a gold border. At one point it also had a green harp and a shamrock.

The battle flag of Batoche of the mid-1880s has recently been recreated by the Gabriel Dumont Institute. It has as symbols the head of a wolf and an upraised hand with an accompanying motto in French reading "maisons . . . . autels" above the symbols and "Surtout Liberté" below the symbols. These words mean "homes . . . . . altars" and "Above all Freedom".

At the Batoche Museum there is a marker that provides the following explanation of the symbols of this battle flag:

> The hand and wolf denote 'We lift our hand in prayer to the Lord that he may grant us the courage of the wolf to defend our homes'.

Apparently an open hand in Irish heraldry denotes faith, sincerity and justice. A wolf represented perseverance in struggles and in combat. A battle flag was intended to uplift the morale of the rank and file and instill in them a patriotic ardor.

The Union Nationale Metisse St. Joseph du Manitoba, formed in 1887, adopted a flag consisting of a white field with the Union Jack in the top left hand corner and gold-colored fleur de lis in each of the other three corners.

Today the flag of the Metis Nation of British Columbia has at the top a triangular field of red lying above a triangular field of blue with a horizontal white figure eight straddling them. Beneath this is a Red River cart which overlies images of the mountains, the sun and the ocean.

The figure eight in the Metis flag signifies "infinity", representing the coalescence of two great cultures forever. Today, the flag with the blue background and horizontal figure eight has been adopted as the flag of the Metis National Council and is the one most frequently displayed at gatherings of the Metis as an emblem of their patrimony, their persistence and their pride.

2. Voyageur and Metis Clothing

Contemporary observers in the 19th century have left sometimes varying descriptions of the type of clothing worn by the voyageurs and the historical western Metis.

In the book *The Voyageur* author Grace Lee Nute gives the following quote from an 1832 entry in the diary of the missionary Sherman Hall:

> My man dressed himself in the habit of a voyageur, that is a short shirt, a red woolen cap, a pair of deer skin leggins [sic] which reach from the ancles [sic] a little above the knees and are held up by a string secured to a belt about the waist, the azion ["breech cloth"] of the Indians, and a pair of deer skin moccasins without stockings on the feet. The thighs are left bare. This is the dress of voyageurs in summer and winter.

The belt referred to may have been the arrowhead sash since voyageurs invariably wore one. Nute also mentioned an old voyageur "dressed in his blue capote, wearing his ceinture fléchée (sash) and his sac-á-feu (beaded bag)."

An article in *Harper's Magazine* of October 1860 discussed two dances that took place at Pembina, one at Joe Rolette's house. It stated that;

> The men wore shirts, trousers, belts and moccasins; and the women wore gowns which had no hoops. A black-eyed beauty in blue calico and a strapping Bois Brulé [Metis] would jump up from the floor and outdo their predecessors in figure and velocity.

In his 1879 book *The Great Fur Land* H. M. Robertson wrote the following of "half-breed" clothing:

> A pair of corduroy trousers, a cotton shirt, a capote, moccasins and a fur cap, constitute his winter costume. His hands are encased in mittaines [sic], but in lieu of under clothing he ties his trousers tightly about the ankles, and the sleeves of his capote closely about the wrists. This, with the gaudy sash always wrapped around his waist, divides his clothing into two air-tight compartments, as it were.

In 1875 the Earl of Southesk wrote of his visit in the 1860s to the Red River Settlement in his book *Saskatchewan and the Rocky Mountains*. In it he gave a description of the prominent Metis James McKay when he first saw him at St. Paul. Among other matters Southesk wrote of McKay:

> He was dressed in Red River style - a blue cloth 'capot' (hooded frock-coat) with brass buttons; red-and-black flannel shirt, which served also for waistcoat; black belt round the waist; buff leather moccasins on his feet; trowsers [sic] of brown and white striped home-made woollen stuff.
>
> I had never come across a wearer of moccasins before, and it amused me to watch this grand and massive man pacing the hotel corridors with noiseless footfall, while excitable little Yankees in shiny boots creaked and stamped about like so many busy steam engines.

In his Memoirs, that inimitable and highly entertaining Metis raconteur Louis Goulet described clothing worn by Metis men and women in the 19th century. The men usually wore navy blue trousers made of heavy English cloth and sometimes corduroy. They were held up not by suspenders but by the Metis sash.

Goulet also said that the trousers of many winter hunters were known as "culottes à bavaloise" which opened at the hip. These were accompanied by grey flannel shirts (made by the Hudson's Bay Company), leggings, sash and moccasins. Cotton shirts when worn were brightly colored. In winter a hooded light wool coat, a "capot du craint-rien" (a kind of short fur -lined jacket), and an old cap were worn.

Some of the stylish young men wore mitts embroidered in bright and gay colors, sometimes with beadwork, with fur at the wrist. The intricately stitched leggings ("mitasses"), made of leather or cloth, were like over-stockings of long cuffs worn on the legs. As well the Metis also used fancily decorated clothing such as shirts and leather vests and jackets. These items were often embellished with attractive needle and bead work and were fringed along the seams.

Moccasins, which Goulet described as "simply mittens for the feet" were usually worn without socks. There were several different types. The mitten style was fashioned from two leather strips stitched together. Another variety had pointed toes without any decoration. Another example was a moccasin ornately adorned with colorful beads or other ornamentation such as needlework, horse hair, or porcupine quills. A *housse* (literally translated as a "covering") made from a wool blanket or rabbit skin with the fur inside was worn on the foot in place of socks.

The Metis women, according to Goulet, wore a dress with the skirt extending to their ankles. Over top they wore a kind of jerkin (called a *basque*). This *basque* had puffy sleeves. Moccasins were commonly worn by the women as well as the men. Velvet was a favorite material for women's clothing.

In his novel *Dot-It-Down* written in 1871 Alexander Begg, a writer and historian living in the Red River Settlement, wrote of a family on their way to Red River from Canada. The family saw a number of peculiarly dressed men standing in groups upon the platform. It was the first time the family had encountered French "half-breeds". The following description of them and their clothing is given:

> All of them had sashes round their waists, some of which were of the brightest hues. A few, spotted leggings highly ornamented with beadwork. One or two wore long blue coats, with bright buttons, while others were in their shirt sleeves; and the most of them had moccasins on their feet. As a general thing, they shewed [sic] great strength and activity of body; their features were chiefly dark, but regular - mild and pleasant in appearance. As a rule they were what could be considered handsome, although many of them gave indisputable signs of Indian origin.

Of all the historical clothing worn by the Metis of the past, the sash (dealt with in the next section) has continued as the most enduring symbol of today's Metis.

3. Metis Sash

This woolen belt is one of the prime symbols of Metis identity. It was originally known as the Assomption sash after the town of L'Assomption near Montreal where a cottage industry had developed early in the 19th century to produce this hand-woven type of belt.

In the west the sash developed under the influence of the fur trade, particularly due to the voyageurs of the North West Company. Voyageurs wore them and often brought additional sashes from the east to barter for furs.

It was also called a "ceinture fléchée" i.e. arrow sash, due to its pattern. In due course many of the fur traders' mixed-blood children also became voyageurs. Because the sash became so popular among the Metis of Red River, the word Assomption was dropped in favor of the name "Metis Sash".

The Metis sash is usually about three meters long. A work of art, it is a finger-woven belt with a blend of bright-colored fibers woven into a decorative pattern. Each end of the sash has long fringes. This sash is truly a North American creation with the designs representing the diversity of the French Canadian, First Nations, and Celtic heritage of the Metis.

This sash was adopted by the Metis; it was not only an

attractive addition to their clothing, it served a number of functional purposes. It was used in a variety of ways such as:

- a belt wrapped around a coat to keep it closed;
- a scarf and muffler to keep warm in the winter;
- a tumpline (an Algonquian word) - a strap or a sling passing across the forehead and over the shoulders to support a load on the back;
- a rope for such purposes as pulling a Red River cart out of the mud when mired;
- a wash cloth and towel;
- a first-aid or emergency sewing kit; and
- a saddle blanket and emergency bridle.

One humorous use was described by the Metis Louis Goulet in his memoirs *Vanishing Spaces*:

> The men wore their pants without suspenders, counting on the ceinture fléchée to prevent a descent !

Today the colors of the sash are said by some Metis to represent some aspects of their history, such as the following:

- red is for Metis blood shed over the years in fighting for their rights;
- blue is the depth of their spirit;
- white is the connection with the Earth and the Creator;
- white and blue are the colors of the Metis Nation national flag;
- black represents the dark period when the Metis suffered dispossession and suppression;
- green signifies fertility and growth; and
- yellow represents prosperity for the Metis Nation.

The sash is worn to this day by Metis people, usually at ceremonial and festive gatherings and cultural celebrations. It is traditionally wrapped around the waist and tied loosely to one side over the hip. Some Metis women wear it across the chest and tied at the shoulder. Other Metis women prefer to wear a small ribbon replica of the sash.

Although one of the authors of this book normally wears his sash around his waist, he has used it on occasion as a scarf while on a winter speaking tour.

When Nelson Mandela, the President of South Africa, visited Canada in 1998 he was presented with a Metis sash that he proudly subsequently wore when he addressed the Canadian Parliament.

In March 2006 Bruce Dumont, President of the Metis Nation of British Columbia presented a Metis sash to Governor General Michaelle Jean at a luncheon hosted by Premier Gordon Campbell. The Governor General wore the sash around her neck during the preliminary ceremonies.

In December 2001 Senator Thelma Chalifoux, the Metis Matriarch, introduced in the Senate of Canada a private member's Bill No. S-35. One of the provisions of this Bill read:

> The arrowhead sash is hereby acknowledged as the recognized symbol of the Metis people.

This Bill died on the order paper. However, that clause indicates the esteem in which the sash is held by the Metis people.

The intricate design of the sash integrating many patterns, yarns and colors reflects the weaving together of the lives of the Metis people from a composite of different cultures, traditions and heritages. In each case this intermixture results in a uniqueness that is found nowhere else in the world.

The self-esteem of the Metis people in their identity is evident when they wear the Metis sash with confidence, pride and dignity.

4. Red River Cart

In the 19th century this storied cart was a unique means of transportation on the Prairies that combined and modified aspects of similar vehicles found in Scotland and France. Its prime utilization was in connection with the buffalo hunt, but it was also used to convey products to various markets.

For a number of decades, the Metis drove many hundreds of carts west across the Prairies and to the northern Great Plains to the site of the buffalo herds. The meat from the animals slaughtered during the hunt was packed in these carts and after processing it at the camp site pemmican, dried meat, bags of grease, hides, and buffalo robes were conveyed back to the Red River Settlement.

When a cart was towed by a horse it could transport a load of 500 pounds some 50 miles in one day. However the vehicle was usually pulled by an ox which could haul twice as much cargo as a horse, but the distance traveled was then reduced to about 20 miles per day.

The Red River cart inaugurated the use of the wheel on the northern Great Plains. It was made wholly of wood and shaganappi, a native word meaning flayed cord or tong made of rawhide. The French Canadian term derived from Algonquian for wet raw hide is babiche. This shaganappi was used to bind the parts of the Red River cart together. The wet raw hide was wrapped around the rims of the wheels. As it dried the shaganappi tightened up, stuck fast and was solid and firm. Wooden pegs, not nails were used in the construction.

A cart had two high-dished wheels with spokes, and two shafts that were fastened to the axles. It stood as tall as a man. Because of its all-wood construction, repairs were easily made from trees found en route. As well when the wheels were removed, this wooden cart became buoyant allowing it to be used as a raft when fording a river.

Because of its light weight it was relatively easy to pull a cart out of muddy spots when it got stuck. Frequently the owner's trusty Metis sash was used as rope to pull it out of the mire.

The saucer-shaped wheels could not be oiled, otherwise clouds of prairie dust raised on the trail would congeal, become glued to the axles and prevent the wheels from rolling. This lack of lubrication caused the greaseless wheels of the Red River cart to emit an ear-piercing screeching noise as it traveled the Great Plains. Because of its creaking squeal, the nickname "the Northwest Fiddle" was applied to the cart.

En route to the buffalo herds the scouts traveled well in advance of the cart train. When they sighted a buffalo herd or unfriendly Indians, the scouts would warn their party to stop, thus preventing the shrill squeal of the wheels from broadcasting the presence of the oncoming entourage.

The two shafts to which the draft animal was attached served another purpose. For example in the Battle of the Grand Coteau they played an important feature in protection against the warring Sioux tribe. When "circling the wagons" the shafts were pointed outward and upward, acting like spears and presenting a daunting obstacle to a breach of the circle by the enemy.

Another use of the Red River cart was in conveying furs, robes, hides and other products to markets such as St. Paul, Minnesota along the Crow Wing Trail (also known as the Woods Trail and the Chemin St. Paul). Other freighting destinations included locations such as St. Peter's in Montana and Edmonton House via the Carlton Trail. The cart parade would then return to Red River with trade goods acquired from the sale of its products.

As a result of the outcome of the Sayer Trial in 1849 (discussed in another chapter of this book) the Hudson's Bay Company's monopoly on trade in and from the Red River was broken. This ushered in free trade with the United States. The North-South trade routes that then flourished witnessed a small explosion in the construction of Red River carts necessary to ply these routes and carry freight back and forth. By the late 1860s Metis entrepreneurs constituted most of the traders of furs and buffalo hides to St. Paul and elsewhere.

In the winter, without its wheels, the cart became a horse-drawn sleigh also known as a carriole. It could then be used to transport a family to church, to visit friends, to go to socials, and for other purposes. The functional use of the Red River cart was superseded later in the 19th century by the arrival of the steamboat and the railway.

In the highly entertaining *Memoirs* of Louis Goulet, he described the Red River cart as "a magnificent invention". He stated that with a few tools such as an axe, a saw, and a small number of other items, a man could construct a cart in a week. In an obvious reference to the barely tolerable shriek of its wheels, he wittily added that the cart "would play music as a bonus" any time it moved.

Paul Kane in his book *Wanderings of an Artist* described the Red River cart as follows:

> Their cart is a curious-looking vehicle, made by themselves with their own axes, and fastened together with wooden pins and leather strings, nails not being procurable. The tire of the wheel is made of buffalo hide, and put on wet; when it becomes dry, it shrinks, and is so tight, that it never falls off, and lasts as long as the cart holds together.

In the summer of 2002 a Red River cart trip, sponsored in part by the Manitoba Metis Federation, was re-enacted between Pembina, North Dakota and St. Norbert, Manitoba. The carts then participated in the opening ceremonies of the North American Indigenous Games in Winnipeg. From time to time other Metis organizations are instrumental in promoting similar cart trips.

Today replicas of the historical Red River cart are regularly seen at Metis festivals and other gatherings. It is a continual reminder and symbol of the identity and culture of this unique aboriginal people.

5. Birchbark Canoe

The birchbark canoe was a superlative accomplishment of First Nations culture. It played an indispensable part in opening up the fur trade for the captivating voyageurs who manned it.

This canoe was also a vital means of transportation in the exploration of the far-flung western and northern lands of North America and southward as far as the Gulf of Mexico.

The voyageurs, who manned these canoes, also played a fundamental role in sowing the seeds leading to the birth of the historic Metis people of Western and Central North America. This marvelous birchbark canoe and its fascinating operators were trailblazers in major aspects of the history of North America.

The voyageurs, and their aboriginal children born in the hinterland, became as adept as the natives in building the birchbark canoe and in its utilization. Eventually they made them larger and they even added features such as sails.

There is a prevailing image of the colorful voyageur in a birchbark canoe which captures the imagination. He is pictured as a brave young man whose life was full of adventurous romance, exuberant camaraderie, hard work, and hazardous expeditions. It pictures him and his comrades plying the waters leading from Quebec westward to the thickly-forested fur trade country and on to the mighty Columbia and Mackenzie Rivers.

In New France, as the fur-trade expanded further into the hinterland, the use of the birchbark canoe became more prominent as a means of transportation.

The voyageurs who manned the canoes to provide the supply line from Montreal to Grand Portage and later Fort William were dubbed "mangeurs du lard" or "pork eaters" because of the salt pork provisions they ate.

The voyageurs were originally adventurers from Montreal and the surrounding areas who made up the brigades that traveled west and south to the fur-bearing lands in the 17th, 18th and 19th centuries to trade in furs with the natives.

They journeyed to the Indian country bearing trade goods (such as beads, coarse woolen cloths, kettles, cutlery, and liquor) to barter for furs and wintered over and took female Indian mates. They did so not only for amorous reasons but also for trade contacts and assistance in adapting to life in the wild.

The craft which a voyageur and his confreres paddled, through many precarious rapids and swirling waters en route, to the interior was the historic birchbark canoe. When they stopped for the night, the voyageurs would often use an overturned canoe as protection against the elements while they slept.

The birchbark canoe was made of birch wood without nails or metal. It was the principal means of water transportation for voyageurs because it was light and maneuverable. It was ideal for summer travel through streams, lakes and rivers amid the thick forests in the lands abounding with beaver, mink, marten and other fur-bearing animals.

The canoe's light weight made it easy to portage between rivers or around navigable water. Simple to handle, it was just right to shoot some fast flowing white-water rapids. It could transport men and cargo disproportionate to its own weight.

One drawback was that it was not durable, but it could easily be repaired with new bark from the birch tree. Wattape (the fine root of a coniferous tree) was used for sewing on the patches and pine-gum used for waterproofing the seams. In his memoirs, Alexander Henry wrote of a birchbark canoe being damaged beyond repair in the depths of the wilderness, and the voyageurs built another one in four days.

The fur brigades in due course consisted of up to 20 or more canoes. The canoes were frequently painted and ornamented at the front with the picture of a rearing horse, a company flag, or other feature.

There was more than one type of birchbark canoe. The canot du nord was about 30 feet long and had a crew consisting of a steersman, a bowsman, and up to six tripmen or middlemen. The canot du maître was about one-third longer and was manned by about 14 voyageurs, carried a heavier load, and plied the waters between Montreal and the Great Lakes.

In their search for furs the North West Company (NWC) men also explored northward to the Arctic Ocean and westward to the Pacific Ocean. The Company encouraged this activity and in some cases the explorers, such as David Thompson, claimed the lands they traversed for the NWC and for England. Although it was part of the HBC's mandate to explore the land, they initially remained rooted at their forts on Hudson's Bay expecting the natives to come there to trade with them.

The inland penetration by the NWC and its voyageurs in their fur brigades into what is now Western Canada and Pacific North America enabled them to get to the natives first. This forced the HBC to abandon its policy of waiting for the natives to bring furs to it at Hudson Bay. They realized that they would have to emulate their NWC competitors by going into the Indian country or lose the commercial fur trade war. In due course the HBC used York boat brigades as an alternative to the canoe.

The voyageurs were colorfully and quaintly attired. Many had a feather in their cap, others wore red woolen caps. The arrowhead (Metis) sash was common among them, as were moccasins without stockings. Deer-skin leggings frequently covered their legs beneath the knee, and many wore capotes (or long coats). They invariably smoked a pipe at rest stops.

En route the indefatigable voyageurs, while paddling 12 to 14 or more hours per day, would sing amusing ballads, lively chansons (rollicking songs), and poetic verses. They would also sing about their lives, their sweethearts, and even about their beloved birchbark canoe. They were water-born traveling troubadours.

The rhythm of the voyageurs' songs matched the rhythm of their rapidly moving oars as they and their Metis voyageur descendants and the birchbark canoe paddled into the history of Canada.

6. York Boat

The York boat was developed by the Hudson's Bay Company (HBC) in the late 18th century to carry heavy loads on Northern inland waters. It was used with a crew of mostly Metis middlemen to transport furs and other goods, frequently on long hauls, to Hudson Bay and other points. On its return from these destinations it would bring back supplies, merchandise, and other products.

For many years during the 19th century, brigades consisting of several boats traveled yearly between Portage la Loche (in what is now Northern Saskatchewan and lying between the Saskatchewan and Athabaska River systems) and York Factory.

A picture in the mid-19th century by the noted artist Paul Kane depicted over one dozen York boats in a brigade, but it is more likely that the usual brigade consisted of from four to nine boats.

The York boat received its designation because one of its destinations was York Factory. York Factory was the trading post owned by the HBC at the mouth of the Hayes River on the shore of Hudson Bay in what is now Manitoba.

This huge inland boat had its antecedents in the Orkney fishing boat and in the Viking galley. After the amalgamation of the North West Company with the HBC in 1821, Hudson Bay replaced Montreal as the main port for overseas shipping of furs and the York boat gradually displaced the birchbark canoes on the main water systems in the northwest.

This boat had advantages over the birchbark canoe, particularly in its capacity to transport much heavier loads (up to twice that of the canoe); in its greater safety on stormy lakes; and in its economics relating to the number of crew to the size of the load. However the major disadvantage of the York boat was that its size and weight made portaging between water routes more difficult.

Many of the rivers navigated were shallow. As a consequence, rather than being deep-keeled, these boats had a shallow draft. The boats had a minimum keel length of 24 feet, but many were over 40 feet long and had an 8 foot beam. It was made of soft woods that grew in the region. Each boat had one large sail. Depending on its size, a boat could carry freight consisting of 70 to 100 pieces of cargo, each weighing 90 pounds. In time, the Red River Settlement and Edmonton House became centers for construction of the York boat by HBC shipbuilders.

Each boat carried appropriate equipment as well as food, a tool chest and a medical chest. A York boat had 6 to 8 tripmen (middlemen), a bowsman who guided the boat, and a steersman who controlled its direction with a sweep (a long oar fastened to the stern of the boat).

Because of climate conditions, York boat trips were seasonal in nature. Consequently the Metis tripmen would return to the Red River in the off-season. There they would spend the winters with their Metis relatives enjoying the life and the winter festivities in the community.

On the inland return from Hudson Bay, the York boat transported a variety of goods. Some of the unusual cargo included pianos, cathedral bells for St. Boniface, church bells for St. Andrews, cannons, wheeled carriages, cattle, and even live young buffalo.

In the book *Women of Red River,* Christiana Ross tells of traveling to Oxford House. While en route she first heard, then saw, the Portage la Loche brigade of four York boats of voyageurs coming at great speed under the command of Baptiste Bruce. She said:

> .... the boatmen were all wearing bright-colored shirts and each of the four boats, one after another, went over the brink of the tumbling water [rapids], and the last we saw of each was the steering oar.

That same book mentions the:

> .... voyageurs with their brightly colored shirts and feathers

> and gay streaming ribbons .... with their canoes, or boats, decorated with fluttering little flags.

It quotes Mrs. W. R. Black:

> We could hear them singing around the bend of the [Red] river long before we could see them.

The same Baptiste Bruce mentioned above was referred to in an article titled "York Boat Brigade" in the *Beaver Magazine* of December 1940 which gives the experiences on that trip of HBC Chief Trader W. Cornwallis King. King told of being on an 1863 brigade of nine York boats from Red River bound for Fort Simpson, and from there to York Factory.

He mentioned that Baptiste Bruce "the celebrated boat guide of the North was in charge" and that once en route and until the boat touched shore no one, not even the Governor of the HBC, dared interfere with Bruce. The lives of the voyageurs and the cargo were entrusted to his care. King added that:

> At the helm, Bruce was a Viking of old come to life .... the great pilot [with] muscles like whipcords alive on his body.

As for the paddling voyageurs King stated:

> Beads of sweat stood round and silvery on their hairy breasts and between their powerful brown shoulders.

He said of the voyageurs their physiques would do credit to the ancient Greeks. He also said:

> How they could sing! In Scotch, French, English and Indian of many dialects .... The men sang in time to their oars.

Ashore he mentioned one voyageur waving his fiddle and he "stepped out a vigorous jig ...." while the others kept time with their hands.

King concluded:

> I sometimes wonder if there are men anywhere today - men of the breed of these Red River voyageurs.

At the height of their employment, there were close to 200 York boats operated by more than 1,200 voyageurs, mostly Metis. The death knell of the York boat was wrung with the arrival of the steamer which was a faster and far more capacious vessel. The steamer Anson Northup arrived in the Red River in 1859 and by the 1870s the HBC was using steamers on Lake Winnipeg and making plans to do so on the Saskatchewan River.

As with their more romantic adventures in the birchbark canoe, the Metis tripmen in the York boats made immense contributions to the development of Canada.

7. Michif Language

Michif is a unique language of the Metis people. It evolved over 200 years ago as a result of the strong ties which were developed between the voyageurs and the fur traders with the First Nations people of the Great Plains and western Canada.

The Metis were the original intermediaries between the Europeans from Quebec and the Indians, and they frequently spoke Indian languages. This led to a creative new tongue, Michif, which represented the blending not only of aboriginal and French languages but of two cultures. This resulted in both a unique tongue and a unique identity. In French the word Michif is frequently used to designate Metis people as well as the Metis language.

The primary Michif language combines French nouns, Cree verbs and related grammar. However, Saulteaux and Ojibway words may be involved since some Metis can trace their ancestry to these tribes that could also speak Plains Cree. There were several Michif languages such as Michif French, Michif Cree and others.

Although this aboriginal language has its roots in fur trade alliances, the Metis spoke it among themselves when they ventured out on the buffalo hunt to the northern Great Plains. They also talked it when they wintered over on the Great Plains after the hunt rather than returning to the Red River area and the White Horse Plain.

In the 1830s the Roman Catholic priest Georges Antoine Belcourt, who was a gifted linguist, wrote a Michif dictionary while in charge of the mission at Baie St. Paul, a short distance from St. François Xavier.

The Michif language is documented in a dictionary at the Turtle Mountain Reservation in North Dakota, which is close to the Manitoba border. This Reservation has many residents who are descendants from the Red River Valley and one of their towns bears Father Belcourt's surname.

Since the United States Government does not officially recognize the Metis, many of its residents identify as natives in order to obtain reservation benefits, among other reasons. The term "reservation" is used in the United States for the area of land reserved for occupancy by Indians, whereas the Canadian term is "reserve".

The Michif dictionary of Turtle Mountain states that:

> An observation of available evidence shows that far from being a random mixture of elements from a lot of languages, Michif is dominated by two, French and Cree, and in a pattern of combinations which is most unusual and in its way, very rigorous.

There are those who fear that the Michif language is a dying legacy. Many Metis lost the ability to learn Michif some generations ago because churches and schools were unsympathetic and wanted only French or English spoken. However, although not widely spoken today, Michif does live on in the Turtle Mountain Reservation and in areas of Manitoba and Saskatchewan, as well as several other Provinces and States.

To ensure its survival, different Metis organizations are developing learning programs and language projects. There is an Aboriginal Language Initiative to develop revitalization strategies and to promote such projects in Metis communities. In addition National Michif Conferences have been held in Canada for a number of years to deal with language preservation and revitalization.

People who speak Michif are coming forward and providing classes in this language to Metis groups. A school in the primarily Metis community of St. Laurent, Manitoba teaches Michif. As a result of these initiatives the future looks bright for the preservation of this unrivaled Metis tongue.

Chapter Reference Sources

1. **Metis Flags**

- *Creation of Manitoba, or a History of the Red River Troubles,* by Alexander Begg, p. 167-170.
- *Cuthbert Grant of Grantown, Warden of the Plains of Red River* by Margaret Arnett MacLeod and W. L. Morton, p. 32; 43.
- *Flags of the Metis,* by Calvin Racette, *passim.*
- *Life of Louis Riel, The,* by Peter Charlebois, p. 42; 46.
- *Metis Legacy,* editors Lawrence J. Barkwell et al, p. 25; 443.
- *Strange Empire, Louis Riel and the Metis People,* by Joseph Howard, p. 165.
- "Battle Flag of Batoche, The" by Shaun Redmond *Metis Voyageur* Newspaper, June 2002.

2. **Voyageur and Metis Clothing**

- *Dot it Down, a Story of Life in the North-West,* by Alexander Begg, p. 47-48.
- *Great Fur Land or Sketches of Life in the Hudson's Bay Territory, The,* by H. M. Robinson, p. 229-230.
- *Saskatchewan and the Rocky Mountains ...,* by the Earl of Southesk, p. 9; 44-45; 348.
- *Vanishing Spaces, Memoirs of Louis Goulet,* by Guillaume Charette, p. 47-49.
- *Voyageur, The,* by Grace Lee Nute, p. 13; 42.
- *Women of Red River,* by W. J. Healy, p. 206-07.

3. **Metis Sash**

- "Metis Sash, The", Manitoba Metis Federation web site.
- "Metis Sash, The " *Red River Telegraph,* Sept. 1999, p. 28.
- *Museum Called Canada, The,* by Charlotte Gray, p. 385.
- "Sashes for the Fur Trade" by Marius Barbeau, *The Beaver,* June 1941, p. 24-27.
- "Significance of the Metis Sash" by Brian Muloin, *Red River Telegraph,* March 2000.
- *Vanishing Spaces, Memoirs of Louis Goulet,* by Guillaume Charette, p. 47.

4. **Red River Cart**

- *Caesars of the Wilderness,* by Peter C. Newman, p. 164-165.
- *New Peoples - Being and Becoming Metis in North America, The,* by Jacqueline Peterson and Jennifer S. H. Brown, p. 105-106.
- "North West Fiddle to once again travel down city streets", by Bruce Cherney, *Winnipeg Real Estate News,* July 26, 2002, p.10-11.
- "Red River Cart, The" by James Marsh, *Canadian Encyclopedia,* p.

1983.
- "Red River Cart, The" *Red River Telegraph*, July 1999, p.10.
- *Trials & Tribulations, The Red River Settlement and the Emergence of Manitoba*, by J. M. Bumsted, p. 149-150.
- *Vanishing Spaces, Memoirs of Louis Goulet*, by Guillaume Charette, p. 77-78.
- *Wanderings of an Artist among the Indians of North America*, by Paul Kane, p. 51.

5. **Birchbark Canoe**
- *Caesars of the Wilderness*, by Peter C. Newman, p. 32-33; 40-42.
- *Canadian Frontier 1534-1760, The*, by W. J. Eccles, p. 5; 145-46; 203 (note 22).
- "Canoe, Birchbark" by James Marsh, *Canadian Encyclopedia*, p. 392.
- *Building the Canadian Nation* Vol. 1, 1492-1849, by George W. Brown, p. 194-203.
- *History of the Canadian People, A*, Vol. I New France, by Morden H. Long, p. 206-207.
- "On Building a Birch-bark Canoe", by Albert Burger, *The Beaver Outfit*, Summer 1973, p. 50-53.
- *New Peoples - Being and Becoming Metis in North America, The*, by Jacqueline Peterson and Jennifer S. H. Brown, p. 105-106.
- *Voyageur, The*, by Grace Lee Nute, p. 23-32.

6. **York Boat**
- *Caesars of the Wilderness*, by Peter C. Newman, p. 228-229.
- "H.B.C. Inland Transport" by A. A. McDonald, *The Beaver*, Oct. 1923 p. 19-21; Nov. 1923, p. 52-53; Dec. 1923, p. 92-93.
- *Homeland to Hinterland, The Changing Worlds of the Red River Metis in the Nineteenth Century*, by Gerhard J, Ens, p. 43-46.
- *Honourable Company, The*, by Douglas MacKay, p. 248-49.
- *Manitoba a History*, by W. L. Morton, p. 59; 82-84; 167.
- "York Boat, The" by John E. Foster, *Canadian Encyclopedia*, p. 2561.
- *Trials & Tribulations, The Red River Settlement and the Emergence of Manitoba*, by J. M. Bumsted, p. 148-149.
- *Women of Red River*, by W. J. Healy, p. 184-85; 203.
- *York Boat Brigade*, by W. Cornwallis King, *The Beaver*, December, 1940, p. 24-26.
- "York Boats, The", by R. Glover *The Beaver*, p. 19-23.

7. **Michif Language**
- *New Peoples, Being and Becoming Metis in North America, The*, editors, Jacqueline Peterson and Jennifer S. H. Brown, p. 231-41.
- "Michif" by Jennifer H. S. Brown, *Canadian Encyclopedia*, p. 1482.
- "Michif: a dying legacy?", *Metis Voyageur*, Newspaper, Sept/Oct. 1999, p. 14.
- "Michif Language of the Metis, The" by Peter Bakker, *Metis Legacy*, editors Lawrence J. Barkwell et al, ch. 13.
- "Michif, The Spoken Word" by Bruce Dumont, *Metis Nation Magazine*, Issue 1, Vol. 1, March, 2005, P. 18-20.

Chapter V

GOOD TIMES and OTHER TOPICS

The historical Western Metis people loved to party, feast and celebrate whenever an opportune occasion presented itself, and many did. Like the people themselves, these activities were an amalgam of French, Scottish, Irish and Indian roots.

Festivities consisting of good food and drink, rousing music, energetic dancing, lively singing and jovial socializing would usually start in the early evening and continue until the morning hours. During this merrymaking, and continuing to this day, the Red River Jig and the fiddle were at the core of Metis identity. The primary source of this music came from the Scottish winterers of the North West Company.

In the 19th century the Christmas and New Year period was the main festive season in the Red River with activities extending over ten days to two weeks. Those away from Red River on the winter buffalo hunt didn't miss out on the celebrations. An example is given by Norbert Welsh in *The Last Buffalo Hunter.* In his narrative, Welsh said that at New Year's (1865) they had a good time:

> We would dance the old-time dances and the Red River Jig, reel of four, reel of eight, double jig, strip the willow, rabbit chase, Tucker circle, drops of brandy, and all the half-breed dances. There were always lots of fiddlers. Nearly every man could play the fiddle. Then we would go to another family. I tell you, we had a regular good time. We had lots to eat and drink .... This feasting lasted about ten days.

The prominent Metis entrepreneur James McKay (who was born at Edmonton House in 1828 and died in 1879 at St. James, Manitoba) invariably gave a fun-filled New Year's Party at his home in the Red River Settlement. His home was called Deer Lodge and was a frequent gathering place for the Metis, Indians and other residents in the area.

His New Year's Day festivities consisted of dancing, music, songs, eating and socializing, and began in the late afternoon. The young men were gussied up in their best homespun, while the young ladies wore their finest dresses and close-fitting bodices. All wore moccasins, making fast-foot shuffling easy while dancing.

In an article titled "Red River New Year", historian Margaret A. MacLeod wrote that when the dance at McKay's home began "Four fiddlers played in relays of two to give the exhausted ones a chance to recover. Four sets for the square dance formed in that big room and to the music of 'The Buffalo Girl' or 'Soldiers' Joy', they were off at the dancing in earnest." A late supper was served while the spirited dancing carried on long into the night.

There were other convivial happenings during the Christmas - New Year Holidays. Joseph James Hargrave wrote in his book *Red River*:

> Much driving about and visiting take place, and balls, family parties and celebrations of a kindred nature are set on foot.... One of the principal events in the holidays is the celebration of a midnight mass in the cathedral of St. Boniface, on Christmas eve.

Weddings were very common at this time of year and lasted several days with much feasting, dancing and drinking. The son of Cuthbert Grant (profiled elsewhere in this book) was married to a Metis girl at St. François Xavier in 1843. As quoted in the Spring, 1961 issue of *Beaver Magazine*, Robert Clouston a guest at the wedding wrote in an 1843 letter that:

> We reached Mr. Grant's about 12 o'clock and found them all dancing; and Mr. G. himself, in that happy state, which is sometimes called glorious; we had something to eat, and then joined the dance .... We had dancing all day and till 4 o'clock next morning - and by 9 the following day left them - heartily tired of the scene, but thinking the bridegroom a very happy fellow.

In the morning a breakfast was served. It was a custom that one had to sing a song to the bride to receive a piece of the wedding cake.

Another event held on New Year's Day witnessed horse-racing on the Red River. Woolen-capped men in carrioles galloped their ribbon-adorned steeds along the frozen river, with many spectators cheering on their favorite team.

In his book *Homeland to Hinterland,* Gerhard Ens gives a brief description of "The Social and Seasonal Round" of the Red River Metis. This account includes the winter festive season, a Christmas dinner, a dance, and New Year's Day.

In his Memoirs Louis Goulet gave a verbal picture of a Metis feast in the 19th century. He stated that everyone tried to surpass all others in preparing the tastiest dinner. During the festivities, a singing competition was held. This was followed by exhilarated dancing to the music of fiddles, guitars, drums, mouth organs, and other rhythmic instruments at hand. Each dancer, each musician and each singer animatedly tried to outshine the others while the onlookers watched the joyous rivalry with enthusiasm. An event such as this carried on for many hours and the most energetic jiggers might find at the end of the festivities that the soles of their moccasins had seen their last days.

The Metis in other communities carried on the same festive tradition. Goulet mentioned a house dance in the Judith Basin. This was an enclave on the Missouri River in present day Montana where many Metis people reside today. He mentioned that men pounded madly on a drum "to the rhythm of the Red River Jig ....The dancers kept time by clapping and snapping their fingers over their heads."

Fort Langley, British Columbia was established in 1827 by the Hudson's Bay Company with the help of, among others, the Metis. Members of the Metis community participated in dances at this Fort. There is a plaque on the walls of the reconstructed Fort that contains the following quote from C. C. Gardiner (identified as a gold-seeker invited to a ball at Fort Langley in 1858):

> .... There were English, Scotch, French and the Kanackas [Hawaiians] present, and their offspring all .... thoroughly mixed with the native Indian blood ....

An article in the October 1860 issue of *Harper's Magazine* recounts that the writer could here "the jiggish fiddle" before he arrived at a log house in Pembina (Dakota

Territory) where a brisk dance was underway. He added:

> The fiddle did not cease its scraping, nor the heels of the dancers for a moment intermit their vibrant thumps on the plank floor .... Jigs, reels, and quadrilles were danced in rapid succession, fresh dancers taking the place of those on the floor every two or three moments.

There was also loud laughter and fiddle-shrieks of the trembling strings. The other dance mentioned in the article was held the next night at Joe Rolette's Pembina house. The author wrote:

> .... here we saw the aristocracy of Pembina. There was a better fiddle and a better fiddler and better dancing.

Harriet (the daughter of the Scottish Metis James Sinclair of Red River Expedition fame) was considered one of the belles of the ball that was held at Red River in March 1848. Dr. John Bunn, a Metis physician who was in attendance, wrote:

> Polkas, gallops, waltzes, quadrilles, cotillions, country dances, reels and jigs employed the heels and talents of the assembly.

Metis music was based on the fiddle. It was, and is, the principal instrument used in the Red River Jig. This Jig is the most renowned Metis musical piece. The fiddle has become one of the symbols of the Metis Nation. The Red River Jig is lively and upbeat. It is performed and danced in two parts - in the high pitch section the dancers do basic two steps and move clockwise in a circle; when the fiddle changes to a lower pitch, the jiggers face each other across the circle and try to outdo one another with fancy footwork. In the early days in the West a bagpipe sometimes accompanied the fiddle, whereas today it is usually a guitar.

The convivial Metis gatherings of the past have continued to this day. One of the authors of this book, George Goulet, remembers as a child being taken by his parents to outdoor barn dances at the farm of his Metis McDougall grandparents. The farm at Prairie Grove (near Winnipeg) consisted of 240 acres, the size of the land grant given to each of the children of Metis families under the

Manitoba Act of 1870.

George's uncle, Pete McDougall, lived on a separate area of the farm with his wife. Not far from his house Uncle Pete had built an outdoor dance floor. Every Saturday night during the summer, Metis and other people would come from all over the area for a night of dancing and revelry. Pete's brother George would play his fiddle like a virtuoso. The author's father and others would perform the Red River Jig and other dances with lively abandon. Beer and potent potables (some of it home-brewed) were not in short supply. The partying lasted well into the night.

As for Metis songs, most of them were from bygone days. They came from the repertoire of the voyageurs that brought them West with the fur trade. Louis Goulet lists a number of songs in his Memoirs. As noted elsewhere in this book, voyageurs sang ballads, poetic verses, songs about their sweetheart and their canoe, and others.

After the Battle of Seven Oaks in 1816, the Metis minstrel Pierre Falcon wrote of this Metis victory a song titled *La Grenouillère*. Parts of this ballad are quoted in the chapter of this book that profiles Falcon.

Louis Riel wrote both songs and poetry. Chapter 12 of the book *Metis Legacy* written by Lynn Whidden gives a description of Metis music and songs, and one of the songs Riel wrote is reproduced.

Riel was also a fine poet. The depth of his sorrow on hearing of his father's death in Red River in 1864, while Louis was a student in Montreal, poignantly shines through in the following poem that he wrote shortly thereafter:

> In the midst of the crowd
> which ebbs and flows,
> When the mob sees a man
> with a pensive look,
> And an air of sadness,
> they throw him a
> Glance of suspicion.
> They whisper:

"Brother, who is that one?"
This attention which he arouses
is a cause for his worries.
He goes on aloof,
Sadness in his heart
So full of sighs,
Alone with his sorrows,
An exile from pleasures.
In sorrow he consumes his life,
His days are full of sadness.

The translation of this poem in the 1920s from French to English was done by Phillip Boyer de la Giroday, father of the author Terry Goulet.

Today grand festivals celebrating the traditions and heritage of the Metis are held every summer at Batoche, (Saskatchewan) , Big Valley (Alberta), near Victoria (British Columbia), at Lewiston (Montana), and at other locales. Over a few days large crowds of Metis and other guests participate in these festivals.

Common to all gatherings are Metis sashes, Red River carts, historical dress, jigging and fiddling. Depending on the location one may find a buffalo hunt camp, tepees, traditional voyageur games, Metis foods and food preparation, fiddling and jigging contests, craft exhibits, genealogical services, knife and hatchet throwing, historical re-enactments and more. The authors' have given talks relating to the history of the Metis at each of the festivals named above.

Historically the buffalo and the products that they produced from it, were the main food staple of the historic Metis. They also consumed prairie chickens, geese, ducks, rabbits, bears, deer, elk, and other wild game. They picked various berries and many were mixed with dried buffalo meat in the making of pemmican. Tea was their main beverage; it and tobacco were considered two special treats by the Metis.

Bannock, derived from the Celtic word "bannach" for flat bread, was a main element in the Metis diet. Originating in Scotland and brought to the West by the fur traders, bannock was round unleavened flat bread made from flour, water and fat and cooked over a fire. The Metis called it "galette" when they were speaking in French.

Food served at the New Year's party held by the Metis squire James McKay included such items as buffalo tongues and hump, smoked deer, beaver tail, roasted ducks and geese, hot joints of beef and pork, pemmican, bannock, and strong black tea.

At Metis festivals today food servings may include buffalo burgers, chicken burgers, fry bread, bannock (a leavened variation), game stews, homemade jams, tea, and coffee. No alcohol is allowed.

Historically the name "beadwork people" was attributed to the Metis. They fashioned coats, leggings, moccasins, mittens, gloves, pouches, saddles, and other clothing and accessories from the skins of deer, elk, moose and other animals. To these items they added creative and decorative features such as colored beadwork with a floral motif.

An informative article on the clothing and decorative arts of the Metis by Sherry Farrell Racette is found in chapter 14 of the book *Metis Legacy*.

The tradition, heritage and culture of the Metis, and the good times and handiwork described herein, are alive and well today across the historic Metis Nation homeland.

Chapter Reference Sources

- *Homeland to Hinterland, The Changing Worlds of the Red River Metis in the Nineteenth Century,* by Gerhard J. Ens, p. 46-50.
- *Last Buffalo Hunter, The,* by Norbert Welsh, p. 37-38.
- *Metis Legacy,* editors Lawrence J. Barkwell et al, ch, 12 by Lynn Whidden; and ch. 14 by Sherry Farrell Racette.
- *Red River,* by Joseph James Hargrave, p. 171.
- "Red River Gossip, A" by Elaine Allan Mitchell, *The Beaver,* Spring, 1961, p. 4-11.
- "Red River New Year" by Margaret Arnett MacLeod, *The Beaver,* Dec. 1953, p. 43-47.
- "Sound of Tradition, The" by Cherie Dimaline, *Metis Voyageur* Newspaper, June 2002, p. 9.
- *Vanishing Spaces, the Memoirs of Louis Goulet,* by Guillaume Charette, p. 43-47.
- *Women of Red River,* by W. J. Healy, p. 206-07.

SECTION B

MEMORABLE EVENTS

BUFFALO HUNTING

Sketch by Henri Julien

(Provincial Archives of Manitoba N.4035)

Hudson's Bay Company Archives, Archives of Manitoba N.8281

BATTLE OF SEVEN OAKS, 1816

by Charles Jefferys

Chapter VI

THE BATTLE OF SEVEN OAKS

In 1812 Lord Selkirk established the Red River Colony with a grant of land from the Hudson's Bay Company (HBC), of which he was a major shareholder. The North West Company (NWC) feared that the Colony might adversely affect a vital transportation route of their canoe brigades to the fur-bearing country, while the Metis were worried that the Colony would be a threat to their way of life.

The NWC was also concerned that the establishment of the Colony was a stepping stone that would lead the HBC to the rich fur-bearing Athabaska Country where the NWC had enjoyed exclusive trade for over 20 years. With respect to the Metis and their concerns, it should be noted that Selkirk in his plans and programs never wrote of, or acknowledged, the existence of the Metis people.

At first, the settlers and the NWC got along well. In fact Alexander Greenfield Macdonell, the head of the NWC in Red River, furnished provisions to the settlers to get them through their first winter. At the same time he invited his cousin Miles Macdonell, whom Selkirk had appointed Governor of the Colony, to spend that winter at the NWC fort and also gave him a horse.

However, an incident not long after made the initial concerns of the NWC and of the Metis a reality. The ire of the NWC and the mixed-blood people was aroused by an embargo known as the Pemmican Proclamation. It was issued, without consultation with the NWC or the Metis, on January 8, 1814 by Governor Miles Macdonell. It read in part:

> .... it is hereby ordered that no .... persons whatever shall take any provisions either of flesh, fish, grain, or vegetable .... by water or land carriage .... The provisions procured and raised .... shall be taken for the use of the colony.

This Proclamation also provided for the arrest and prosecution of transgressors. It also stipulated that there would be forfeiture of their provisions, vehicles, and cattle involved in conveying the provisions out of the settlement at Red River.

This ban, ostensibly to ensure a food supply for the colonists that winter, outraged both the Metis and officials of the NWC. Eventually this unilateral Proclamation led to what has been referred to as a "Pemmican War".

The Metis, as provisioners of pemmican to the NWC and its forts and canoe brigades, saw it as a direct interference with their economic well-being and an attack on a core element of their way of life. This threat to their freedom and very existence as a people spurred a greater awareness of themselves as a distinct entity.

The NWC viewed it as a scheme by the HBC, controlled by Selkirk, to prevent its fur traders, engagés, and canoe brigades from receiving the essential pemmican food required for their operations.

Governor Macdonell's Act also effectively amounted to a declaration of his jurisdiction and authority, and Selkirk's ownership, over the Red River lands and the people who lived there. This was a claim unacceptable to the Metis who were born in these lands, and unacceptable to the NWC who had explored these lands and built and manned the posts that were on it.

Not many months later, Governor Macdonell announced another edict which further angered the Metis. This imported upstart was purporting to further meddle in their way of life. This latest pronouncement enjoined the use of horses in "running" the buffalo during a hunt, a matter the Metis considered their birthright.

The misgivings of the Metis and the NWC were realized when Governor Macdonell commandeered from them huge quantities of pemmican. He also issued a notice to the HBC posts to eject the Nor'Westers from the lands which Governor Macdonell claimed jurisdiction over. As well, in October 1814 a notice was given to Duncan Cameron (officer in charge of the NWC Fort Gibraltar) to leave that

Fort.

The two wintering partners of the NWC, the said Duncan Cameron and the Governor's cousin Alexander Greenfield Macdonell, attended the subsequent great summer rendezvous held at the NWC headquarters in Fort William. At this annual meeting they were instructed by the NWC partners to take measures to expel the settlers from the Colony and to counter the HBC threat to their business operations.

These two NWC officials determined to enlist the Metis to assist them in these objectives. They talked to them and encouraged the Metis to appreciate what the Metis already instinctively knew in their hearts, and what the arrival of the Selkirk Settlers helped to crystallize, about their identity. This was the realization by these indigenous people that they were unique and distinct with shared experiences and with their own cultural, social, racial, religious, and language ties.

In 1814 Duncan Cameron had appointed Cuthbert Grant, an intelligent educated Scottish Metis only 21 years old, as Captain of the Metis. With the furtive support of the NWC the Metis harassed the Selkirk Settlement by trampling on crops, confiscating equipment, slaughtering livestock, and frightening the settlers.

The Pemmican Proclamation was ignored by the NWC and the Metis; and Cameron talked many colonists into abandoning the Colony by offering them free transportation to, and free land in, Upper Canada. Governor Miles Macdonell himself was arrested by the NWC and sent to Montreal for trial. In the summer of 1815, the Selkirk Settlers had abandoned the Settlement and it was put to the torch. This attempt at colonization was seemingly at an end.

However a few months later a group of settlers (old and new) under Colin Robertson, acting on HBC instructions, restored the Colony. In November the new governor of the Settlement, Robert Semple, arrived with an additional group of 84 colonists. Several months later Semple found out that the Metis and the Nor'Westers intended to resume harassing the Colony.

It was in this poisoned atmosphere that momentous and lethal fireworks were soon to erupt. The prelude to the open violence that ensued saw Cuthbert Grant and Alexander Greenfield Macdonell spending the winter of 1815-16 in the Qu'Appelle River area, where they undoubtedly discussed how to deal with the HBC and the return of the colonists to the Selkirk Settlement.

Although he was not the catalyst behind Metis ethnogenesis, Alexander Greenfield Macdonell inspired the Metis to recognize their aboriginal rights in the land, in the buffalo hunt and in their way of life, and in seeing themselves as a "New Nation". He was their ally in pursuing common objectives. In his letter of March 13, 1816 to Duncan Cameron, Alexander Greenfield Macdonell specifically referred to the Metis as a "new nation" when he wrote the following:

> .... the new nation under their leaders are coming forward to clear their native soil of intruders and assassins.

In May 1816, Governor Semple and Colin Robertson had the NWC Fort Gibraltar seized, and had it destroyed on June 1, 1816. They also had Duncan Cameron arrested.

As a result of the destruction of Fort Gibraltar, the Metis retaliated by capturing the HBC's Brandon House. They were led in this venture by Cuthbert Grant, who now bore the title of "Captain-General of all the Half-Breeds."

Brandon House was seized while the Metis were en route with supplies of pemmican for NWC traders at Lake Winnipeg. At Brandon House, the Metis party under Grant expropriated the HBC's store of pemmican, which they believed they were entitled to as a result of seizures previously made by the HBC.

The group then set out for Lake Winnipeg, some 50 miles north of the Forks, the confluence of the Red and the Assiniboine Rivers, to provision the NWC brigades - the voyageurs and bourgeois (wintering partners) waiting there.

In heading east, several dozen Metis horsemen were on each side of the Assiniboine River protecting the large supplies of pemmican being transported on the River. On reaching Portage la Prairie, the pemmican was transferred to three Red River carts for carriage overland from there.

Grant had intended that he and his men would surreptitiously bypass the Forks and nearby Fort Douglas. They did not want to endanger their mission to get the pemmican and other supplies to the NWC men. However the Saulteaux Chief Peguis alerted Governor Semple to their presence in the area. As a result on June 19, 1816 they were noticed by a lookout at the Fort. The resulting incident led to the historic Battle of Seven Oaks.

Governor Semple, then inside Fort Douglas, was determined to block the well-armed Metis (of whom there were five or six dozen, and not just the 15 or so that had first been seen) from proceeding further. Semple and a couple of dozen armed men left the well-fortified Fort, where he and the others would have been safe, in order to confront the Metis.

While en route to challenge the Metis, Semple realized that he was outnumbered and sent John Bourke back to the Fort to get their cannon. However, the impetuous Semple decided not to wait for the cannon and forged ahead.

The opposing groups met at a grove known as Seven Oaks, also known by the Metis as La Grenouillère (the name of a nearby swamp). The Metis horsemen fanned out into a half crescent around Semple's men. Grant sent a Metis, François Fermin Boucher, to talk to Semple. Angry words were exchanged, Boucher shouting that Semple was a "damned rascal"; Semple in turn labeling Boucher a "scoundrel", while simultaneously grappling for Boucher's gun and the reins of his horse.

Boucher promptly jumped off his horse and dashed back to his comrades, when a gunshot rang out. There has been some debate as to which party fired first, although two specialists in history, Professor W. L. Morton and

Margaret Arnett MacLeod, wrote that it was Semple's side that did so.

More significantly W. B. Coltman (who was appointed by Canada as a Royal Commissioner to investigate the occurrence) stated in a letter of May 14, 1818 to Lieutenant-Governor Sir John Sherbrooke that "next to certainty" the first shot was fired by Semple's side. Coltman also expressed the view that "the two parties met accidentally". Soon after the first shot was fired, volleys erupted back and forth. Semple was wounded in the thigh by Grant, who did not intend to kill him. However while Grant was otherwise engaged one of his men shot Semple in the head and he died.

Venting their pent-up rage at the interlopers, whose sponsors had unilaterally imposed decrees on the Metis and intruded into their way of life and their native land, the Metis showed no mercy. The Metis killed most of Semple's entourage, twenty-one in all including Semple, in an encounter that lasted less than half an hour. Only one of Grant's men perished in the conflict. Fort Douglas surrendered to Grant and he allowed the colonists to leave the Fort and the area without harm.

Under the spirited and determined young leader Cuthbert Grant, the Metis had completely vanquished their opponents. Some Eurocentric historians, such as E. E. Rich, refer to the confrontation at Seven Oaks as a massacre.

Lord Selkirk also referred to it as a massacre in a letter of September 3, 1816 to Sir John Sherbrooke. Use of the term "massacre" often depends on one's point of view. If one's supporters are killed in battle some might call it a massacre but if the reverse occurred, it would more likely be called a glorious victory.

Selkirk futilely pursued criminal proceedings against many members of the NWC. Although Cuthbert Grant was charged with murder neither he nor a number of other NWC employees including Duncan Cameron were ever brought to trial. In an unrelated incident, Charles de

Reinhard (a former De Meuron sergeant who had been employed by the NWC) was convicted of the murder of Owen Keveny, an HBC agent. François Fermin Boucher of the NWC was charged with the murder of Governor Robert Semple, but was acquitted.

However the Battle of Seven Oaks was unpremeditated, and as the eminent historian Gerald Friesen in his book *The Canadian Prairies* has written:

> the metis were not ruthless, thoughtless renegades .... but soldiers in what they believed to be a just cause.

In a letter of March 14, 1818, only a few years after this Battle, William McGillivray (a principal of the NWC) wrote of the Metis and their influential early leader Cuthbert Grant that notwithstanding their association with the NWC:

> they one and all look upon themselves as members of an independent tribe of natives entitled to a property in the soil, to a flag of their own, and to protection from the British government.

In fact the Metis believed that they had aboriginal rights in their native land.

In his September 3, 1816 letter to Sir John Sherbrooke, Lord Selkirk also stated that Alexander Macdonell of the NWC was "the author and the instigator of the massacre of 19th June." Macdonell was an interesting personality in his own right.

Also known as Alexander Macdonell of Greenfield, he was born in 1782 at Greenfield in the Highlands of Scotland to a prominent family whose roots extended back to the legendary Robert the Bruce of Bannockburn fame. Alexander's parents moved the family to Upper Canada when he was still a laddie.

He joined the NWC in the early 1800s. Since the NWC had many Scottish personnel with the same or similar names, it became necessary to include the area that they came from as part of their names in order to differentiate one from another, thus the use of Greenfield in his name. In addition in the Celtic tradition the names Macdonell and Macdonald were frequently interchangeable, and the manner in which Macdonell was pronounced was the same as Macdonald without the letter "d".

Alexander Greenfield Macdonell was the Nor'Wester in charge of the Red River Department when his cousin, Miles Macdonell, arrived as Governor with the Selkirk Settlers to establish the Red River Colony. As noted previously, although their dealings initially were amicable they soon deteriorated due to Governor Macdonell's high-handed treatment and his Pemmican Proclamation. As a result, their relationship was not that of "kissing cousins".

Alexander Greenfield Macdonell became a partner of the NWC in 1814. While in the West, Alexander took a young Metis country wife, Suzette Laurin. Their Metis daughter Marguerite Macdonell (born in 1820) is the great-great grandmother of George Goulet, one of the authors of this book.

Macdonell wrote "A narrative of transactions in the Red River country, from the commencement of the operations of the Earl of Selkirk till the summer of the year 1816". This provides a contemporary insight of relevant events during this period from the point of view of an insider of the NWC.

He was never put on trial for his involvement with the Metis in opposing the HBC and the colonists, or in relation to the Battle of Seven Oaks. Several years later, on the amalgamation of the HBC and the NWC in 1821, he was purposely excluded from the merged Company. No doubt this was due to the lingering HBC animosity towards him.

He left the West for Upper Canada in 1821, leaving behind his country wife and daughter, a not uncommon practice in those days. He became Sheriff of the Ottawa District and was successfully elected from the constituency of Glengarry to the House of Assembly. He died in Upper Canada in 1835 at Toronto.

The episode of the Metis, the bois brûlés, at Seven Oaks was celebrated in a ballad "a Metis national anthem", composed by the bard of the Metis and Grant's brother-in-law, Pierre Falcon. This song is discussed later in this book in the profile of Pierre Falcon.

The site of the Battle of Seven Oaks is in what is now the north part of Winnipeg and it is commemorated by a cairn that was erected in 1891 by the Manitoba Historical Society through the generosity of the Countess of Selkirk.

The Battle of Seven Oaks was a paramount defining moment in the evolution of the Metis as a people. They had established themselves as a cohesive force that would not back down in pursuing their rights. They had fought for and won political rights and freedoms for themselves against foreign intruders, including the right to run the buffalo and the freedom to carry on their lives in accordance with their customs and traditions.

The Battle of Seven Oaks was the awakening of a new consciousness for the Metis. Their momentous ordeal by fire crystallized their awareness of themselves as a New People, a "New Nation".

Chapter Reference Sources

- "Battle of Seven Oaks - Semple, 20 settlers and one Metis killed" by Bruce Cherney, *Winnipeg Real Estate* News, November 28, 2003, p. 4-6.
- *Battle of the West, Fur Traders and the Birth of Western Canada*, by Daniel Francis, p. 117-122.
- *Birth of Western Canada, a History of the Riel Rebellions, The*, by George F. G. Stanley, p. 11-12.
- "Bloodshed at Seven Oaks" by Joe Martin, *The Beaver Outfit 297*, 1966, p. 36-40.
- *Canadian Prairies a History, The*, by Gerald Friesen, p. 75-80.
- *Caesars of the Wilderness*, by Peter C. Newman, p. 169-176.
- *Cuthbert Grant of Grantown, Warden of the Plains of Red River*, by Margaret Arnett MacLeod and W. L. Morton, ch. IV; and p. 70.
- *Fur Trade and the North West to 1857*, by E. E. Rich, ch. 12.
- *Fur Trade Wars, The Founding of Western Canada*, by J. M. Bumsted, p. 141-52.
- *HBC Archives* Vol. XXII , p. 318-29.
- *Lord Selkirk of Red River*, by John M. Gray, p. 138-48.
- *Manitoba: A History*, by W. L. Morton, p. 50-55.
- *Narrative of transactions in the Red River country, from the commencement of the operations of the Earl of Selkirk till the summer of the Year 1816, A*, by Alexander Greenfield Macdonell, *passim*.
- "Seven Oaks Incident", by J. E. Rea, *Canadian Encyclopedia*, p. 2144.

Chapter VII

EVENTS AFTER SEVEN OAKS

Several months after the Battle of Seven Oaks, Cuthbert Grant and a number of Metis returned to the Qu'Appelle area. However Lord Selkirk had not given up on his Colony. With a band of about 100 Swiss and German mercenaries mostly from the de Meuron Regiment, Selkirk headed west to retake his Colony.

En route he seized Fort William, the North West Company (NWC) headquarters. He then decided to winter there while his soldiers pushed on to the Forks where they retook the undermanned Fort Douglas in 1817. They did so without resistance and the Selkirk Settlers returned once again. The soldiers had also captured the NWC's Pembina Fort.

In June 1817, Selkirk arrived at Fort Douglas and saw crops growing in the Settlement. Shortly after his arrival, legal proceedings were initiated by the NWC, namely a warrant for Selkirk's arrest. He ignored the warrant. This decision later caused him a great deal of consternation and led to events that likely contributed to his premature death three years later.

The Hudson's Bay Company (HBC) and Selkirk exchanged charges and counter-charges with the NWC. During this period of conflict, not one Metis was even convicted as a result of the Battle of Seven Oaks. Although the Colony itself was no longer threatened, the British Colonial Office established the commission to investigate the violence. William B. Coltman was sent from Canada to the Colony as commissioner. The British Government, weary of the conflicts, was becoming fed up with the frontier battles of the two fur-trading companies.

Lord Selkirk died in 1820, and the British Government finally decided that to end the turbulence the HBC and the NWC must merge. They did so in 1821 under the continuing name and charter of the HBC.

The merger of the HBC and the NWC, resulting in a HBC trading monopoly, saw a significant reduction in its staffing needs in the fur trade and in its provisioning requirements. Many Metis no longer had work.

In 1818, a few years before the merger, a Roman Catholic priest Father Joseph Norbert Provencher (later to become a bishop) established a mission church at St. Boniface, across the Red River from what is now downtown Winnipeg. Over the ensuing decades, the area around St. Boniface and its parish were the heart and soul of the Catholic Metis homeland and the center of Metis educational, cultural, and political activities.

Louis Riel, the great Metis hero, was born in these lands in 1844. Formation of a parish at St. Boniface attracted the Scots, Irish and French Metis who had inherited the Roman Catholic faith through their Euro-Canadian ancestors.

Many Metis, who were not already there, settled in the Red River area in the vicinity of the Forks, along the Red River Valley, and at Pembina. A number of them took up farming but continued to participate in the annual buffalo hunts. For some years they found a ready market for their products in the Settlement. English Metis and retired employees of the HBC were also drawn to this Settlement.

At this time many Metis, the largest identifiable group in the area, already lived in the Red River Valley near the banks of the River. However, they often combined modest residences in this location with their semi-nomadic life wandering the plains in search of the buffalo. As freemen they also acted as guides, huntsmen, or trip-men on fur brigades.

It is rather ironic that the Red River Settlement (including the area on one side of the Forks which the Metis had so vigorously harassed in prior years) eventually became the center of the Metis homeland.

Another Metis location soon developed at White Horse Plain, on the north bank of the Assiniboine River, about 30 kilometers west of the Forks. Cuthbert Grant had received from the HBC a large tract of land on this Plain. Grant, a Roman Catholic Scottish Metis, decided to establish a Metis farm settlement at this location. In 1824 approximately 100 Metis families living at Pembina in the Dakota Territory (which had recently become part of the United States) were induced to move to the White Horse Plain, although quite a few other Metis families remained behind.

Father Provencher was very supportive of Grant's venture. It provided an opportunity for him to minister to the faithful. Pembina had been an important base for the buffalo hunt and continued as such after it became part of the United States. In 1823 the HBC relocated their Pembina operations to Fort Garry (formerly Fort Douglas).

In the new settlement at White Horse Plain established by Cuthbert Grant each settler received a river lot, and the community became known as Grantown after its founder. It subsequently became the parish and mission of St. François-Xavier, the name of the community today. Grantown immediately became a safeguard against the unfriendly Sioux warriors for other communities that developed along the Red and Assiniboine Rivers such as St. James, Kildonan, and St. Andrews.

The history of White Horse Plain carries with it an old Indian legend of a beautiful daughter of the chief of the Assiniboine people and the white horse on which she and her Cree suitor tried to flee Sioux warriors. They perished in the attempt, and legend has it that the horse was never captured but freely roamed the Plain. The white horse is said to wander the Plain to this day. A larger-than-life statue of the white horse has been erected along the Trans-Canada highway at the Highway 26 turn-off that leads to the town of St. François-Xavier.

With the influx of retired employees of the HBC, many of whom were of "mixed-blood" (a term incidentally not beloved by some anthropologists) the Red River area was to become primarily a Metis society by the mid 1830s. About that time, the HBC had reacquired Assiniboia from the estate of Lord Selkirk. Thereafter the Governor and

Council of Assiniboia, effectively controlled by the HBC, continued on. A General Court presided over by Recorder Adam Thom was inaugurated but, as will be seen in a following chapter, there was no established force to carry out any order if perchance the Metis strongly opposed it.

Chapter Reference Sources

- *Canadian Prairies a History, The,* by Gerald Friesen, p. 82-90.
- *Cuthbert Grant of Grantown, Warden of the Plains of Red River,* by Margaret Arnett MacLeod and W. L. Morton, ch. V.
- *Lord Selkirk of Red River,* by John Morgan Gray, ch. 6; ch. 7.
- *Manitoba: A History,* by W. L. Morton, *passim.*
- *North West Company, The,* by Marjorie Wilkins Campbell, *passim.*

Chapter VIII

THE BUFFALO HUNT

For a number of decades in the 19th century the annual Metis buffalo hunts, besides being an essential food-gathering and mercantile expedition, provided an opportunity for an extended convivial get-together. The Metis hunt was a large-scale and grand socio-economic affair in which the hunters were accompanied by their wives and children. The hunt was an integral part of the Metis way of life and their freedom to roam the plains.

During these excursions onto the northern Great Plains of America, the Metis were semi-nomads in search of the hump-backed furry bovines with huge heads and short horns. The North American buffalo (also called a bison) was generally over five feet high, ten feet long, and weighed well over 1,000 lbs.

The natives, of course, were the first plains buffalo hunters. They originally funneled the beasts into a sturdy corral where they were easy prey, or stampeded them over a steep cliff. A famous one of these jumps is the aptly named Head-Smashed-In Buffalo Jump, a tourist attraction and United Nations World Heritage Site in Southern Alberta.

The buffalo were indigenous only to the plains. As a result some Indians from the west, such as members of the Kootenay and the Snake tribes, would cross the Rocky Mountains to hunt buffalo and to steal horses and women from the plains Indians, such as their enemies the Blackfoot.

The buffalo was a source of food from its meat and fat, shelter and clothing from its hide, and tools from its bones. Tallow from the buffalo was a trading commodity that was used for making soap and candles. For the Metis it was a major economic enterprise to obtain food and furs for themselves, and to supply and sell these items to the traders and servants of the fur trading companies and to the settlers of the Red River Colony.

The Metis buffalo hunts, one in late spring and a smaller one in the fall, frequently saved the Red River settlers from near starvation. In many years the settlers experienced crop failures due to floods, drought, frost, and other natural disasters. In such instances they had to rely on the Metis to supply food in order to survive. As G. Herman Sprenger wrote in an article in the book titled *The Other Natives - the Metis*:

> .... buffalo hunting was also essential for the survival of the people of the Red River Settlement and the success of the fur trade economy.

In June of each year for several decades commencing in the 1820s, Metis from various places in the Red River area met at a rendezvous, such as Pembina, for the large summer hunt. From there they traveled several hundred kilometers to find the buffalo herds. Each trip lasted up to three months.

A hunt brigade frequently had over 1,000 men, women and children; almost as many Red River carts; hundreds of horses, oxen, dogs and other animals. Tents, clothing, hunting equipment, lodgepoles, spare axles, frame drying materials, rifles, ammunition, butchering implements, and other paraphernalia, were also carted along by the Metis on the hunt.

Each day's journey towards the sometimes elusive herd covered only a small part of the trip. Consequently a gigantic camp of tepees and lodges encircled by the carts was set up every evening.

This cart corral served a dual purpose - as a defensive enclosure for protection against any hostile natives, and as a common area for the business of the hunt, for socializing, and for religious services. Subsequent to the arrival of clergy in the west, a priest invariably went along on the hunt to minister to the people most of whom, both French and English Metis, were Roman Catholics.

An almost festive atmosphere prevailed in the prairie

encampment. The rollicking fellowship and merry-making enhanced the sense of camaraderie among the Metis. The pervasive jovial atmosphere in the camp was filled with music and song, storytelling, fiddling, dancing, gambling, gossip and lively conversations. During this time lovers were married and babies were born.

However in addition to the fun and games within the camp, business relating to the hunt had to be attended to. Much of this was done prior to the departure at the rendezvous, which usually lasted several days. The organization of the hunt and the establishment of rules and regulations were essential to its success and to maintaining order. Strict discipline had to be enforced.

There was no room for a hunter to act on his own behalf. The buffalo could easily be stampeded by a willful or wayward hunter. As well, the job of packing up and moving such a large brigade of people and animals to a new hunting ground would have to be unnecessarily repeated. In addition, a watch had to be maintained against a potential attack from hostile natives, and if matters such as disruptive quarreling and pilfering occurred they had to be firmly dealt with.

After the women and children had withdrawn to their sleeping quarters, the organization of the hunt took place. The hunters democratically voted at a great council to elect 10 captains, one of whom was named Chief of the Hunt. In turn each of the 10 captains elected at the council selected 10 or more scouts or soldiers and a guide to be under his command.

To be elected Chief of the Hunt was a high accolade. The hunt epitomized democratic principles at work, principles which were not then being practiced in eastern Canada. The democratic principles of the hunt were subsequently used as a model in the formation of the provisional government headed by Louis Riel during the Red River Resistance and on other occasions.

This command structure had the responsibility of ensuring compliance with the customary rules and regulations of the hunt and to ensure security for the camp. Throughout the night, sentries stood guard to ensure safety. These traditional rules and regulations were approved by the council. They became the laws of the hunt, and had to be observed by everyone.

The guide of the day was entrusted with the flag of the camp. His raising of the flag in the morning was the signal to all that it was time to break camp and prepare for departure. The men and older boys mounted their horses, the women and children road in the carts, and the march was on. The procession, some six miles long, was not uniform; it was staggered to minimize the prairie dust, but nothing could diminish the continuous piercing screech from the dry wooden axles of the Red River carts.

En route the designated guide was in charge, but when the caravan stopped to make camp for the night, the Chief of the Hunt assumed command with his captains and their soldiers who were under his authority. With the measured discipline of a militia, the Chief and his captains oversaw the setting-up and security of the campsite, discussed business including the next day's destination, and dealt with any issues that may have arisen that day.

It usually took more than a week to locate the buffalo, particularly because of the slow pace of the cavalcade, much of which was drawn by plodding oxen. About 25 to 30 kilometers were traveled each day.

When on a hunt, scouts were sent in advance of the group to look for herds. Scouts were the eyes and ears of the camp both for locating the buffalo and for detecting potential harm to the expedition, such as hostile natives. Once the buffalo were sited, the scouts swiftly road back to the main party shouting "la vache, la vache", the French term for a cow.

The plains buffalo cows were smaller in size and their average weight was about 700 pounds, whereas the average weight of a bull was significantly higher. The Metis considered the meat of the cow to be more tender, than that of the bull.

Upon hearing the call of the scouts the camp was swiftly set up, after which the captains immediately marshaled the hunters. The Chief gave the signal to proceed and they started out as slowly and quietly as possible. They approached up-wind because, although the buffalo had poor vision, they had a keen sense of smell.

When all were in position, the Chief gave the "battle cry". Immediately the Metis charged, with their colorful Assomption sashes streaming in the wind, and with exuberant shouts, sparkling eyes, and spirited horses trained to respond to the slightest pressures from their masters. In the words of Father Georges Belcourt, a missionary priest who accompanied the 1845 fall hunt, the thrill of the hunt had them "beaming with the keenest joy."

When the buffalo became aware of the hunters closing in for the kill, they took off in a thundering rush and the buffalo run was on. The pounding of the ground by the hoofs of the fleeing buffalo and of the galloping horses caused the very earth to tremble and clouds of choking dust to be raised.

Each hunter knew the dangers to be faced. He might be thrown from his horse and trampled on or, if he fell on a buffalo, be tossed and tossed again into the air by an infuriated animal. If a bullet was improperly loaded, his gun barrel could explode causing him great harm. He could even be hit by a stray bullet.

Each hunter, on his fleet horse, breathtakingly dashed in and out among the stampeding beasts with bullets in his mouth and his rifle at the ready. He would shoot a cow at almost point-blank range, and while going full tilt would reload with remarkable agility, losing no time in continuing his headlong chase to bring down another animal. This process was repeated by a hunter several times during a run.

Father Belcourt also wrote that "some of them managed to discharge their pieces as many as five times during the course of a chase."

The cumulative effect of the blazing guns witnessed

hundreds of dead and dying animals strewn across the plains. At the end of the attack, each hunter would then check for the buffalo he himself had killed. The pursuit of a particular herd could extend over a number of days in which the spectacular and hazardous attacks would be replicated again and again.

Alexander Ross in his book *The Red River Settlement, Its Rise, Progress, and Present State* noted these rules, when he accompanied the largest hunt ever held, that of the summer of 1840:

> 1. No buffalo to be run on the Sabbath day.
>
> 2. No party to fork off, lag behind, or go before without permission.
>
> 3. No person or party to run buffalo before the general order.
>
> 4. Every captain with his men in turn to patrol camp and keep guard.
>
> 5. For the first trespass against these laws, the offender to have his saddle and bridle cut up.
>
> 6. For the second offence, the coat to be taken off the offender's back and be cut up.
>
> 7. For the third offence, the offender to be flogged.
>
> 8. Any person convicted of theft, even to the value of a sinew, to be brought to the middle of the camp, the crier to call out his or her name three times, adding the word 'thief' at each time,

Ross also wrote:

> No less than 400 huntsmen, all mounted and anxiously waiting for the word, 'Start!' took up their position in a line at one end of the camp, while Captain Wilkie, with his spy-glass at his eye, surveyed the buffalo, examined the ground, and issued his orders. At 8 o'clock the whole cavalcade broke ground, and made for the buffalo; first at a slow trot, then at a gallop, and lastly at full speed.

This 1840 buffalo hunt was an immense undertaking. It consisted of:

- over 1,600 people made up of 620 hunters, 650 women, and 360 children;
- 403 buffalo runners (horses), 655 cart horses, 586 draft

oxen, and 542 dogs;

- 1,210 Red River carts; and
- 740 guns and the extensive ammunition required for the hunt itself as well as for protection on the journey.

On the hunt there were also:

- poles, axes, tools, and other implements;
- butchering knives and other utensils;
- harnesses, saddles; and
- numerous other items.

The Chief of the summer hunt of 1840 was Jean Baptiste Wilkie, whose daughter some years later was to marry Gabriel Dumont (who was destined to become a renowned Metis hunter and military strategist).

The fall hunt occurred later in the year and was smaller than the summer hunt. The 1845 fall hunt started on November 9th and Father Belcourt wrote of it that the camp consisted of about 60 lodges, a wagon train and some 300 horses and over 100 oxen. He stated the carts transported "such things as fire-wood, spare axles, lodge poles, drying frames and hide-stretchers." He also said the following as to the size of a buffalo:

> I measured a medium sized bull and found him to have a girth of eight feet nine inches, a length of nine feet two inches, twenty inches from muzzle to top of forehead, tail one foot three inches, and fourteen inches between the eyes.

In 1850 Father Lacombe accompanied a hunt from Pembina. In the book *Father Lacombe* by Katherine Hughes there is a description of the hunt in which Father Lacombe stated that the Chief of the Hunt, after receiving approval of the regulations, solemnly declared:

> If any of you do not approve of these laws, let him leave our camp and come not with us, for once we set out together from this encampment no one will be free to separate from us.

A crier announced this and, when required, other information to one and all in the encampment.

Each morning Father Lacombe celebrated Mass at an early hour. He reckoned that the 1850 hunt consisted of over 1,000 men, women and children; 800 to 1,000 carts; oxen; numerous dogs; and hundreds of buffalo runners and cart horses. His report of the organization and establishment of the regulations was similar to that reported by Alexander Ross with respect to the 1840 hunt.

Ross, while expressing some negative qualities about the Metis such as their being "unsteady as the wind in all their habits" and "fickle in their dispositions" wrote at the same time that:

> They are generous, warm-hearted and brave .... believing all men were born free .... They cherish freedom as they cherish life.

Major Samuel Woods was in the Red River area in 1849 to check out the establishment of a military fort on behalf of the United States Secretary of War. In Woods' report referred to in *The Voyageur* by Grace Lee Nute, he wrote briefly of the Metis buffalo hunt and stated of the Metis that they had;

> mild and gentle manners, great vivacity, generous and honest in their transactions, and disposed to be a civil and orderly community. They are hale and hearty, robust men, evidently accustomed to hardships and exposure, to which they submit cheerfully.

In the 1840 hunt witnessed by Alexander Ross 1,375 buffalo were killed, while Father Lacombe noted that close to 800 met the same fate in the 1850 hunt that he accompanied.

In the book *The Last Buffalo Hunter* by Mary Weekes, Norbert Welsh gave a first-hand account to the author of being a member of a buffalo-hunting brigade in the 1860s. He narrated the shooting by him of a buffalo from his 'runner', detailed how he skinned the buffalo, and how pemmican was prepared. He stated that in the winter of 1868, the "buffalo were beginning to get scarce" an omen of their near demise little more than a decade later.

During the hunt, the wives of the men demonstrated that they were an indispensable part of this Metis way of life. It was the women who actually processed the buffalo to make the pemmican, the robes, and the other commodities produced from the hunt.

Besides being faithful companions and spouses, bearing and looking after the children, the wives made clothing and ornaments, cooked meals, and generally supported their men. This was no more evident than on the buffalo hunt when wives and children accompanied the hunters.

On completion of each buffalo run, the women rode to the site in the Red River carts and would find the hunters already butchering the slaughtered animals. In addition to skinning the beasts, the choicest meat portions were removed, of which the tongue in particular was considered a delicacy as were the humps. The entrails and other inedible parts were left on the field to be gorged upon by wolves, coyotes, and other wild life.

The meat was loaded into the carts and the women returned with it to the camp. That evening a banquet was held at which many of the choicest cuts of meat were consumed. Over the next number of days, the women tanned the hides and dried the meat. These women were of immense assistance in making buffalo robes. Made from buffalo skin, the hide was tanned and the fur retained. Tanning and preparation took days of hard work by the Metis women to make the robes soft and pliable.

The book *The New Peoples: Being and Becoming Metis in North America* refers to the following personal experience of Clemence G. Berger on a hunt:

> Every night we had prayer meeting and just before a buffalo hunt we would see our men on bended knee in prayer. Our men did all the hunting, and we women did all the tanning of the buffalo hides, jerky meat making, pemmican and moccasins.

The women cut the meat into long thin strips and stretched it on poles to dry in the sun. When dry the meat was bundled in packages of about 70 pounds, and each package was bound with buffalo sinew.

The women made pemmican with the dried meat by

placing it on a buffalo hide and pounding it until it was powdery. Melted buffalo fat and marrow were mixed with the meat, and frequently flavorful berries were added. This melange was put in sacks made of buffalo hide and the sacks were sewn up.

Pemmican was a principal source of food to carry the Metis, as well as many of the residents of the Red River Settlement, through the winter months. Pemmican kept well and was also an essential staple for those engaged in the fur trade. As previously noted, tallow for making candles and soap was another product derived from the buffalo.

In his 1849 report to the United States Secretary of War, Major Woods told of the nomadic Metis hunting train returning to Pembina with the products derived from the hunt. These consisted of 1,776 cows consisting of 228 leather bags of pemmican; 1,213 roles of dried meat; 166 bags of grease; and 556 bladders of marrow grease. These products were conveyed in Red River carts.

With respect to the June 1840 hunt documented by Alexander Ross, the Metis came home with 1,200 Red River carts each loaded with 900 pounds of meat. This amounted to 200 pounds per capita for each person residing in the Red River Settlement.

He also pointed out that the HBC bought a huge supply of meat and many buffalo robes from the Metis for an amount significantly greater than the Settlement's farmers received during that season for their entire farm produce.

Because the Metis preferred the hunt to farming some Eurocentric historians suggested that the Metis were indolent and improvident. The facts belie this prejudice. In fact, the energetic Metis endeavors on the hunt frequently saved many a settler, his wife and small children from going to bed with an empty stomach.

As Joseph Howard wrote in *Strange Empire - Louis Riel and the Metis People,* the Metis (whose trips to the prairies were deplored by the Anglo-Saxon farmers) did more work on a hunting venture lasting a few months "than the farmers did in a year, and braved more hardship than the farmers did in a lifetime."

In the 1840s and for several decades after, the open American market led to an increased demand for buffalo robes and furs. As a result, more Metis cut back on their subsistence agriculture in the Red River area to follow the buffalo to the western plains now known as Saskatchewan, Alberta, North Dakota and Montana.

Many Metis and their families stayed in these areas over the wintertime after the fall hunt. They established small communities and became known as "hivernants". The value of the trade in furs and buffalo robes increased a hundredfold in a twenty year period from about $3,000 in 1845 to some $300,000 in 1865. A number of Metis traders became quite successful as a result. Many of them returned to the Red River Settlement for the summer but a number remained permanently in the West, in places such as in the community of Spring Creek, now called Lewistown, Montana.

The hazardous conditions of the buffalo hunt were even more dangerous during the fall or winter hunt. For example Alexander Ross in his book told of the winter hunt of 1825-1826 that ".... there was a fearful snow-storm" that came on suddenly and lasted several days and killed most of the hunters' horses. Of the men, women and children on the hunt "Thirty-three lives were lost."

A further example of the danger is that of the Missionary George McDougall who was accompanying a winter hunt. He was lost in a prairie blizzard north of Calgary and froze to death on January 25, 1876.

The arrival home from the hunt was a happy occasion for the Metis and called for a grand party. It was a time for one and all to eat, drink and be merry, and to dance-up a storm with lots of exuberant fiddling and jigging.

There may have been upward of sixty million buffalo before European contact was made on the western plains. There were vast numbers of buffalo during the decades of the most prolific of the Metis hunts. In his book

Wanderings of an Artist among the Indians of North America, Paul Kane (the noted Canadian artist who painted hundreds of sketches of western scenery and aboriginal life) wrote of his 1846 journey:

> During the whole of the three days that it took us to reach Edmonton House, we saw nothing else but these animals covering the plains as far as the eye could reach, and so numerous were they that at times they impeded our progress, filling the air with dust almost to suffocation.

William Bleasdell Cameron, in his book *Blood Red the Sun,* wrote that in 1884 the Indian warrior Meeminook told him that in earlier days:

> the buffalo were like grass on the plains and with your ear to the ground you could not sleep for the thunder of their hoofs.

Both during the height of the hunt's existence, and for some time after, many Metis earned their livelihood as voyageurs and from fur-trapping, freighting, fishing, and tripmen for the HBC. The less nomadic Metis had small farms on which they grew crops, planted vegetables and owned livestock.

Archbishop Alexandre A. Taché of St. Boniface wanted the Metis to change their way of life to a more agricultural lifestyle. With this end in view, in 1874 he prohibited priests from accompanying the winter buffalo hunts. Nevertheless the Metis realized the economic importance to them of the buffalo hunt, and continued with it as an essential aspect of their regular lifestyle.

In the last half of the 19th century, there was a movement for white agricultural settlement of the western plains both in Canada and the United States, a situation incompatible with buffalo hunts over prairie ranges.

Other influences that affected life on the prairies included the United States government policies with respect to American natives; the coming of the Union Pacific Railway which split the herds of buffalo (they would not cross the tracks); and the wholesale slaughter of this food staple by commercial hunters and sports marksmen such as Buffalo Bill Cody.

There was indiscriminate killing of the buffalo in order to subdue the natives into submissiveness and to force them onto reservations. It is estimated that this carnage may have killed many millions of buffalo.

It was these factors that brought the buffalo to near extinction by the early 1880s. The glory days of the buffalo hunt were over. An aboriginal, a Metis way of life had been forever lost.

Chapter Reference Sources

- "Buffalo Hunt", by G. A. Belcourt, *The Beaver*, Dec. 1944, p. 13-17.
- "Buffalo Hunt", by John E. Foster, *The Canadian Encyclopedia*, p. 323.
- *Caesars of the Wilderness*, by Peter C. Newman, p. 158-63.
- *Cuthbert Grant of Grantown, Warden of the Plains of Red River*, by Margaret Arnett MacLeod and W. L. Morton, p. 108-113.
- *Father Lacombe The Black-Robe Voyageur*, by Katherine Hughes, p. 23-33.
- *Hold High Your Heads (History of the Metis Nation in Western Canada)*, by A. H. de Tremaudan p. 202-04.
- *Homeland to Hinterland, The Changing Worlds of the Red River Metis in the Nineteenth Century*, Gerhard J. Ens, p. 39-42.
- *Last Buffalo Hunter, The*, by Norbert Welsh as told to Mary Weekes, p. 56-60.
- *New Peoples, Being and Becoming Metis in North America*, by editors Jacqueline Petersen and Jennifer S. H. Brown, p. 124-25.
- *Other Natives: The Metis, The Vol. I*, Lussier, Antoine S. and Bruce Sealey editors, p.130.
- *Red River Settlement: Its Rise, Progress and Present State with some account of the Native Races and its general History to the Present Day*, by Alexander Ross, p. 101; 242-74.
- *Wanderings of an Artist Among the Indians of North America*, by Paul Kane, p. 89.

Chapter IX

RED RIVER EXPEDITION to the OREGON COUNTRY

One of the most spectacular feats in the history of the Metis people occurred in 1841. In that year a group of families led by their intrepid Metis leader James Sinclair (who is profiled in a later chapter) journeyed overland from the Red River Settlement to the Oregon Country in an attempt to save that disputed territory from being taken over by the Americans. They traveled to this destination by crossing the majestic and lofty Rocky Mountains through passes previously unknown, and never before traversed, except by natives.

The initial seed leading to this epic four month journey was sown in 1803 when Thomas Jefferson was President of the United States. In that year he agreed to Napoleon's offer and approved the Louisiana Purchase from France. Overnight the geographical size of the United States grew immensely by this acquisition of lands lying between the Mississippi River and the Rocky Mountains and stretching from the Gulf of Mexico to Canada.

President Jefferson had a great interest in the West and was keenly intent on learning more about it. He commissioned his private secretary Captain Meriwether Lewis and William Clark to explore the Missouri River and to find a practical and overland route to the Pacific Ocean. He also instructed them to study the flora, fauna, animals, and natives they encountered on their travels.

In May 1804 Lewis and Clark with their Corps of Discovery commenced their unprecedented western journey. When Lewis and Clark arrived at the Mandan Village in North Dakota they hired as guides and interpreters Toussaint Charbonneau (a French-Canadian fur trader whose mother is believed to have been a Sioux Indian) and his teenage wife, the legendary Sacagawea (a full-blooded Shoshone Indian). The Corps included at least three other Metis men - George Drouillard, Pierre Cruzatte, and François La Biche.

During the entire expedition Sacagawea carried her new-born Metis baby, Jean Baptiste Charbonneau (nicknamed Pomp by the Corps) strapped to her back on a cradle-board. She was invaluable to Lewis and Clark in obtaining horses from native tribes, an essential requirement for crossing the mountains.

In his journal entry of October 13, 1805 William Clark wrote:

> The wife of Shabono [sic] our interpreter we find reconsiles [sic] all the Indians, as to our friendly intentions, a woman with a party of men is a token of peace.

As a result of her inestimable services to the Corps of Discovery, statues of Sacagawea have been erected in Oregon and elsewhere to serve as memorials to her. A Washington State Park has been named after her, and not far away is the federal Charbonneau Park next to Lake Sacajawea, as her name is spelled there and as the authors discovered when personally visiting these Parks.

The United States Mint has issued a golden dollar coin in her honor. The representation of Sacagawea on this coin shows her with Pomp on her back.

The Corps of Discovery successfully crossed the Continental Divide and the Rocky Mountains in August of 1805. The Continental Divide, also called the Great Divide, is the spine of the Rocky Mountains and the watershed dividing the waters flowing west from those flowing east.

On the western side of the Rocky Mountains to the Pacific Ocean lay what the Americans then called the Oregon Country. It encompassed the lands stretching from modern-day northern California to just south of present-day Alaska. This area today consists of Oregon, Washington, British Columbia and parts of Idaho and Montana. At the time southern California was Spanish Territory, while Alaska belonged to Russia.

Lewis and Clark with a crew from the Expedition reached the mouth of the Columbia River, where it empties into the Pacific Ocean, on November 18, 1805. Not far from present day Astoria, Oregon they built a fort which they named after the local Clatsop tribe, and they wintered there.

After that winter the Expedition returned east arriving at the Mandan Village on August 14, 1806. Sacagawea, Charbonneau and their Metis baby Pomp remained at the village while the Corps of Discovery returned to St. Louis.

It was in 1806 that David Thompson, a surveyor, explorer and partner with the North West Company (NWC), sought a route west of the mountains with a view to developing fur trading with the Indians in that area, and to establish trading forts on the Pacific slope. He commenced exploration west from the Saskatchewan and Athabasca Rivers through passes over the Rocky Mountains from what is now Alberta into British Columbia.

He not only explored but also charted the lands through which he traveled. For this reason, he was referred to as "the man who looks at stars". In addition he is credited with creating the "batteaux" as a replacement for the birch bark canoe, in areas in the west where birch bark was not readily available.

He crossed the Continental Divide not only with his men, but with his Metis wife Charlotte Small, whose father was Patrick Small of the NWC, and with their three young children. Shortly after, their group reached the Columbia River.

An objective of Thompson was to find a southern trade route to the Pacific Ocean in order that the NWC could develop its fur trade in the lucrative Asian market. Two other NWC explorers, Alexander Mackenzie and Simon Fraser, had previously tried to find the elusive North West Passage to the Pacific. These three extraordinary explorers all had crews that were primarily Metis who assisted and guided them in their ventures.

Alexander Mackenzie's first attempt was in 1789 when he took a wrong fork in the river (that was to be subsequently named after him) and followed it north ending up at the Arctic Ocean. His second attempt was made in 1793 and although he took the correct fork in the river and headed south, he did not actually reach the Pacific Ocean. However he did see it from a distance from King Island at the top of Fitz Hugh Sound, where hostile natives threatened the party causing them to return east.

The other NWC explorer who had searched for this route to the Pacific Ocean was Simon Fraser. He successfully followed a more southern route along the river that now bears his name and arrived at the mouth of the Fraser River in the Gulf of Georgia in 1808. Due to the dangerous rapids along this River it was considered, at that time, not to be an appropriate fur trading route.

After his arrival in the west in 1806, David Thompson spent the next several years surveying and mapping the entire Columbia River. He eventually reached the Pacific Ocean on July 15, 1811.

This was several months after the arrival there of the ship Tonquin, which had sailed around Cape Horn, bearing traders of John Jacob Astor's Pacific Fur Company. Astor's traders had erected a fur trading post there at what is now Astoria, Oregon.

En route to the Pacific in the early part of 1811, Thompson nailed to a tree a document claiming territory including Mount Hood, the Dalles and the Willamette River, for the NWC and Great Britain.

During the time that Thompson was west of the mountains, he built a chain of fur trading posts for the NWC in many of the areas that he explored and surveyed. These included Kootenay House (also known as Kootenae or Kootenai) below Windermere Lake near Invermere, British Columbia in 1806. There is a cairn marking the spot today, as well as a sign reading "Kootenae House, David Thompson Historic Site".

At Invermere in the Windermere Valley (not far from the Columbia River) there has been erected a larger-than-life statue of David Thompson and his Metis wife Charlotte, dressed native-style, with eyes upraised looking towards the mountains.

In 1810 Thompson built Spokane House, a fort near present day Spokane. There is a cairn at this site stating in part "First permanent white settlement in present State of Washington". Thompson also constructed a post near Pend d' Oreille Lake in Idaho as well as other places.

Because of the War of 1812 in which the United States was involved, Fort Astoria was sold to the NWC in 1813. Oregon Country at this time was not under the sovereignty of any nation and, of course, in addition to resident fur traders, there were many native tribes (some unfriendly) who had inhabited it from time immemorial. The term "Oregon" itself is derived from the Amerindian word "ouragan", which means a birchbark dish and was the name that the natives used for the Columbia River.

Because of fur-trading interests and rivalries of both American and British traders, a ten-year treaty of joint occupation of the Oregon Country was entered into in 1818 by the United States and Great Britain. Under the Treaty, members of each of these nations were free to trade there.

However, with respect to British subjects the Hudson's Bay Company (HBC) was granted a trade monopoly in that land by Great Britain. No such monopoly was granted by the American government to any United States group, leaving American free traders to compete against the HBC.

In 1821 the NWC and the HBC merged under the continuing name of the Hudson's Bay Company. This brought the extensive interests and posts which the NWC had cultivated in the Oregon Country and elsewhere under the HBC umbrella. The northern part of the NWC legacy west of the Rocky Mountains was called New Caledonia and the southern part was called the Columbia Department by the HBC.

Three years later the HBC appointed Dr. John McLoughlin, who had been born in Quebec, as the Chief Factor at Fort Vancouver. He was also made Superintendent in charge of the Columbia Department. His responsibility in this capacity was to preside over the vast wilderness of the Oregon Country. In addition he oversaw the construction of the new headquarters of the HBC at Fort Vancouver located on the north side of the Columbia River at present day Vancouver, Washington.

In a message to the American Congress in 1823, President James Monroe announced the Monroe Doctrine. This unilateral declaration stated that the United States would consider as a potentially hostile act any activity by a European nation to intervene in the affairs of the Americas, or to add to its possessions on the American continents. Nevertheless this pronouncement did not prevent the Joint Occupation Treaty of the Oregon Country from being renewed in 1827.

In the 1820s and for two decades thereafter, the American free traders became more aggressive in their search for furs on the western side of the Rockies. The Americans William Ashley, Pierre Chouteau Jr., and John Jacob Astor had an early mutual interest in triumphing over the HBC in the Rocky Mountain area and in the Oregon Country. In the 1820s one of Ashley's parties had found the South Pass through the Rockies from which one could proceed to the Columbia River region. This led to a number of Americans moving to the west.

In 1835 the HBC reacquired the Red River lands from Lord Selkirk's estate. The HBC governor George Simpson soon realized that the influx of American settlers to the Oregon, including the Columbia and Willamette Valleys, would imperil not only the pretensions by the British to the area but also the fur trade of the HBC.

At the time it was believed that the international boundary of the Oregon Country might well be determined by which nation had the most citizens settled and living there. To offset the effect of a number of American wagon trains bearing immigrants to these lands, the HBC knew that countermeasures would have to be taken by the HBC and Great Britain.

Governor Simpson, with the support of HBC headquarters in London, decided to send a group of Red

River residents to settle in the Oregon Country and establish farm communities there. The Puget's Sound Agricultural Company was formed for this purpose. Simpson's first choice for a leader of this trans-mountain expedition was Alexander Ross.

Ross, who lived in the Red River Settlement, had previously been in the service of both the Pacific Fur Company and the HBC in the Columbia River area. He is the same person who wrote about the 1840 buffalo hunt referred to in another chapter of this book. However Ross declined because of his age, requiring Simpson to look for another leader who was up to this momentous task.

Simpson also realized that he could achieve not one but several objectives by arranging for a number of Red River settlers to travel to the Oregon Country. Such an expedition would serve the HBC in a number of ways:

- It would create a larger population of British subjects in the Oregon with a view to enhancing HBC and British claims to the area. At the time the non-native population in the area was less than 500 of whom about 150 were Americans. The Red River Settlers together with the existing HBC population would be a significant majority percentage of the total population.
- It would reduce excess population in the Red River Settlement.
- It would provide an opportunity to arrange for settlers unsympathetic to or competitive with the HBC to leave.

The latter objective was achieved, at least temporarily, by the selection of a prominent Scottish Metis free trader James Sinclair as leader of the Red River Expedition to the Oregon Country. Sinclair, together with Andrew McDermot, was one of the leading private traders and freighters in the Settlement.

By sending Sinclair off to the Oregon, Simpson would be removing one of the HBC's principal competitors. However Simpson also knew that Sinclair was an outstanding individual, a born leader, an intelligent and well-educated person who could take charge and successfully complete the arduous journey that lay ahead. In Governor Simpson's absence, Chief Factor Duncan Finlayson of the HBC at Red River negotiated terms with the proposed emigrants. He also finalized the arrangements for their journey.

No one in the Sinclair party kept a journal of this Expedition. However John Flett, who was a member of the Expedition, wrote an account of it some 44 years after the event. His report appeared in an article in the *Tacoma Daily Ledger Newspaper* of February 18, 1885.

In this report Flett stated that in addition to James Sinclair being named Captain of the venture the terms of the Agreement made by the HBC with the emigrants were to the effect that each family head was to receive £10 sterling in advance, goods for the journey, and horses and provisions at the forts en route.

On arrival at Puget Sound the Company was to furnish them with houses, barns, fenced fields, 15 cows, one bull, 50 ewes, one ram, and oxen or horses, farm implements and seed. In turn, the colonists were to deliver to the Company one-half of their crops yearly for five years and, at the end of that period, one-half of the increase in their flocks.

This arrangement with the settlers meant that they would lease the land from the Company on halves - i.e. they would be required to give the Company half of what they produced. Effectively they would be sharecroppers and not land owners.

Because of the unsettled state of the Oregon Country, the Agreement did not provide that the HBC would sell the lands to the settlers. Although the HBC were occupants of the land and to a large extent governed the trading in this area, under its Charter the HBC did not have title to these lands. As a consequence a crucial element in successful colonization was missing - the right to own the land, to dispose of it or bequeath it was unavailable to the settlers.

These factors undoubtedly caused the proposed

emigrants to have serious concerns with respect to this venture. As a result Finlayson took it upon himself to promise them that when the international border was finalized the HBC would sell the farms outright to the settlers.

This adventurous group, mainly Red River Metis many of whom were rugged buffalo hunters, consisted of 23 families. Many no doubt treasured the prospect of leaving behind the frigid Red River winters for an evergreen land with a mild climate where roses bloomed year-round. Many of the men were known personally by Sinclair. Some had familiarity with farming and livestock, a definite asset for this first attempt by the HBC to settle farmers in the Columbia region.

The party left Fort Garry on June 5, 1841 and met up with additional emigrants at White Horse Plain. In all there were 121 men, women and children, although a plaque erected by the British Columbia Government in 1966 near Radium Hot Springs, BC states that Sinclair "guided 200 Red River settlers" to the Oregon.

Each family had Red River carts and brought along dogs, horses and cows. The women and smaller children rode in the canvas-topped carts, the men and older sons on horses.

The women wore sensible homespun dresses, shawls, with bright head-coverings or neckwear, and moccasins. The men clothed themselves as they did on the buffalo hunt - i.e. buckskin jackets and shirts, homespun pants, and moccasins. They brought along with them capotes and fur robes for the cold mountain passes that they were to encounter.

En route to Edmonton House, some 1500 kilometers distant, they were frequently attacked by swarms of mosquitoes and other insects. They hunted wild fowl and game along the way. These were a welcome change from the pemmican that they had brought with them.

At night they usually slept in or under the Red River carts which had been circled for protection, although some slept under the starry skies on buffalo robes. Sentinels were posted each night to provide for the security of the party.

The journey to the Oregon Country took so long that three babies were born. River crossings were often dangerous particularly the Saskatchewan where the River was sometimes almost a mile wide and the current was very swift. While fording with their carts and belongings on a large raft of dry logs, one family was swept towards the rapids. In a moment of high drama they were saved by their compatriots who threw a rope to them and dragged them to shore.

The Expedition arrived at Fort Carlton in the last week of June. From there on, they had to keep guard night and day for warring Indian tribes. They arrived at Fort Pitt on July 10th and, after resting for a couple of days, they continued on to Edmonton House arriving towards the end of July. They had taken this indirect somewhat circuitous route for safety reasons.

At Edmonton House, Governor Simpson had left specific instructions for James Sinclair (the leader of the Expedition) as to the route that the party was to take to cross the Rockies. Simpson was able to leave these instructions for Sinclair at Fort Edmonton because he himself had been there a number of days earlier while en route to Fort Vancouver on the Columbia River a short distance inland from the Pacific Ocean.

Unlike the Red River Expedition Governor Simpson traveled with the finest horses, express canoes, a number of attendants and no families. As a result his small entourage traveled at a much faster pace.

After receiving Simpson's orders, Sinclair promptly ignored them. He was determined to discover new paths across the formidable mountains, paths that no one other than the natives had previously traversed.

When the cavalcade left Edmonton House it had to wend its way through perilous territory that the Blackfoot, Assiniboine, Peigan, and Cree frequently fought over. John Flett reported that when he and his younger brother had been out hunting they had a hair-raising experience. They found themselves amid unfriendly Indians. They hid out until nightfall and then, with their horses, swam across a frigid river and escaped danger.

After traveling south the Expedition rested at Lake Minnewanka (near present-day Banff). They next reached an area close to what is now Canmore, Alberta and saw the majestic Three Sisters Peaks, below which today an upscale residential and resort development has been built.

After crossing the Bow River they approached the east side of the towering Rocky Mountains, some of them still snow capped. They realized that soon they would have to abandon the Red River carts. The mountainous terrain would have been impassible with the carts.

Their effects were then loaded on the backs of the horses and oxen. The women and children rode on the horses, while the men and older boys walked and climbed the mountainous trails.

With the pack train assembled, the group started on the daunting high-country challenge. What happened next is best described by John Flett in a *Tacoma Daily Ledger* article:

> The oxen, however, were unused to this mode of traveling, and were frightened, and a stampede ensued. Then what a sight, oxen bellowing, kicking, running; horses neighing, rearing, plunging; children squalling; women crying; men swearing, shouting and laughing; while the air seemed full of blankets, kettles, packs of pots, pans and jerked buffalo. At last the cattle were again secured, all our goods that could be found were gathered up, and the remnant repacked and we again started.

Shortly after entering the mountains the Metis guide James Bird left the party. Sinclair had arranged for Mackipictoon (a Cree Chief also called Crooked Arm in reference to his physical deformity) who knew the various mountain passes, to escort them through the towering peaks and beyond. Because of the lofty heights and majestic views, it was a breathtaking experience.

Crooked Arm successfully led them through the

Continental Divide at White Man Pass, not far from the headwaters of the Kootenay River. The party emerged from the Rocky Mountains nine days after they had entered them.

On the west side of the Continental Divide, the exhilarated group followed an old Indian trail and nearby stream southwestward to the Kootenay River. A little further along as they traveled west they came to a wondrous site along the trail. It was a narrow canyon of red rock precipitously carved by nature through the looming mountains.

Four years later in 1845 a Belgian pioneer priest, Father Peter J. De Smet, who was associated with St. Louis University, crossed the Rocky Mountains from west to east. He reached this same site and in his writings described it as:

> .... a narrow mountain defile where the light of day almost vanished from view amidst the huge, bold barriers of colossal rocks.

Wending their way through this confining dark gorge, Sinclair and the Expedition emerged into the Columbia River Valley, into the Great Lone Land of the west. They were at the Kootenai Plain. It should be noted that Kootenay is spelled a number of ways.

The great explorer and map-maker David Thompson wrote of this Plain:

> Here among their stupendous and solitary wilds covered with eternal Snow, and Mountain connected with Mountain by immense glaciers, the collection of Ages and on which the Beams of the Sun makes hardly an impression when aided by the most favorable weather, I stayed fourteen days more ....

In defying Governor Simpson's orders, Sinclair pioneered his own trans-mountain path to the Columbia, a path which was easier going than that dictated by the Little Emperor (Simpson). In fact in a letter dated November 25, 1841 to the HBC headquarters in London, Governor Simpson wrote that the Red River party pursued a pass that was:

> .... not only shorter [than the one Simpson had taken] but better in every respect, so that even with families and encumbered with baggage as they were, they effected the passage of the Mountains with infinitely less labor and in a shorter time than we accomplished it.

The Expedition next traveled south alongside Lakes Windermere and Columbia. Father De Smet wrote that in 1845 he found numerous swans, cormorants, ducks, cranes, and other birds on these Lakes. He also saw salmon spawning and witnessed eagles, coyotes, deer, wild goats, and bears nearby.

The Red River emigrants soon reached Canal Flats. Canal Flats, named McGillivray's Portage by David Thompson in 1808, connected Columbia Lake to the Kootenay River. The Portage was later made a canal by the North West Company prior to its 1821 amalgamation with the HBC.

After leaving Canal Flats the emigrants arrived at and followed the route of the Kootenay River southward. They passed by Moyie Lake and through rich grassy lands until they reached Lake Pend d'Oreille in present day Idaho. In his account of their journey, John Flett told of a horse and a female rider accidentally falling into Lake Pend d'Oreille and being rescued with some difficulty.

The Expedition reached Fort Colvile (now called St. Paul's Mission near Kettle Falls, Washington) on the Columbia River, where they rested and stocked up. Their next destination was Fort Walla Walla (also called Fort Nez Perce) at the junction of the Walla Walla and Columbia Rivers. As much as possible, the authors of this book followed the route of the Red River Expedition and found cairns for the historic Fort Walla Walla at this junction. The Fort was destroyed in the great Columbia River flood of 1890 and is presently under the waters of Lake Wallula. Its location was some 20 miles west of present day Walla Walla, Washington and the military fort of the same name.

The Sinclair party entered Fort Walla Walla on October 4th but the original buildings of this Fort were burned in a fire the very next day. The settlers quickly moved on. It was a wise move since Walla Walla was in an area of hostile Indian tribes who resented the intrusions of the white man and Metis into their native lands and ruthlessly showed it some years later during the Indian Wars.

Heading west along the Columbia River towards their Fort Vancouver destination, the Expedition pushed on past the Dalles and the Cascades. Fort Vancouver was on the north side of the mighty Columbia River across from what is now Portland, Oregon. They finally arrived at the HBC's impressive western headquarters on October 13, 1841. Fort Vancouver, Washington has been reconstructed and today is a United States National Historic Site open to the public.

More than four months after their departure from Red River the Sinclair entourage of men, women and children (including newborn infants) had successfully reached the Oregon Country, their Promised Land. However, they were in for a big shock. Governor Simpson was then at Fort Vancouver. He delivered a crushing message to the adventurous colonizers.

His devastating news was that neither the Company nor Dr. John McLoughlin (the powerful head of the HBC's Columbia District and the Chief Factor of the Fort) were able to honor the glowing promises that the HBC had given the colonizers prior to their leaving Red River. The HBC commitments had enticed them to leave their homes, their friends, and their way of life. Under frequently hazardous conditions, they had traveled half a continent away through uncharted territory to reach a land of broken promises.

Several years earlier McLoughlin had made a suggestion that the HBC send settlers to the Puget Sound area. This fit in with Governor's Simpson's plan of making all the HBC trading posts self-sufficient with respect to produce. Because of HBC bureaucratic red tape, a requirement for authorization from London, and organizational time in Red River, it had taken several years to implement the plan.

During this time McLoughlin had become friendly with

the American settlers who were immigrating to this area overland along the Oregon Trail. His views with respect to the HBC settlers had dampened. He had come to believe that an eventual American takeover of the area was inevitable.

As John Flett wrote in his article the Company failed to provide them with houses, cattle, plows, and other items. This was not their Promised Land after all. After their arduous overland journey, the emigrants were disappointed, dismayed, disheartened and discontented to hear the calamitous news from Governor Simpson.

Simpson did state that some help would be provided to those who went to Fort Nisqually and Cowlitz, and a number took him up on this proposal arriving there in November 1841. However, Dr. McLouglin himself acknowledged that the land at Nisqually was "very indifferent". Its light, sandy soil was not conducive to abundant crops.

Others refused to go to these places and left on their own for the rich farm lands of the Willamette Valley southeast of what today is Portland, Oregon. As well most of those who initially went to Nisqually and Cowlitz abandoned those areas in less than two years to also go to the Willamette Valley. Many descendants of the Red River Expedition live there today. The end result was that due to crop failure and lack of HBC support most of the Red River emigrants dispersed, and contrary to the HBC's plan, eventually became American citizens.

Simpson's early bold design of enhancing British claims to the Oregon Country did not survive. His enthusiasm for an agricultural settlement there faded quickly and in addition wagon trains of Americans started streaming into this area in the early 1840s.

Simpson's change of heart may have been precipitated in part by the 1840s American movement for territorial expansion labeled "Manifest Destiny". This cause was inflamed by British interference in a number of areas such as Texas and California.

In relation to the Oregon Country, Manifest Destiny meant expansion to the Pacific Ocean. In his inaugural address in 1845, President James Polk declared American title to the disputed Oregon Territory to be "clear and unquestionable". An American slogan at the time was 54° 40' or fight.

This may have cowed Great Britain into submission. Its foreign secretary Lord Aberdeen set out to convince (or manipulate) by the use of propaganda the then adverse British public opinion into accepting the preconceived decision of the British government. This decision was to cede to the Americans that part of the disputed territory which today is Oregon, Washington, northern California and the lands east of these States to the Rocky Mountains.

Lord Aberdeen succeeded in his propaganda. This was so not withstanding that an earlier British foreign secretary George Canning had presented a convincing argument for resisting American claims to the area due to Britain's more authoritative claim to this land under international law. Canning also stated that the issue raised a question of British national honor.

An 1846 article from *The Topic* (London) that was reprinted in the *Oregon Historical Quarterly* issue of March/Dec. 1935 advocated the British side of the Oregon situation. This article stated that under doctrines of international law, territorial or sovereign rights could only be acquired by discovery and settlement, conquest or cession. The analysis in the article is convincing and indisputably established the much stronger claims of Britain over that of the Americans to the disputed lands in the Oregon Country.

In effect, Great Britain gave away its superior right to this enormous area of land which it ceded to the United States. Great Britain did so in return for the northern boundary of the United States being set at the 49th parallel. This happened pursuant to the Oregon Treaty of 1846.

Thankfully for Canadians today, the British did not also surrender the land now encompassing British Columbia.

This was probably due to the fact that the British and the HBC needed a shipping port on the Pacific Ocean to service the lucrative Asian market.

After retiring from the HBC in 1846, Dr. John McLoughlin with his Metis wife Marguerite settled in the Willamette Valley in Oregon City, a suburb of present day Portland, Oregon. His house has been designated a National Historic Site. McLoughlin is known as the Father of Oregon, a title conferred on him by the House of Representatives and the Senate of Oregon in 1957, the centennial of his death.

When the HBC reneged on its promises to the Red River emigrants in 1841, James Sinclair was outraged with Governor Simpson and with the deplorable outcome faced by the courageous men, women, and children who had made their monumental and valiant trans-mountain trek. However they were later reconciled.

Notwithstanding the ultimate failure of its prime purpose, the Red River Expedition of 1841 was a stupendous achievement It was a trail-blazing undertaking by a stout-hearted, mostly Metis, people forging their way west close to 2,000 miles under daunting and primitive conditions.

They were spearheaded by a leader par excellence, James Sinclair. This Metis stalwart led the historic mission overland through fair weather and foul, through glorious lands, hazardous back-country, threatening water, hostile tribes, and in some instances uncharted mountainous terrain on which no foot other than that of a native had ever before trod. This Red River Expedition to the Oregon country was truly an adventure of epic proportions.

Chapter Reference Sources

- "British Side of Oregon Question 1846", by Charles H. Carey, *Oregon Historical Quarterly*, March/Dec. 1935, vol. 36, p. 263-294.
- *David Thompson, Fur Trader, Explorer, Geographer,* by James K. Smith, ch. 5.
- "From Red River to the Columbia, the story of a migration", by William J. Betts, *The Beaver*, Spring 1971, p. 50-55.
- *Fur and Gold in the Kootenays,* by Clara Graham, ch. VI; VII, and

VIII.

- *Fur Trade and the Northwest to 1857*, by E. E. Rich, p.278-283.
- *Hudson's Bay Company Archives*, vol. XXII, p. 696-699; vol. XXIX, p. xxxiv-xxxvii; Ref. D.4/111, p. 47-48.
- *Hudson's Bay Company as an Imperial Factor 1821 -1869,* by John S. Galbraith, ch. 9; 10.
- *Lewis & Clark, Legacies, Memories, and New Perspectives*, editors Chris Fresonke and Mark Spence, p. 75; 99; 184.
- *Lifeline of the Oregon Country, The Fraser-Columbia Brigade System, 1811-1847*, by James R. Gibson, p. 4-5; 102-03.
- *Manifest Destiny and Mission in American History*, by Frederick Merk, *passim*.
- *North West Company*, by Marjorie Wilkins Campbell, ch. VIII.
- "Routes Through the Rockies", by Irene M. Spry, *The Beaver*, Winter 1960, p. 26-39.
- "Sketch of the immigration from Selkirk's Settlement to Puget Sound in 1841, A", by John Flett, *Tacoma Daily Ledger*, Feb. 18, 1885.
- *West of the Mountains, James Sinclair and the Hudson's Bay Company*, by D. Geneva Lent, *passim*.

Chapter X

FREE TRADE and the SAYER TRIAL

As time progressed after the 1821 merger of the North West Company and the Hudson's Bay Company (HBC), the Metis found the monopolistic practices and enforcement tactics of the HBC and their undemocratically appointed Council aggravating and vexatious. They became increasingly discontented with the manner in which they were governed and with the exclusive right and authority of the HBC over the fur and pemmican trade.

The Metis wanted the freedom to follow the way of life that they felt entitled to as native-born inhabitants of the west. They knew that the HBC's domineering practices were directed by a group of men from a foreign nation far across the Atlantic Ocean, who had little knowledge of the Metis or their culture.

At first a number of Metis fur traders and entrepreneurs ignored the HBC monopoly. They acquired furs and robes directly from the Indians and transported them to northern areas of the United States, such as St. Paul, to trade them for money or goods. The HBC was not concerned if colonists obtained furs and other items for their own use, but balked at their trafficking in them with third parties.

The smuggling continued, spurred by the fur trading post that had been established at Pembina in 1844 by the trader Norman Kittson, who worked for the American Fur Company owned by John Jacob Astor. The situation was aggravated by the fact that HBC prices were unduly low compared to those paid by the United States traders and merchants.

During this period the Metis, both French and English, were pressing for rights and remedies. In 1845, two dozen Metis (including Alexis Goulet, the author George Goulet's great grandfather) submitted a series of questions to the Governor and Chief Factor with respect to their rights.

The following year further documents (one in French

and one in English) were prepared by the Metis in which they petitioned for representative government and free trade. They were taken to England by the Metis leader, James Sinclair (who was a prominent free trader and the same person who led the 1841 Red River Expedition to the Oregon Country). A Scottish Metis Alexander Kennedy Isbister, who resided in London where he became a lawyer, presented the 1846 petitions to the English Government which failed to take any action.

In an attempt to stop what they considered to be illicit trading, the HBC:

- checked the settler's mail;
- searched Metis homes;
- seized furs from trains of Red River carts that were traveling to and from Pembina and St. Paul;
- penalized those who breached its monopoly;
- imposed an import duty on American products; and
- through Governor Simpson requested that the Catholic Church withdraw Father Belcourt from the Red River area for his participation in drafting the 1846 Metis petition.

These measures ultimately failed to suppress the Metis trading in breach of the HBC's monopoly. In 1846 a regiment had been sent to Red River at the request of Governor Simpson. They had been sent allegedly because of Simpson's concerns over the Oregon boundary dispute, but in reality over the mounting unrest in the Colony. During the regiment's occupation, martial law was effectively imposed.

In 1848, this Imperial regiment withdrew from the Colony. They were replaced by the Chelsea Pensioners, who proved to be nothing more than an unruly and undisciplined tiger without teeth.

Unrest in the Colony came to a head in 1849 with the laying of charges against four Metis men for illegally trafficking in furs. These men were Pierre Guillaume

Sayer, Andre Goulet, Hector McGinnis, and Norbert Laronde. Led by the "miller of the Seine", Jean-Louis Riel (father of Louis Riel, who was not yet five years old), a committee of Metis was set up to respond to these charges.

Jean-Louis Riel traveled to Pembina to discuss the matter with Father Georges Antoine Belcourt. Father Belcourt had previously been the pastor at a mission at Baie-St. Paul on the White Horse Plain. His pro-Metis activities landed him in trouble with Governor Simpson and Bishop Provencher.

It was Belcourt who had urged the Metis to draw up the 1846 petition that Alexander Kennedy Isbister presented to the Government in the United Kingdom. He also accompanied the Metis on buffalo hunts, rather than encouraging them to settle down as Bishop Provencher preferred.

Father Belcourt was eased, or pushed out, of his mission at Baie-St. Paul, and in turn in 1847 he established one at Pembina, beyond the jurisdiction of Simpson and Provencher. He ministered to the Indian, Metis and white people in Pembina and St. Joseph for the next eleven years. In 1859 he moved to Rustico, Prince Edward Island to be the priest of St. Augustine Parish. While serving in that capacity he established the Farmer's Bank of Rustico, a predecessor of the Credit Union movement in Canada.

The clergy in the West generally both Catholic and Protestant did not favor the semi-nomadic pursuits of those Metis, whether French or English, who followed this type of lifestyle. Many clergy, witless or unfamiliar with that life, felt that it was one of indolence. They would have much preferred the Metis to follow an agricultural, sedentary livelihood where the clergy could inculcate "civilizing and Christian" values in them. However this way of life held no appeal for many of the Metis.

The contemporary writer Alexander Ross pointed out:

> They [half-breeds] take no delight in cultivating the soil. Their thoughts, their ideas, their energies are all limited to buffalo-hunting, fiddling, and horse-racing.

With respect to the charges against Sayer and the others, another leader of the Metis protest was James Sinclair (who had taken the 1846 petition to London). Sinclair and Andrew McDermot (an Irishman) were the two most prominent private traders and freighters in the Red River Settlement. They had also run into trouble with the HBC.

The Sayer trial was to proceed first. Shortly before it was to commence, a formidable assembly of hundreds of armed Metis convened at St. Boniface Cathedral. The Cathedral was on the opposite side of the Red River from the HBC post of Fort Garry at the Forks.

It was there that Jean-Louis Riel made a stirring speech to the assembled Metis. The aroused group then crossed the Red River with their rifles and congregated in front of the courthouse where Recorder Adam Thom was to preside over the high-sounding General Quarterly Court of Assiniboia.

Alexander Ross wrote of Thom:

> People said that he possessed the gift of twisting and untwisting his interpretations, so as always to fit his own cause. .... the more diligently he showed that he could split hairs, the more readily did the many believe that he would split them whether they needed splitting or not.

Ross also wrote that the "multitude" was inspired "with a notion that Mr. Thom could turn black into white and white into black".

The Metis were justifiably suspicious of Thom and his anti-Metis bias. Ross wrote a detailed summary of what he termed a "mock trial". Not long after Sayer's trial, Thom lost his position as Recorder of Rupert's Land.

In the trial itself James Sinclair, styled by many at the time as Chief of the Half-Breeds, acted as Sayer's counsel. According to a report of the trial in the *Western Law Times*:

> On the defendant being called to answer the charge against him a considerable time elapsed before he could be found .... but in place of the defendant coming to the bar of the court, James Sinclair, Peter Garrioch and many others presented themselves as Delegates from a great number of armed Half-

> Breeds who were outside the court.

When Recorder Thom asked them in what capacity they appeared, Sinclair answered "As delegates of the people." The Recorder replied that they could not act in the court in that capacity. Sinclair then argued before the court that there was great doubt as to the validity of the HBC's Charter, which purportedly gave that Company the exclusive right of trade. This argument was not accepted, but the court did agree that Sinclair could plead on behalf of Sayer as his counsel.

One of the witnesses for Sayer was Alexis Goulet, a prominent trader. He stated he had bought a horse from Chief Factor Harriott. In his testimony Goulet said that he told Harriott that he would pay him with furs.

The only direct evidence against Sayer was that given by his son Louison, who testified that his father had traded furs. As Alexander Ross, who was one of the members of the court presiding over the Case, later wrote of Louison's testimony:

> .... the defendant's son, who, under the stern injunction of one parent, told the whole truth, without any attempt at delay or equivocation .... In what court of England or Scotland could the moral beauty of this scene have been surpassed?

Sayer stated in his testimony that Harriott advanced him credit in the winter and forbade him from trading with Indians but said nothing about Half-Breeds. This evidence was disputed by Governor and Chief Factor John Ballenden, but not by Harriott who was not called as a witness.

Sayer was found guilty but the jury recommended mercy. Ballenden, aware of the menacing armed Metis presence looming outside the walls of the courtroom, realized that prudence was the better part of valor. He told Recorder Thom that he was contented with the verdict, asked that there be no punishment imposed on Sayer, and further asked that the charges against the other three accused be abandoned. Recorder Thom followed these instructions.

When Sayer and the others left the courthouse as free men the assembled Metis immediately concluded that failure to pass sentence on him, as well as the charges against the other three Metis being dropped, meant that henceforth trade would be free.

They were electrified and erupted in glee, firing their rifles in the air. Amidst this jubilation arose a shout from Jean-Louis Riel "Le Commerce est Libre. Vivé la Liberté" (Trade is Free. Long Live Freedom). The monopoly of the Company of Adventurers, the Hudson's Bay Company, which had no means of enforcing it, had been effectively broken. It was the end of an epoch - the HBC trade monopoly. Henceforth, trade would be free.

After the trial, the Governor of Assiniboia W. B. Caldwell wrote Chief Factor Donald Ross stating:

> About nine o'clock this morning May 17, 1849, the French-Canadians and half-breeds, all armed and from every quarter, began to assemble at Fort Garry, giving revolutionary indications. The immediate cause of this demonstration was to prevent the punishment of certain persons who, including one man by the name of Sayer, had been arrested for illicit trafficking in furs with the natives.

In that letter Caldwell also wrote:

> Had it not been for the calm conduct of Mr. Sinclair and the influence of Mr. Macallum and Pascal Breland, the half-breeds would have rushed. Some of them came right into the courtroom, with their powder horns on and gun covers dangling from their belts. Some even sat in the jury box with powder and shot pouches on.

In writing about the trial, Alexander Ross stated:

> The half-breeds of the country, considering [sic] and always have considered that they have a right as natives of the soil to trade, traffic and barter furs among themselves and also from the Indians ....

After this trial, the trade with Pembina, St. Paul and the Upper Missouri grew. Many more Metis freeman traders emerged in addition to those such as James Sinclair, his nephew Peter Garrioch, Pascal Breland, Andrew McDermot, and the four men who had been charged with illegal trafficking.

In due course, many hundred of Red River carts would travel annually along the Crow Wing Trail over 1,000 kilometers to St. Paul to sell or barter various goods. For example 1,400 carts made the trip to St. Paul in 1865. The carts carried with them furs, pemmican, buffalo robes and hides, tallow, and leather goods such as saddles, embroidered coats and moccasins.

The Metis actions at the Sayer trial had brought about free trade with the United States nearly one and one-half centuries prior to the implementation of a Free Trade Agreement between the Canadian Government and the United States Government.

While their longing for a representative government of which they would be a part would have to wait for another day, the paramilitary supremacy of the Metis buffalo hunters had prevailed. They had successfully defied the HBC trade monopoly and the Government of Assiniboia and had victoriously championed the right of the Metis to free trade.

Events outlined in this chapter, such as the petitions of 1845 and 1846 and the Sayer Trial, together with other events such as the 1841 Red River Expedition to the Oregon Country, evidence the significant cooperation between the English and French speaking Metis. At this time there was interaction, not enmity, between them, many of whom were friends and over the years many of their members had intermarried. These efforts had united them in a common cause.

The concerted and triumphant political action of the Metis who participated in the Sayer trial reinvigorated their sense of collective identity as a people, their sense of being a "New Nation".

Chapter Reference Sources

- *Cuthbert Grant of Grantown*, by Margaret Arnett MacLeod and W. L. Morton, 131; 134-137.
- *Four Recorders of Rupert's Land*, by Roy St. George Stubbs, p. 26-30.
- *Fur Trade and the Northwest to 1857*, by E. E. Rich, p. 265-66.

- *History of the Canadian West, A,* by Arthur S. Morton, p. 814-17.
- *Hudson's Bay Record Society,* Vol. XIX, p. lxxxii-lxxxiii; xc-xcvii.
- *Manitoba A History,* by W. L. Morton, p. 74-78.
- *Metis in the Canadian West, The,* Vol. II by Marcel Giraud, p. 239.
- *New Peoples, Being and Becoming Metis in North America, The,* editors, Jacqueline Peterson and Jennifer S. H. Brown, p. 108-13.
- *Prairie West to 1905, The,* general editor Lewis G. Thomas, p. 56-58.
- Provincial Archives of Manitoba, Ref. No. M389-MG2 B4; Ref. Box 1361, File A52-53(AM-P 1361).
- *Red River Settlement, Its Rise, Progress and Present State, The,* by Alexander Ross, p. 372-86.
- *West of the Mountains: James Sinclair and the Hudson's Bay Company,* by D. Geneva Lent, ch. X.
- *Western Law Times, The,* Vol. 2, 1891, p. 12-15.

Chapter XI

BATTLE of the GRAND COTEAU

The most astounding and dramatic military triumph in Metis history is the relatively unknown Battle of the Grand Coteau. This epic event in the annals of the Metis people pitted an overwhelming force of Sioux warriors against a gallant but heavily undermanned group of Metis. This conflict occurred in July 1851 while the Metis were on a buffalo hunt.

The Metis had set out on a peaceful hunt for the shaggy-haired denizen of the North American plains. Since they would be traveling into the territory of the unfriendly Sioux Indians, who wanted the buffalo for themselves, they knew in advance that it was essential to be prepared for any unforeseen combat.

The Sioux were ferocious adversaries in battle. Alexander Ross in his 1856 book about the Red River Settlement wrote:

> The Sioux are a bold and numerous race, whose very name has been the terror of every other nation .... War is their profession; horses, guns, and hunting, their delight.

This summer Metis hunting venture was made up of three different brigades - from St. Boniface, Pembina, and the White Horse Plain (St. François Xavier). In June 1851 the St. Boniface group, accompanied by Father Albert Lacombe, left the Red River area to meet up with the Pembina group.

These two bands, which included women and children, numbered about 1,300 people of whom about 315 were hunters. There were over 1,000 Red River carts as well as horses, oxen and dogs. The two parties then headed west from Pembina to rendezvous with their brethren from the White Horse Plain at a point in what is now northern North Dakota.

Since they were going to hunt in the Grand Coteau area,

this rendezvous was held so that the three brigades could plan on providing each other with mutual help and protection if the Sioux should attack one of the brigades hunting at a distance from the others. There was no love lost between the Sioux and the Metis (whose mothers were primarily Cree and Ojibway) and in addition the Sioux looked on the Grand Coteau as their historical stomping grounds.

Initially all parties hunted in proximity to one another, but towards the end of June the White Horse Plain group parted company from the others. There is speculation that the White Horse Plain Metis, from the Grantown area, may have left to hunt on their own because the Metis from the other groups were still unhappy at Cuthbert Grant's sympathy (as warden and magistrate of Assiniboia) towards upholding the monopoly of the HBC during the Sayer Trial.

The White Horse Plain group arrived at the eastern ridge of the Grand Coteau (also known as the Coteau du Missouri) on July 12, 1851. The word "coteau" is derived from the French language. It is elevated land such as a butte, a plateau, or a divide between valleys. The Grand Coteau is extensive and extends over many kilometers. The eastern ridge of the Coteau is a long escarpment signaling the second steppe of the North American plains. The White Horse Plain group consisted of only 67 hunters and an indeterminate number of women and children.

Although the Grand Coteau was in Sioux territory, it is not known exactly where the Metis encountered them on this hunt. It may have been a short distance south of present day Minot, North Dakota.

Five Metis scouts discovered that there was a huge encampment numbering between 2,000 and 2,500 Sioux not far away from their own camp on the Coteau. They immediately alerted their group and throwing caution to the winds they approached the Sioux, presumably to parley. The scouts were taken hostage, but two of them were able to escape and fled on their speedy steeds back to their Metis camp.

When they reached the safety of their camp, they found that hasty preparations were being made under the Chief of the Hunt Jean Baptiste Falcon (son of the Metis minstrel Pierre Falcon). Under his leadership, they were taking measures to defend themselves against the attack that they knew was imminent.

The Red River carts had been formed into a circle, axle to axle, and slightly angled up from the ground. The shafts were pointed outwards like spears. Poles were shoved through the wheels of all the carts to ensure their immobility and to make penetration by the enemy formidably difficult.

Pemmican and other supplies were placed between the carts to fill the gaps and fortify the hastily assembled bulwark. Rifle pits were dug by the men in front of the carts to provide the hunters with protection while sniping at their attackers. Meanwhile trenches were dug under the carts by the women and children to provide them with shelter, and the livestock were placed inside the circle. The Metis had literally “circled the wagons”.

A number of Sioux approached the Metis barricade stating that they would release the remaining three prisoners the following day, and indicated they would like to receive something in return, presumably a peace offering. The Metis did not believe them. Metis riflemen would not allow a subsequent Sioux delegation to come near their bulwark. The Metis were determined to conceal from the Sioux the military preparations they had made in their makeshift fort.

That night (in which an eclipse of the moon occurred) an attempt was made by the Metis to furtively dispatch scouts to the St. Boniface and Pembina hunting parties to ask them to urgently come to their assistance. These scouts were seen, but sometime later two other Metis were able to elude the Sioux and make it to the other brigades.

The next day July 13th while Father Louis Laflêche (the priest from the White Horse Plain who was accompanying them) was administering the sacraments, the Metis scouts warned that a multitude of Sioux warriors were rapidly approaching. Thirty armed Metis huntsmen road out to meet the lead band of oncoming Sioux, offering them gifts and asking them to turn back. The Sioux refused and, as they continued to approach, the Metis scouts raced back to their camp, corralled their horses, and jumped into their rifle pits.

The remaining three Metis captives of the Sioux made a break for freedom. Two were successful; the third Jean Baptiste Malaterre, who was riding a slower horse, was unable to make it to safety. His dismembered body was later found with three bullet holes and 67 seven arrows in it.

The Indians, painted and decked out for war, did not charge the Metis fortification en masse. Undoubtedly this would have seen the Metis ramparts breached. Instead the Sioux used hit and run tactics, firing off bullets and launching countless arrows at their low-lying, well-protected opponents. This method of attack, which they repeated after an initial fallback, was a failure. In the meantime the Metis sharpshooters picked off a number of Sioux, while the Metis women and older children continually reloaded the rifles.

During the attacks by the Sioux Father Laflêche urged on the Metis. He went among the carts with a crucifix raised in his hand, energizing the Metis hunters and soothing the children. His bravery played a part in discouraging the Sioux. His staunch spirit (together with the eclipse of the moon the night before and a sudden thunderstorm that day) made the Sioux believe that the Metis were supported by a Manitou, a supernatural being.

Among the 77 riflemen, which now included the teenage boys, was not only the senior Isadore Dumont but also his two sons 17 year old Isadore and 13 year old Gabriel. Young Gabriel was destined to become the great military leader of the Metis during the North-West Uprising of 1885 over 40 years later. Many of the lessons he learned at the Battle of the Grand Coteau, particularly the effectiveness of the rifle pits, he later used during that Uprising. Gabriel Dumont is profiled in a later chapter of this book.

The Sioux onslaught on the first day of the Battle continued for six hours until a heavy downpour, coupled with their losses, caused them to withdraw. However they continued to whoop and shout all night long, indicating that they were not yet done with the Metis.

Before sun-up the next morning (July 14th) and the return of the Sioux, the Metis decided to make a run for safety to the other Metis parties some 25 or 30 miles away. Sentries were dispatched to watch for the approach of the native warriors, while the Red River carts were hastily readied, after which they quickly departed.

However, it was not long into their flight before their sentinels warned them that the Sioux were in hot pursuit. The same procedures of circling the wagons, as they had used the day before, was quickly implemented by the Metis.

The Sioux charged, again using their hit and run technique. This method of attack was of no value against the fortified barrier of the Metis and their rifle power. The Metis marksmen were deadly accurate with their rifles, and continued to gun down their opponents while suffering no casualties themselves, except for some livestock.

After five hours of attack on this second day, the Sioux had sustained enough carnage. In a gesture of peace, a chief approached and conceded victory to the Metis.

The Sioux retreated just as another torrential downpour erupted. Almost immediately after, a large group of Metis hunters from the Red River and Pembina parties belatedly galloped on to the scene. It was decided not to pursue and seek revenge from the unsuccessful native adversaries, but to carry on with the buffalo hunt.

The exact number of Sioux casualties is not known, but has been estimated at 80 killed, numerous wounded, and the loss of dozens of their horses. They had been emphatically repulsed. This Battle, resulting in both bloodshed and a watershed, forever ended warfare between the Sioux and the Metis. This triumph made the Metis the undisputed Lords of these Plains and of the buffalo herds in this and the nearby Turtle Mountain areas.

Astonishingly, the Metis did not lose one man, woman or child during the lengthy onslaughts. However several were wounded and a number of their horses and oxen were killed and the unfortunate Malaterre had been killed by the Sioux before the battle started.

The results of Metis fighting skills against the Sioux may be compared with what happened at the Battle of Little Big Horn in Montana just 25 years later. In that Battle the United States Army and its cavalry, under the command of General George Custer, attacked the Sioux led by Chief Sitting Bull, the most feared Aboriginal brave in North America. The renowned Indian Chief Crazy Horse, who played a significant role in this Battle, was with Sitting Bull.

The Sioux opposed the United States order of 1875 to compel them to settle on reservations. They fought for their home and native land against General Custer's army and completely annihilated him and his soldiers in this Battle of the Little Big Horn in 1876.

To escape retribution from the Americans, Sitting Bull and thousands of Sioux fled to the Wood Mountain area in southwest Saskatchewan. Although the nearby resident inspector of the North West Mounted Police, James Walsh, befriended Sitting Bull, the Canadian Government was not sympathetic and he and most of his fellow natives returned to the United States in 1881.

Margaret MacLeod and the noted historian Professor W. L. Morton, in writing of the Battle of the Grand Coteau in their book *Cuthbert Grant of Grantown*, stated that Metis battle tactics "were brilliant by any standard of warfare"; that it was "perhaps the proudest memory of the Metis nation"; and it "symbolized their highest endeavour as a people"; and added it was "the apex of the Metis nation, their supreme achievement as a people".

The Metis who fought for their lives at the historic Battle of the Grand Coteau figuratively wore badges of honor and courage. Their valiant actions in this dramatic conflict were an accomplishment par excellence and vividly exemplified the fighting spirit of this unique people.

Chapter Reference Sources

- *Cuthbert Grant of Grantown, Warden of the Plains,* by Margaret Arnett MacLeod and W. L. Morton, p. 142-151.
- *Father Lacombe,* by James A. MacGregor, p. 46-53.
- *Gabriel Dumont,* by George Woodcock, p. 55-62.
- *Lord of the Plains,* by Alfred Silver, ch. 2.
- Provincial Archives of Manitoba, Ref. No. M389-MG2 B4; Ref. Box 1361, File A52-53(AM-P 1361).
- "Blood on the prairie" by Bill Redekop, *The Winnipeg Free Press,* Nov. 4, 2001, p. B1.

Chapter XII

THE RED RIVER RESISTANCE

The Metis reached the pinnacle of their political power and recognition as a unique people - a "New Nation" - in the Red River Resistance of 1869-70. The Resistance was not a 'rebellion' against the Government of Canada. At the time it occurred the Red River Settlement was a part of Rupert's Land, not a part of Canada. Canada then had no legal jurisdiction or authority over Rupert's Land or its peoples.

Prior to the Resistance the creation of Canada had occurred in 1867 pursuant to the *British North America Act*. This Act only united the two Provinces of Canada (which became Ontario and Quebec), Nova Scotia and New Brunswick into a Confederation of four provinces. It established a federal government of which John A. Macdonald became the first prime minister.

The Metis Resistance movement had its antecedents in a campaign to annex Rupert's Land to Canada. That campaign originated in the Toronto and Ottawa valley areas in the mid-1850s, and continued into the 1860s. Under a Royal Charter issued on May 2, 1670, King Charles granted Rupert's Land to the Hudson's Bay Company (HBC) which was led by his cousin Prince Rupert.

This gigantic grant comprised lands in the Hudson Bay drainage system. It roughly encompassed much of the modern day Prairie Provinces (Manitoba, Saskatchewan and Alberta), northern areas of Ontario and Quebec, the southern Northwest Territories, and part of Nunavut. This land mass equaled in total about 40 per cent of modern day Canada. It also originally included uncharted parts of the United States such as northern Minnesota, North Dakota and Montana before they became part of the United States. Rupert's Land is sometimes referred to herein as the North-West (indicative of those lands which later became part of Canada).

The instigators of the movement in the 1850s to annex

Rupert's Land to Canada were primarily English-speaking Anglo-Saxon Protestants, many of whom were Orangemen. At the time the remaining undeveloped arable land in Upper Canada was minimal, due to the Canadian Shield.

The expansionists in Canada saw Rupert's Land, with the North-West, as a *lebensraum* - as a golden opportunity to enlarge their hinterland and extend their commercial frontiers. They also saw it as a pathway to the Pacific Ocean and from there a gateway to the riches of the Orient. They were inspired by a sense of being a part of the British Empire, of an imperial community. They wished to populate the West with agricultural settlers who adhered to the same British values and British traditions that they themselves observed. The expansionist movement to annex Rupert's Land to Canada was fueled principally by Toronto and Upper Canada, not by the inhabitants of the West.

However this aspiration would require a transcontinental railway and immigrants to the North-West to build the infrastructure for the railroad and to settle there. To attract settlers it was essential that the prevailing image in Upper Canada of the North-West as that of a cold, sub-arctic wilderness, suitable only for the fur trade, be transformed.

The North-West had to be mentally metamorphosed into that of a fertile land capable of producing abundant crops in climatic conditions which, while on the brisk side in winter, were generally salubrious and refreshing. It was necessary to create the notion of an agricultural "fertile belt" in the West. This would have the added advantage in the expansionists' minds of developing a settlement base for further movement west to the Pacific Ocean.

Another necessary step was to attack the HBC's monopoly on government and trade in Rupert's Land. The expansionists campaigned on all fronts:

- to change the perception of the North-West from a barren harsh wilderness into a plenteous land suitable for farming and settlement in a healthy climate;

- to lobby the federal government for a transcontinental railway to the Pacific;
- to portray the HBC as a monopolistic oligarchy whose interest was protection of its fur trade monopoly even at the expense of thwarting expansion of the British Empire into the North-West; and
- to push for annexation of Rupert's Land by Canada.

Proponents of annexation equated it with nationalism and imperialism. They saw the West for what it could do for them and for Canada in the future and they saw the Red River Settlement as the home base for spreading westward.

The annexationists had little consideration or concern for the Metis, the Indians, or the heritage, culture and lifestyle of these inhabitants of the prairie plains, particularly those in the area of the Red River Settlement. One of their main thoughts was about the grand future that would result from the civilizing and other benefits their western intrusion in the name of imperial progress would bring to the Indians and to the Metis. A cultural kismet of Ontario and British values would descend on Rupert's Land when it became part of Canada.

The Canadian mercantile interests also witnessed the prosperity that had accrued in the United States as a result of its western frontier expansion and settlement. Completion of the railway and large-scale immigration increased Minnesota's population by 30 times in the 1850s.

Canada also perceived that with construction of a railway to the west accompanied by an abundance of immigrants who would settle in and cultivate the western lands, the North-West would not only create additional markets for Canadian products, but would protect the West from being absorbed by the United States. In the West wheat would become the chief commodity in place of furs and buffalo. This scheme would require settlement and an agricultural plan and, in due course, private land ownership in the West.

In pursuit of these objectives a large group of

newcomers, primarily Anglo-Saxon Protestants, came from the East to the Red River Settlement in the 1860s and a few years earlier. Some of them styled themselves the "Canadian Party" and staunchly supported the annexation by Canada of Rupert's Land (of which the Settlement was a part). They also vehemently opposed the control of the local government by the HBC.

The leader of the Canadian Party was John Christian Schultz, an Ontarian by birth. The renowned Manitoba historian W. L. Morton suggested in his book *Manitoba, A History* that the Canadian Party "was in fact John Schultz and such Canadians as were under his influence at any given time".

Schultz had forsaken the medical profession and arrived in the Settlement about 1860. He was an Orangeman - headstrong antagonists of the 'Papists' (Roman Catholics), harshly anti-Metis, and vigorously anti-HBC. Professor Morton also noted that Roderick Campbell (an acquaintance of Schultz) said that in Schultz:

> Fate had manufactured a scoundrel out of material meant by Nature for a gentleman.

A similar assessment of this obnoxious individual was made by Professor Arthur S. Morton in his book *History of the Canadian West* in the following statement:

> Grasping by nature and utterly unscrupulous, he followed a policy which was not simply purely personal, but mean.

In 1865 Schultz acquired ownership of the Nor-Wester, a newspaper in the Red River Settlement. This organ was used by him to push his annexation agenda.

After Confederation in 1867 more voices were added to the push for western expansion. In 1868 a Canada First movement was founded, led by the Ontarian Charles Mair, who had recently arrived in the Settlement and who soon married Schultz's niece. The movement espoused Anglo-Saxon imperialistic views, pushed for extensive immigration from Ontario, and looked down on the French Catholic Metis with whom they would have no truck, nor trade. There was unrest in the Settlement in large part due to the opposing views of the annexationists and those, not keen on annexation by Canada, who did not know what the future held.

By the late 1860s nationalism and expansionism had become intertwined. An ardent Canadian nationalist, Thomas D'Arcy McGee, said in 1868 that "the future of the Dominion depends on our early occupation of the rich prairie land." This sentiment was not uncommon in Canada.

Some months after Confederation William McDougall, Minister of the Interior in John A. Macdonald's Canadian government and a leading proselytizer of national expansion, had tabled resolutions in the House of Commons which led to the request to Britain to transfer the HBC lands to Canada. Shortly after that, the Canadian Government entered into serious negotiations with the British Colonial office concerning acquisition of Rupert's Land from the HBC.

In July of 1868, the British Parliament passed the *Rupert's Land Act* to authorize the surrender of the HBC lands and privileges and to transfer them to Canada. After much negotiation in England involving Canadian delegates, including William McDougall, terms of transfer were settled in April 1869. There included a payment to the HBC of £300,000, extensive land grants to the HBC, and other matters. The official transfer was to occur on December 1, 1869.

However no one, especially McDougall, had thought to discuss the terms of transfer with the inhabitants of the West. As Professor W. L. Morton wrote:

> One of the greatest transfers of territory and sovereignty in history was conducted as a mere transaction in real estate.

Lands which many of the Red River inhabitants had previously purchased from the HBC, and which the HBC no longer had a right to, were included in the lands being sold by the HBC to Canada.

Without consultation with or warning to the

inhabitants, a Canadian survey party commissioned by William McDougall appeared in the Red River area in August 1869. At that time Canada had no legal right to make surveys there since the Settlement and the North-West were not then part of Canada.

Under John Stoughton Dennis (whom the notorious Schultz befriended), the survey followed the American system of dividing the lands into rectangular townships. This system was contrary to the narrow river-front lots occupied and worked by the Metis, who also enjoyed water rights and land stretching back several miles from the river, the back part of which was for hay privileges for livestock.

Matters came to a head when on October 1, 1869 a Canadian crew ran the survey lines across André Nault's hay privilege. When the surveyors refused to leave the land Nault (a Metis who could not speak English) contacted the fluently bilingual Louis Riel, who is profiled in another chapter of this book. After a verbal altercation with the surveyors, during which Riel stepped on their survey chain, Riel with a group of Metis peacefully but firmly made the trespassers desist and withdraw. This was the start of the Red River Resistance (also called by some a Rebellion).

Only a couple of weeks prior to the Nault incident, settlers in the Red River had learned through the public press that the HBC intended to transfer Rupert's Land to Canada on December 1, 1869, and that the undiplomatic Minister of the Interior (William McDougall) would be appointed Lieutenant Governor.

In a letter to Prime Minister Macdonald of November 13, 1869 the infamous McDougall branded the Metis as "semi-savages and serfs of yesterday". In December 1869 Prime Minister Macdonald referred to the Metis as "miserable half-breeds" and a few weeks later he referred to them as "wild people".

Neither John A. Macdonald nor the HBC consulted or discussed terms of takeover with the local inhabitants.

Macdonald's drive for Canadian ownership of Rupert's Land was accompanied by his disregard for humanitarian concerns of the people who were resident there, a neglect he was to repeat in relationship to settlers' grievances in Saskatchewan prior to the 1885 North-West Uprising that is discussed in another chapter of this book.

Several days after the Nault confrontation, the Metis formed a National Committee with the soon-to-be twenty-five year old Riel as secretary. The Committee was opposed to the unilateral infliction on the community of a Lieutenant Governor with almost despotic powers. Riel made clear that access to the Settlement by McDougall would be prevented unless Canada conferred with the representatives of the Settlement on the terms of the takeover.

On November 2, 1869, true to their word, the Metis on ascertaining that McDougall had crossed the United States border forced him to re-cross the border back into the United States. On the same day a number of Metis under Riel's leadership took control of Fort Garry. This was the HBC's fort in the heart of the Red River Settlement at the junction of the Red and the Assiniboine Rivers. No blood was shed.

Several meetings of English and French speaking inhabitants were held in November. At one meeting Riel told the delegates that a provisional government should be formed "for our protection and to treat with Canada" on terms of union, but that was not done at this meeting.

On December 1 (the day that Rupert's Land was originally to be taken over by Canada), Riel tabled before a meeting of English and Metis delegates a List of Rights. The List set forth terms which Riel and other delegates wanted Canada to accept. This document in effect claimed rights of self-government and control over their local affairs. Its terms called for a local legislature and elections, free homesteads, public lands for schools, use of French and English in the legislature and the courts, Indian treaties, Parliamentary representation, and other matters.

On that very same day, December 1, 1869 (the day that Canada was originally supposed to annex Rupert's Land), Lieutenant Governor designate William McDougall was waiting impatiently in Pembina across the United States Border. Without having received official documents confirming the takeover and not knowing that Macdonald had postponed it, the xenophobic McDougall took it upon himself to draft and issue a proclamation to which he forged the Queen's name.

This falsified document proclaimed that the North-West was now part of Canada and that he was officially the Lieutenant Governor. He stepped across the border and, in bone-chilling cold and snowy weather, he read the fake proclamation to the inhumane elements after which he hied himself back across the border to Pembina. However besides being asinine and comical, McDougall's acts were illegal. They had a most significant effect as well. The Prime Minister, John A. Macdonald, had written a letter dated November 27, 1869 to McDougall reading in part:

> An assumption of the Government by you, of course, puts an end to that of the Hudson's Bay Company's authorities, and Governor McTavish [sic] and his Council would be deprived even of the semblance of legal right to interfere. There would then be, if you were not admitted into the Country, no legal government existing and anarchy must follow. In such a case, no matter how the anarchy was produced, it is quite open by the Law of Nations for the inhabitants to form a Government *ex necessitate,* for the protection of life & property, and such a Government has certain sovereign rights by the *jus gentium* [i.e. the law of nations]...

Professor Stanley in his book *The Birth of Western Canada* quotes a Report of the Privy Council dated December 16, 1869 written by Macdonald to the effect that a proclamation would put an end to the Government of the HBC, but not substitute the Government of Canada. This account added that a state of anarchy and confusion would ensue, which might result in legal status to a *de facto* Government formed for the protection of their lives and property by the inhabitants.

McDougall did not receive Macdonald's letter before his droll escapade. The result, which Macdonald warned him about in his letter, came to pass. On November 24, 1869 the HBC had executed the transfer papers to transfer Rupert's Land to Canada to take effect on an agreed date, originally to have been only seven days later.

Because of the pending transfer, the HBC and its Council of Assiniboia had effectively given up government. Consequently when McDougall made his illegitimate proclamation it was open to the inhabitants of the Settlement by the law of nations (as Prime Minister Macdonald had advised McDougall) to form a government for the protection of the life and property of the inhabitants.

Riel found out some days later that McDougall's proclamation was a fraud. Colonel Stoughton Dennis, who with Schultz and others was opposing Riel's initiatives, made a call to arms at McDougall's request. Riel's men captured Schultz and a number of Canadians who intended to attack Upper Fort Garry and had them imprisoned.

In keeping with his earlier suggestion that a provisional government be formed "for our protection and to treat with Canada", Riel and other inhabitants constituted a provisional government exactly one week after McDougall purported to usurp authority. They did so in a "Declaration of the People of Rupert's Land and the North West", dated December 8, 1869.

The Declaration made reference to the "law of nations" and to the rights and interests of the people "as British subjects". This Declaration opposed the imposition upon them of a "despotic form of government", and proclaimed that a Provisional Government had been established. It added that they were ready to enter into negotiations with the Canadian Government which would be favorable for the good government and prosperity of the people.

In effect this political document amounted to the Metis asserting their right to negotiate the terms on which Canada would acquire control over them and the lands on which they lived. They refused to accept that Canada would treat them as a colony. Riel became president of the Provisional Government two days after Christmas.

This Provisional Government formed "*ex necessitate*, for the protection of life and property" had, at the very least and consistent with Macdonald's advice to McDougall, a color of right and legitimacy.

Macdonald sent Donald A. Smith (the future Lord Strathcona who was then the chief HBC official in Canada) as a secret commissioner to the Red River Settlement and Smith bribed some of the Metis to desert Riel. Riel found out about Smith's commission and assented to Smith addressing a large assembly on January 18, 1870 and on the following day. In his remarks Smith made promises on behalf of Canada to the crowd relating to representation and title to land.

Riel in turn proposed that a Convention of Forty, one-half French and one-half English, be convened to discuss Smith's proposals. This democratic initiative was voted upon and adopted by over 1,000 settlers from various French and English speaking communities.

The Convention met some days later. It struck a committee of six to draft a List of Rights. A couple of Riel's proposals, including provincial status, were voted down by the English members and by several Metis influenced by his cousin Charles Nolin. This led to acrimony between Nolin and Riel which was to have repercussions in Saskatchewan fifteen years later.

Smith now stated that a delegation should be sent to Ottawa to meet with government officials to discuss the territory's entry into Confederation. This offer was received with alacrity.

Riel then proposed formation of a provisional government composed of both French and English speaking settlers, to administer the colony until matters were settled. The Council of Assiniboia had ceased functioning, thanks to the fraudulent proclamation of the hapless McDougall. It was agreed to put the matter of formation of a provisional government to the Governor of

Assiniboia William Mactavish. The ailing Mactavish said he was dying and would not delegate his authority, then said to them:

> Form a Government, for God's sake, and restore peace and order in the Settlement.

The Provisional Government and a legislative council were formed on February 10, 1870, the latter to consist of 12 French and 12 English-speaking members. Louis Riel was elected President and other officers were designated. The result was a democratically formed de facto, valid government formed by the inhabitants of lands not then part of Canada. Lurking in the background were Schultz, Mair and an odious, bigoted and violent Orangeman Thomas Scott. Scott had previously been in trouble with the law. While working as a laborer on construction of the Dawson Road to Fort Garry, he attacked and tried to drown his boss John A. Snow in a row with Snow about wages. Scott was convicted of robbery and assault with violence. Donald Smith himself said that Scott was "a rash, thoughtless man, whom none cared to have anything to do with".

In January 1870 Schultz, Mair and Scott had escaped from imprisonment by the Metis. Thereafter they were trying to get Canadian and English-speaking settlers to take up arms, presumably in order to release other prisoners but in reality to overthrow the new Provisional Government. On February 17 an armed group from Portage la Prairie, led by Captain Charles Boulton, headed for Fort Garry but many were arrested by the Metis and imprisoned, including Boulton and Scott.

Scott showed his contempt for the Metis guards by obscenely vilifying them and shouting that when he was released he would have them hanged. He and another prisoner attempted to overpower a guard but they were subdued.

Riel went to talk to Scott but Scott swore at him. The Metis guards would no longer tolerate Scott's abuse and threats. Riel as President of the Provisional Government ordered the court-martial of Scott. Riel was not a member of the court-martial. After presentation of evidence on March 3 the court-martial by a majority voted for the death penalty. The next day Scott was executed by a firing squad.

Although Riel had suggested mercy, he did not intervene to stop the execution. Perhaps Riel believed it was necessary to demonstrate to the enemies of the Provisional Government that they had better beware of attacks on the Settlement, and also to illustrate to Canada that the Provisional Government was for real.

While it may be substantiated that Scott was legally executed by a legitimate government, the execution was undoubtedly a huge political mistake that eventually caused Riel and the Metis a great deal of grief.

News of the death of Thomas Scott soon reached Orange Ontario. A mighty furor, fueled in speeches in Toronto and elsewhere in Ontario by Schultz and Mair vilifying Riel and praising Scott, erupted over what they saw as the murder of one of their own. Scott's execution was to have serious repercussions on Riel's life both soon after and fifteen years later in Saskatchewan.

The "cabinet" of the new Provisional Government prepared an updated "List of Rights" on March 22, 1870 for its delegates to take to Ottawa. It included many of the provisions in the previous List of Rights and several additional items including, at Riel's insistence, status as a Province. A provision for separate schools among religious denominations was also added.

Father Noel Joseph Ritchot of St. Norbert led the three-person delegation of the Provisional Government to Ottawa, where they were effectively recognized as such by Prime Minister John A. Macdonald and Deputy Prime Minister Georges Etienne Cartier. Riel, by his own choice, was not a delegate since as President of the Provisional Government he had to administer the Red River Settlement and ensure that law and order were maintained.

The end result of the Ottawa discussions was:

- the entry of Manitoba into confederation as a province;
- a grant of 1,400,000 acres of land to be allotted to the children of the Metis;
- bilingualism in the legislature and courts;
- denominational schools; and
- other important provisions, all embodied in the *Manitoba Act.*

Much of this Act was based on the Provisional Government's List of Rights. The section dealing with the allotment of land to the children of the Metis was subsequently expanded to include heads of families.

Manitoba joined Confederation as a province on July 15, 1870. As the driving force behind the creation of Manitoba as a Province, many people consider Louis Riel a "Father of Confederation".

The amnesty of all persons involved in the Resistance, which had been verbally promised by Ottawa to Father Ritchot during the period of negotiations, and also promised to Archbishop Taché, never materialized. Failure to obtain the promised amnesty later proved calamitous to Riel.

It should be noted that the census of 1870, the year in which Manitoba became a province, indicated that there were in the Settlement at that time a total of 12,228 inhabitants of whom there were 5,720 French Metis and 4,080 English Metis.

By means of the Red River Resistance, the Metis achieved most of the spectacular results that they had been aiming for and felt that they were entitled to. This was accomplished through their political determination and savvy. These were exemplified by their establishment of a Provisional Government and in their ability to maintain law and order in the Settlement with their military force.

The delegates of the Provisional Government had

negotiated with representatives of the federal government on a government to government basis. A singular achievement of the Resistance and political action by the Metis was that the Metis were officially referred to and recognized by the Canadian Parliament in the *Manitoba Act*.

However, these heady days for the Metis were not to last long. Within a few months members of the Red River Expeditionary Force (about 1,000 men strong), ostensibly sent on a peaceful mission by Prime Minister John A. Macdonald and his Government, were to act with a vengeance against the Metis in the Settlement.

The brutal treatment the Metis received from this Canadian militia, and the fraudulent and other methods by which the Metis lost or were induced to give up their land rights, led many of them to leave their homes and the Settlement and migrate west – the Metis dispersion.

Chapter Reference Sources

- *Birth of Western Canada a History of the Riel Rebellions, The,* by George F. G. Stanley, passim.
- *Canadian Prairies, a History, The,* by Gerald Friesen, p. 116-28.
- *Correspondence of Sir John Macdonald,* by Joseph Pope, p. 113; 119.
- *Four Recorders of Rupert's Land,* by Roy St. George Stubbs, p. 163-64.
- *History of the Canadian West to 1870-71,* by Arthur S. Morton, p. 863.
- *Louis Riel,* by George F. G. Stanley, passim.
- *Manitoba, A History,* by W. L. Morton, ch. 6.
- National Archives of England Public Record Office, CO (Colonial Office) 42/678, p. 29-31.
- *Promise of Eden - The Canadian Expansionist Movement and the Idea of the West 1856-1900* , by Doug Owram, ch. 4.
- *Snug Little Flock - The Social Origins of the Riel Resistance 1869-1870, A,* by Frits Pannekoek, ch. 8 & 9.
- *Strange Empire Louis Riel and the Metis People,* by Joseph Howard, *passim*.
- *Trial of Louis Riel, Justice and Mercy Denied, The,* by George R. D. Goulet, p. 19-25; 33-36.
- *Trials & Tribulations,* by J. M. Bumsted, ch. 8.

Chapter XIII

THE METIS DISPERSION

While negotiations were going on in Ottawa concerning the Metis List of Rights with respect to Canada's proposed acquisition of the land from the Hudson's Bay Company, Riel busied himself administering the Settlement.

In May 1870 on the orders of Prime Minister John A. Macdonald the British Commander Garnet Wolseley with an army of soldiers and volunteers from Ontario had set off for the Red River to set up a "peaceful" presence. In fact, and as subsequent events proved, it was anything but a peaceful mission.

It was a punitive expedition that brought a reign of terror and intimidation to the Metis. Macdonald's real reason for sending Colonel Wolseley's expeditionary forces to the Red River Settlement was that he mistrusted Riel. According to George Parkin in a biography of Macdonald, Macdonald stated in a letter to John Rose, his friend and former finance minister, he feared that:

> the longer he [Riel] remains in power, the more unwilling will he be to resign it. ... Under these circumstances the preparations for the expeditionary force may not be delayed.

In this letter Macdonald acknowledged that Riel was in power in the Red River Settlement.

On receipt of the news of the execution of Thomas Scott these preparations for an expeditionary force were hurried on. As well, the *Manitoba Act* was introduced by Macdonald "and hurriedly passed through the House." Parkin further states that the long strain on Macdonald had been too great and he became deathly ill and unfit for work for four months.

There is no doubt that the strains and vexations Riel caused Macdonald in Manitoba generated an intense dislike by Macdonald for the Metis leader. Macdonald called Riel "a gone coon" and sometime before the events in Saskatchewan in 1885 he also stated that Riel had:

> ... committed a cold-blooded murder in 1870 which will never be forgotten by the whites, either in Manitoba or

Ontario.

This was obviously a reference to the execution of Thomas Scott. After Riel's conviction for high treason in 1885 and notwithstanding the jury's unanimous recommendation for mercy, Macdonald would treat Riel with a vengeance.

Many of the Wolseley troops sent out by Macdonald to the Red River, ostensibly for peaceful purposes, were Orangemen determined to do Riel and the Metis serious harm. When the troops were almost at Fort Garry in August, the civilian lieutenant governor (Adams George Archibald) to whom they would be subject had not yet arrived.

Riel received word that Colonel Wolseley's men were going to kill him. He fled a few hours before their arrival on August 24. It was a prudent move on his part.

The immediate aftermath of the arrival of Wolseley's "peaceful mission" was as Professor George F. G. Stanley wrote in his book *Louis Riel* "weeks of lawlessness and debauchery."

The streets of Winnipeg were full of quarreling, battling drunks. Numerous criminal acts including murder, arson, assault and rape were committed against the Metis citizens. Among the atrocities committed by Wolseley's troops was the assassination of a prominent Metis Elzéar Goulet, who is profiled in a later chapter of this book.

After Manitoba became a province the expansionist movement saw many more Anglo-Saxon Protestant Ontarians move west. As previously mentioned, 1,400,000 acres had been set aside to be distributed among the children of the Metis. A combination of the violent atmosphere against them, and the federal government's illegal obstructions in relation to their land claims, discouraged the Metis both from taking an active role in the new regime brought in by the *Manitoba Act* and in acquiring the lands that they were entitled to.

Colonel Wolseley's soldiers were still present, and so

were some of the volunteer militia from Ontario. Many of these men, inspired by John Schultz, were motivated by racial and religious bigotry against the Metis.

The Metis were outraged by blatant land grabs by some Ontarians, but Governor Archibald convinced them that, with the presence of the Wolseley troops in the Settlement, it would be dangerous for them and for all the Metis if they fought back against the usurpers. The author Douglas Hill in his book *The Opening of the Canadian West* cites one instance in which Governor Archibald talked the Metis out of the use of force to reclaim their lands located along a stream. On their return home after hunting buffalo, some Metis found that white immigrants from the east had usurped their lands.

The Ontario land-grabbers, many of them Orangemen, then had insultingly renamed this little stream that they had seized "the Boyne". The Boyne was a river in Ireland where in 1690 the Protestant army of William of Orange (William III) defeated the Catholic army of the recently deposed James II. The confrontation is known as the Battle of the Boyne.

In addition, by Orders-in-Council and by flagrant disregard of the provision prohibiting an amendment to the *Manitoba Act* in this respect, the federal government did so in a manner that undermined Metis land rights. These rights, entitling them to land from the 1,400,000 acres set aside for them in the *Manitoba Act,* were further eroded by outright fraud, conflicts with the new settlers from Ontario, unbridled speculation, and Metis inability to obtain agricultural financing to put lands into production.

Many impoverished Metis, who were not cheated out of their entitlements, sold their lands or scrip certificates for a fraction of what they were worth. In addition, the buffalo (a principal source of food and clothing for the Metis) were vanishing from the eastern plains.

As a result a dispersion of the Metis from Red River occurred. Disheartened, many of the Metis picked up and moved to the less populated and less hostile areas further west. Some have called this dispersion a Metis diaspora.

Chapter Reference Sources

- *Correspondence of Sir John Macdonald*, by Joseph Pope, p. 127-28; 317-19.
- *Canada Sessional Papers*, (1871) 34 Victoria (No. 20), p. 15; 51-54.
- "Emergence of the Metis People in Manitoba" , by Fred Shore, *Metis Legacy*, editors Lawrie J. Barkwell et al, ch. 3, p. 74-77.
- *Homeland to Hinterland, The Changing Worlds of the Red River Metis in the Nineteenth Century*, by Gerhard J. Ens, ch. 7.
- *Louis Riel*, by George F. G. Stanley, passim.
- *Louis Riel 1844-1885*, by William McCartney Davidson, p. 95.
- *Opening of the Canadian West, The*, by Douglas Hill, p. 85-86.
- *Riel, A Life of Revolution*, by Maggie Siggins, p. 194.
- *Sir John A. Macdonald*, by George R. Parkin, p.160-161.
- *The Trial of Louis Riel, Justice and Mercy Denied*, by George R. D. Goulet, p. 26-28; 37.

Chapter XIV

THE NORTH-WEST UPRISING

As noted in the previous chapter, the after-effect of the troubles that the Metis encountered in the Red River Settlement (subsequent to the arrival of the Wolseley military forces and numerous Ontarians) was a Metis exodus to what is now Saskatchewan. Many Metis emigrated to the South Branch of the Saskatchewan River, south of Prince Albert. As well as other locations in the West, a number of them settled in the St. Laurent area. A mission was established there by Father Alexis André, an Oblate priest who was later to be a witness at Louis Riel's trial.

In time the South Branch Metis wanted government assurance of their rights to the lands they lived on, land grants (similar to those in Manitoba), and river-lot surveys of their land. The white and English Metis settlers in the Prince Albert area wanted similar rights.

The government did send a survey crew in the late 1870s and, in the first year, river-lot surveys were started. For some reason in 1879, this method was reversed and the square-block principle was followed. The federal government ignored the settlers' complaints in this respect as well as those relating to their inability to obtain title to their land. A number of petitions were sent over the years to the government outlining the grievances but nothing was done.

By 1884 the whites and the Metis in the North-West were fed-up. They had no right to elect members of Parliament and had no representatives in Ottawa to speak for them and to press their case. The North-West was a colony of the Canadian government. This lack of democratic rights was another of their deeply felt grievances.

At a joint meeting in May 1884 of hundreds of Metis and English settlers, a decision was made to send a delegation to Montana to invite Louis Riel to the

Saskatchewan to represent them in dealings with the federal government. At the time Louis Riel was a school teacher of Aboriginal children at St. Peter's Mission in Montana.

Riel was well-known to many of the people at the meeting as the Father of Manitoba, the hero of the Red River Settlement. He had been the driving force behind the acquisition of land, voting, democratic, language and other rights that had brought Manitoba into Confederation as a full-fledged Province.

A delegation of four was sent to Montana and they persuaded Riel to return with them to Saskatchewan to lead them in pursuing their rights. Additional details of their journey are set forth in the profile of Louis Riel in this book.

When Riel arrived in Saskatchewan, he addressed a number of meetings of French Metis, English Metis and whites. His speeches at the outset were moderate, and his endeavors on their behalf were peaceful and constitutional. However, the priests were not supportive of him.

Among other matters Riel advocated on behalf of the people of the area for:

- responsible government;
- parliamentary representation;
- land grants for French and English Metis and white settlers;
- income from land sales for hospitals, schools and farm equipment;
- better provision for the Indians;
- the establishment of Alberta and Saskatchewan as provinces.

The December 16, 1884 petition to the federal government, which Riel drafted after many consultations and public meetings with the local residents, requested the organization of the District of Saskatchewan as a province, among other items. Section 3 of the Bill of Rights of March 8, 1885 called for the provinces of Alberta and Saskatchewan to be forthwith organized with their own legislatures.

Most of the policies advocated by Riel were achieved after his death. The North-West Territories (that is the former Rupert's Land exclusive of Manitoba) achieved voting rights and parliamentary representation in 1886 and responsible government in 1897. Saskatchewan and Alberta were granted provincial status in 1905.

The unrest in Saskatchewan and disregard of settlers' petitions by the federal government in the first half of the 1880s (including the petitions prepared by Louis Riel) led to an uprising, also called a rebellion, in 1885 in this area of the North-West Territories. The Metis formed a Provisional Government on the 19th day of March 1885, which Riel named the Exovedate. In this book the authors have generally used the term "Resistance" with respect to the troubles in the Red River area and the term "Uprising" with respect to the troubles in the North-West Territories.

In his book *Correspondence of Sir John Macdonald*, Joseph Pope noted that on August 28, 1885 after Riel had been convicted of high treason Prime Minister John A. Macdonald [obviously for political reasons] downplayed the North-West outbreak as a "mere domestic trouble ... not to be elevated to the rank of a rebellion."

Because of the importance of the Canadian Pacific Railway (CPR) in events relating to the North-West Uprising, the following is a brief background involving the construction of the CPR. This was the railway which carried the Canadian soldiers from the East to crush the Uprising in the West.

During the 1870s the Eastern-Canadian expansionists continued their push for populating the West with Anglo-Saxon Protestants. They were disappointed with the meager numbers who were immigrating to the prairies. They blamed the absence of a railway into the area. The railway would foster economic activity and a demand for the goods and products of eastern manufacturers; its rails would bind the nation together; and its settlers from Ontario would plant British traditions and values in the West.

These views coincided with those of Prime Minister John A. Macdonald. In the early 1870s manufacturers in the east lobbied Macdonald for tariff protection, and since many were supporters of the Conservative Party, Macdonald was in favor of granting protection. He came up with an inspired euphemism for high tariffs for Eastern manufacturers – the "National Policy".

He pushed for this Policy in the 1872 election as well as for construction of a railway to the Pacific. Macdonald won the election but shortly after corruption in Macdonald's government reared its ugly head.

Sir Hugh Allan, whose company had been granted the charter to build the railway by the Macdonald administration, had made campaign contributions of sizeable amounts specifically, among others, to Macdonald and his Quebec lieutenant Cartier. One of these contributions to Macdonald was made pursuant to a telegram from Prime Minister Macdonald to Sir Hugh Allan marked "Immediate, Private". Macdonald telegraphed

> I must have another ten thousand; will be the last time of calling; do not fail me; answer today.

When the corruption became public in 1873, Macdonald's government resigned in disgrace. In his book *From Sea Unto Sea, The Road to Nationhood 1850-1910,* Professor W. G. Hardy wrote "John A. went on a prolonged drunk." Other historians have also noted the bibulous Macdonald's intemperate drinking habits.

Alexander Mackenzie became Prime Minister of Canada in 1873 but because of a depression, construction of the railway to the west did not proceed during his tenure. Allan's company lost its charter to build the railway. In the 1878 election campaign, John A. Macdonald resurrected his so-called "National Policy". Macdonald's Conservative Party won the election; however he lost his own Kingston seat in Ontario and was parachuted into a seat in Victoria, British Columbia, which he won.

With victory, Macdonald was now able to renew his pursuit of nation building. The National Policy developed beyond tariff protection for eastern manufacturers to embrace greater development policies; western immigration; construction of the railway to the west; etc. This Policy of the Government of John A. Macdonald (who as recently as 1883 had referred to the West as a "Crown Colony"), ignored the West's history and way of life. This way of life of the Metis and the Indians was fading away with the disappearance of the buffalo and implementation of the Indian treaties to settle the Indians on reserves.

The development of Western Canada was to be determined by the interests of eastern Canadian manufacturers and expansionist imperialists (the British Empire and its influence in Ontario were then in their heyday). Hence the federal policies resulted in high tariffs; massive western immigration; movement of Indians to reserves, and frequently keeping them their by means of a policy involving starvation; and a taxpayer bailout of the near-bankrupt CPR.

Federal authorities had continuously disregarded the numerous plaints and petitions by the inhabitants of the North-West relating to land rights; surveys; corrupt officials; lack of representation in Parliament; and other matters. Ottawa's deaf ear to Western grievances, coupled with its eastern-based policies, set the stage for the Uprising that ensued.

With respect to the railway, a charter was again granted for construction of the CPR to a syndicate in which Donald A. Smith (well known in Manitoba in 1870) of the Hudson's Bay Company, and George Stephen of the Bank of Montreal were prominent. The CPR received huge money and land grants, tax exemptions and other benefits from the government. Times were prosperous and, by 1882, railway construction was well advanced. However, in that year the economic boom was dying.

By 1883 the CPR was in financial difficulty. Stephen went to Macdonald and cadged a government loan for the CPR. He pleaded for and received a further government loan of $22,500,000 in 1884.

On March 18, 1885 the canny Scottish-born capitalists and financiers, Stephen and Smith (who were cousins) unashamedly decided to beg Prime Minister John A. Macdonald (also Scottish-born) for a further CPR bailout. These free enterprisers brazenly came with outstretched hands to clamor for a further $5,000,000 loan from the government. The members of the Cabinet had had enough. They rejected the CPR's loan application. The CPR was on the verge of bankruptcy, its principals on the verge of ruin. There was no hope or so George Stephen, Donald A. Smith and Cornelius Van Horne (the CPR triumvirate) thought.

Fortune smiled on Stephen, Smith, Van Horne and the CPR from the most improbable of sources – Louis Riel. Only eight days after the federal cabinet had rejected their loan request, and Stephen, Smith and Van Horne had sunk into the "slough of despond", the battle at Duck Lake in the North-West Territories erupted on March 26, 1885 between the Metis (led by their brilliant military leader Gabriel Dumont) and the troops of Major Crozier of the North West Mounted Police (NWMP).

Blood was shed initiated by Major Crozier's assistant "Gentleman Joe" McKay, who shot dead on the spot Isadore Dumont and Assywin (the Metis and Indian representatives) who had come with a white flag to parley with Crozier in an open field. The slayings of Dumont and Assywin resulted in an outbreak of shooting between Major Crozier's forces and the Metis. There were a number of fatalities on each side before the NWMP forces retreated in defeat. The North-West Uprising had commenced.

Van Horne seized the opportunity. He told the government that he could get the troops from Ontario to the North-West in ten days. It seemed to be a wild pledge. There was close to 90 miles (almost one hundred and fifty kilometers) of track that had not been laid in Northern Ontario. This incomplete mileage was made up of four gaps of icy, barren hinterland.

Macdonald saw a golden opportunity to resurrect his National Dream and coincidentally the CPR. He talked the cabinet into approving Van Horne's proposal. Van Horne responded immediately. The CPR mobilized for the immense mission of transporting troops, matériel, weapons and animals across the country to the North-West.

The gaps in the track north of Lake Superior were bridged by horse-drawn sleighs which carried the troops and supplies to the next point to which track had been laid. It was a remarkable performance. The first detachments made it to Winnipeg within ten days. The CPR had survived due to an unlikely savior, Louis Riel. Under other circumstances the CPR might have erected a statue to him to match the magnificent statue of William Van Horne in the center of the roundabout at the stately Banff Springs Hotel in Banff, Alberta.

With the arrival of the overwhelming forces from the East, the crushing of the Metis and the death knell of Riel were nigh. The actions of Riel had indirectly saved the CPR. The actions of the CPR indirectly, and of Prime Minister Macdonald directly, condemned Riel.

After the humiliating defeat of Crozier's men at Duck Lake, the Prime Minister was determined to crush both the Uprising and Riel. As he had in the Red River Resistance, Macdonald turned to a professional British soldier to take command of the Canadian militia. He appointed Major-General Frederick Middleton as commander of the North-West Expedition.

General Middleton was a paunchy, rotund, 59 year old mustachioed graduate of the Royal Military College at Sandhurst. These credentials didn't impress Lewis Redman Ord, a well-educated surveyor from Toronto, who signed up for service in the North-West Uprising. In his 1886 book titled *Reminiscences of a Bungle by One of the Bunglers* Ord showed his scorn for the pompous English career soldier. He wrote that Middleton deserved:

> .... nothing but contempt for his management of the whole campaign.

Ord refers to Middleton more than once as the "Great I Am". He also called Middleton the "Great Bungler".

Middleton's image was tarnished a few years after the Uprising when a Metis fur trader Charles Bremner succeeded in having the Canadian House of Commons investigate Middleton with respect to Bremner's furs being "confiscated" by Middleton during the Uprising. The best of these furs were consigned personally to Middleton in Eastern Canada. The House of Commons found Middleton's actions illegal, and the scandal caused him to return to England.

Close to 3,000 militiamen were conveyed to Western Canada by the CPR. This overwhelming force was mustered to battle against perhaps 400 Metis, including the young and the old.

With the arrival of Middleton and the troops, the battle at Duck Lake was followed by further battles at Fish Creek and Batoche. These battles are also noted in the profile of Gabriel Dumont in another chapter of this book.

At Fish Creek in the latter part of April, over 800 well-armed soldiers fought against the Metis and, although both sides incurred casualties, the battle was a stand-off.

The cautious Middleton, whose weapons included cannons and the first machine gun (the Gatling gun), did nothing for the next two weeks but on May 9th he had his men mount an attack against the Metis at Batoche. There the Metis had dug rifle pits to shield themselves, a tactic Gabriel Dumont had learned as a teenager 34 years earlier at the Battle of the Grand Coteau. Although they were vastly outnumbered by Middleton's men, who had far superior weapons, the Metis held out for three days. However, bone-weary and lacking ammunition, they were overrun and vanquished on May 12, 1885.

A number of men on both sides were killed, including

the 93 year old Metis fighter Joseph Oullette. Gabriel Dumont and a few other Metis escaped to the United States.

Louis Riel voluntarily and deliberately surrendered, erroneously anticipating that he could use his trial as a showcase to expose the grievances of the Metis and of himself. His trial and execution for high treason are briefly discussed in the profile of him that appears later in this book.

With the rout of the Metis at Batoche, the North-West Uprising was over.

Chapter Reference Sources

- *Birth of Western Canada a History of the Riel Rebellions, The,* by George F. G. Stanley, passim.
- *Correspondence of Sir John Macdonald,* by Joseph Pope, p. 355.
- *From Sea unto Sea - The Road to Nationhood 1850-1910,* by W. G. Hardy, p.261.
- *Hold High Your Heads (History of the Metis Nation in Western Canada),* by Auguste Henri de Tremaudan, p. 112-40.
- *Last War Drum, The,* by Desmond Morton, *passim.*
- *Louis Riel,* by George F. G. Stanley, *passim.*
- *Louis Riel v. Canada,* by J. M. Bumsted, ch.11.
- *Prairie Fire - The 1885 North-West Rebellion,* by Bob Beal and Rod Macleod, *passim.*
- *Reminiscences of a Bungle by One of the Bunglers* , by Lewis Redman Ord, edited by R.C. Macleod p. 39; 46; 54; 71; 93.
- *Strange Empire Louis Riel and the Metis People,* by Joseph Howard, *passim.*
- *Trial of Louis Riel, Justice and Mercy Denied, The,* by George R. D. Goulet, p. 38-43.

Chapter XV

THE METIS - POST NORTH-WEST UPRISING

After the North-West Uprising a large number of the Metis in the West were effectively ostracized politically, socially and economically for decades. Many had no land and had to squat on "road allowances", that is lands abutting the sides of a road reserved as public rights-of-way, or lands retained by government agencies for future road construction.

The Metis receded into the background. Their presence on the national stage went into limbo. They were Canada's "forgotten people". A significant number of Metis moved further west and north to hamlets such as Green Lake, Lac St. Anne, Battle River, Lac La Biche, while others migrated to developing Metis communities (where they often had relatives) in areas such as Spring Creek (Lewistown today), Montana and North Dakota.

Many members of Anglo-Saxon communities looked on those of mixed ancestry as persons of lesser intelligence and beneath them as a social class. Because of the discrimination and prejudice they suffered, a large number of Metis people in Western Canada hid their ancestry and, if able to, chose to become assimilated into the white community and pass as non-Metis.

However, there were others who were determined to maintain their cultural identity. As early as 1887, a group of 15 prominent Metis met at St. Vital (now a suburb of Winnipeg). At this meeting they formed a Metis organization and named it the Union Nationale Metisse St. Joseph du Manitoba. Those attending this meeting included Pierre Delorme (profiled in a later chapter of this book), Joseph Riel (Louis' brother), Martin Jerome, and Elzear Lagimodiere. The purpose of this organization was to protect and promote Metis traditions by means of various educational, historical, and charitable projects with a view to restoring the pride of the Metis people. They chose St. Joseph as their patron.

In 1909 some of these same persons and several others in the Union (including Ambroise Lepine), decided to focus on the history of the Metis and created an historical committee. They wanted to reclaim their own history concerning the Red River Resistance and the North-West Uprising, rather than leave unchallenged biased interpretations of these events presented by anti-Metis and Eurocentric historians and others.

They looked at various Metis documents, a number of which they received from the Riel family. They consulted with participants of the historical events and took their declarations. The goal of this historical committee was to present the Metis point of view whenever the historical role of the Metis was denigrated.

In 1927 the Committee engaged the services of a non-Metis Auguste Henri de Trémaudan to write the Metis history, and they provided him with various relevant documents. It was originally published in French in 1936. An English translation was published in 1982 under the title *Hold High Your Heads (History of the Metis Nation in Western Canada)*. This book was a sympathetic, precedent-setting, methodical history of the Metis people.

All of these activities contributed to maintaining (albeit on a low-key level) the cultural identity, history and traditions of the Metis people, encouraging them to hold high their heads. The French-speaking Union Nationale Metisse St. Joseph du Manitoba is based in St. Boniface and, although not very large, it remains active to this day. This oldest Metis organization in Canada is currently under the leadership of Gabriel Dufault.

In the 1930s two activist Metis leaders, Malcolm Norris and Jim Brady, fought for Metis rights in Alberta and Saskatchewan. Shortly afterwards in that decade, the Metis Association of Alberta and the Saskatchewan Metis Society were formed. The agitation by Norris and Brady contributed to the passage by the Alberta government of the *Metis Betterment Act* in 1938. This Statute benefited squatters on government lands in the north central part of

Alberta by establishing Metis Settlements on these lands.

In 1969 a significant decision was made by the Government of Canada to close the Aboriginal Residential Schools. These Schools had been established in Western Canada in the 1880s by the federal government in conjunction with several churches and religious orders. Their primary intention was to assimilate all young Aboriginal people in their charge into mainstream society. Many of the students were treated shabbily, some were physically and sexually abused, and others were used as cheap labor.

Audrey Poitras (the current President of the Metis Nation of Alberta) in the Foreword to the book *Metis Memories of Residential Schools* wrote:

> Eighteen percent of those who attended residential schools in Alberta were Metis. Across Canada that number is nine percent.

In the Statement of Reconciliation issued on January 7, 1998, the federal government admitted that Canada had mistreated Aboriginal People throughout history. On behalf of Canada an apology was made to all those who suffered physical, mental, and sexual abuse in Residential Schools. The churches involved in running these Schools have also apologized.

Many survivors of the Residential Schools have sued for damages for the harsh treatment that they suffered. The majority of the approximately 12,000 cases have not been settled. On November 23, 2005, the Liberal government offered a compensation package to the victims of abuse totaling $1.9 billion. The Liberal government was defeated in the election of January 2006, but in May 2006 the new Conservative government approved a similar compensation package subject to Court approval.

Metis cultural, historical and political reawakening was heightened in the 1960s with the formation in that decade of the Manitoba Metis Federation and the predecessor to the Metis Nation of British Columbia. These together with the groups formed in Alberta and Saskatchewan in the

1930s resulted in provincial Metis organizations in all the provinces of Western Canada.

Because of restrictive government policies many, but not all, natives who were unable to obtain status under the *Indian Act* identified themselves as Metis even though they were non-status Indians. In the 1970s and early 1980s, the Native Council of Canada (discussed hereafter) acted for many Metis and non-status Indians.

In 1983 the Metis National Council (MNC) was formed and took as its mandate representation of the Metis Nation in Canada, but not those who self-identified as Metis but were not descendants of the historic Red River Metis or were non-status Indians. The result was two national organizations (the Native Council of Canada and the Metis National Council) laying claim to representing people of Metis descent.

In 1993 the MNC recognized a newly formed Metis organization in Ontario and included it in its membership. Currently the MNC, with offices in Ottawa, consists of five Provincial Metis Associations. These are:

- Manitoba Metis Federation (Winnipeg);
- Metis Nation - Saskatchewan (Saskatoon);
- Metis Nation of Alberta (Edmonton);
- Metis Nation of British Columbia (Vancouver); and
- Metis Nation of Ontario (Ottawa).

Representatives from these five provincial associations constitute the membership of the MNC and are the governing members of the Metis Nation. Metis individuals as such are not members; rather, they are members of the provincial Metis organization in the province where they reside and are registered.

Each provincial organization has an executive that manages its affairs and whose principal officers are elected by the provincial membership. A general meeting is held annually at which all registered members are free to speak and debate on resolutions. The provincial organizations have regions and regional councils, with officers elected by the region membership. Many regions have local councils,

It is interesting to note that two descendants of Gabriel Dumont's parents are currently leaders in the Metis Nation movement. Bruce Dumont is President of the Metis Nation of British Columbia, and Audrey Poitras (nee Dumont) is President of the Metis Nation of Alberta,

The Women of the Metis Nation is a women's organization that works within the MNC as an advisory body. It consists of a representative Metis woman from each of the MNC's five governing bodies together with an elected national spokesperson.

There is also a Metis National Youth Advisory Council whose objective is to address the interests of Metis young people. The head offices for this Council and for the Women of the Metis Nation are located in the offices of the MNC in Ottawa.

The Metis National Council limits the definition of who are Metis primarily to persons descended from the historical Metis Nation. This includes but is not limited to descendants of those politically recognized by the federal government in past legislation such as the *Manitoba Act* of 1870 and the *Dominion Lands Act* of 1874. These Statutes provided for land grants to the children of Metis families in the case of the former Act and scrip certificates to the heads of Metis families in the case of the latter Act.

Scrip certificates were issued by the federal government entitling the holder to acquire that number of acres of Crown lands referred to in the certificate. The certificate could also be for a dollar amount and exchanged for that number of acres of Crown lands equal to the face value of its dollar amount - for example, a scrip certificate for $160 could be exchanged for 160 acres of public lands.

With respect to the Native Council of Canada (NCC), it does not purport to act on behalf of the descendants of the Red River Metis, but rather on behalf of others who designate themselves as Metis, non-status Indians and also status Indians living away from reserves, many in urban areas.

In 1993 the NCC changed its name to the Congress of Aboriginal Peoples (CAP). Its view as to who is a Metis is much broader than that of the Metis National Council.

The CAP appears to permit anyone of mixed aboriginal and non-aboriginal ancestry to self-identify as a Metis. The purview of the CAP extends to off-reserve aboriginals including non-status Indians and Metis (in places such as Labrador, Northwest Territories, Ontario, Quebec, the Maritimes and elsewhere). Some of their members have no connection with the historical North-West communities and their history and culture. CAP intends to acquire more members in Western Canada.

As a political organization CAP represents its affiliates on a national level. The independent affiliates of CAP are provincial and territorial organization. Members of these organizations may include Indians not registered under the *Indian Act*, registered Indians, and Metis people. The organizations provide a variety of programs including ones related to Aboriginal justice, youth, women and health. CAP and its associates have received federal and provincial funding for some of their activities.

There are less politically prominent groups that advocate for Aboriginal peoples in Canada. One example out of many is the Friendship Centres. Their organizations and facilities provide services to the Aboriginal peoples in their local urban settings.

In 1972 the National Association of Friendship Centres (NAFC) was formed to represent these associations that today have developed into more than 100 groups all across Canada. The Aboriginal Friendship Centres Program of the NFAC was recognized by the federal government which, in 1988, granted the Program the status of permanent funding.

The purpose of NAFC is to promote the Friendship Centre movement and to advocate for the concerns of Aboriginal peoples in urban environments. It has seven Provincial Territorial Associations that represent the

Friendship Centres within their jurisdiction.

There are also other organizations that have been established to specifically address the interests of Metis women. The Metis National Council of Women states that it is an autonomous organization that represents the interests of all Metis women in Canada wherever they live. It has an office in Ottawa. It is not part of the MNC.

In view of recent momentous legal developments, there will most likely be a number of groups proclaiming Metis status and seeking recognition as such. This will provide these groups with an opportunity to press for participation in whatever rights and benefits may accrue to the Metis people under these recent developments.

As discussed later in this book, the concept of who is a Metis under Constitutional law is not definitive. It may be expected that in the event of a dispute the courts will deal with recognition of community groups on a case by case basis. Among the criteria for recognition, there will undoubtedly be a requirement for an ancestral connection to a distinctive historic Metis community which had developed its own unique way of life, culture, and customs. Self-identification as a Metis by itself will be insufficient. It is also unlikely that the courts will proclaim an all-encompassing determination of who is a Metis under the law.

One may also anticipate that the federal and provincial governments, in an attempt to minimize their future financial outlays, will endeavor to limit the scope of who is a Metis under the Constitution of Canada. However it should be noted that in January 2002 the Province of Saskatchewan adopted a Statute titled *The Metis Act* - Chapter - 14.01. This Act recognizes the contributions of the Metis people to the prosperity and development of Canada. It listed many of the Metis contributions including among others the following:

"(d) the distinctive culture and cultural legacy of the Metis people, as signified by the Metis flag, the Metis sash, the Red River cart, the fiddle and the Red River jig."

Constitutional recognition and recent momentous legal developments with respect to the Metis are discussed in ensuing chapters, as are certain other relevant matters.

Chapter Reference Sources

- *Hold High Your Heads (History of the Metis Nation in Western Canada)*, by Auguste Henri de Tremaudan, p. 153-165.
- *Home From The Hill, A History of the Metis in Western Canada*, by Don McLean, ch. 8.
- *Metis Canada's Forgotten People, The*, by D. Bruce Sealey and Antoine S. Lussier, ch. 10; 11; 12.
- *Metis Legacy*, editors Lawrence J. Barkwell et al, p. 77-78.
- *Metis Memories of Residential Schools*, Foreword by Audrey Poitras (Metis Nation of Alberta, 2004).
- *Prairie Fire - The 1885 North-West Rebellion*, by Bob Beale & Rod Macleod, ch. 18.
- *Who are Canada's Aboriginal Peoples*, editor Paul L. A. H. Chartrand, *passim*.

Chapter XVI

CONSTITUTIONAL and GOVERNMENT RECOGNITION

Over a period of some two centuries the Metis, led by a number of remarkable personalities of unwavering will and determination, experienced many memorable and historic achievements. In doing so they kept alive their history, heritage and culture in the face of recurring hostile opposition from different quarters. The indomitable spirit of the Metis and continual insistence on their native-born identity culminated in their supreme recognition as a "people" of Canada.

In 1982 they were officially recognized as a people in the *Canadian Constitution*, the highest law of the land and a law that takes priority over every other law enacted in Canada whether federal, provincial, territorial, or municipal.

The prelude to this momentous constitutional sanction was the promise made by Prime Minister Pierre Elliott Trudeau to renew the Constitution. This pledge was made during the 1980 battle to defeat the referendum of the Parti Québécois on sovereignty-association. When the referendum was defeated, Quebec Premier René Lévesque called upon Trudeau to carry through on this pledge.

A number of clashes occurred between the First Ministers and federal and provincial officials, as well as with various interest groups. However, the terms of the patriation of the *Canadian Constitution* were finally agreed upon by the federal and provincial governments with one notable exception, the Province of Quebec.

One of the shining provisions for those who cherish a guarantee of individual rights and fundamental freedoms was inclusion of a *Canadian Charter of Rights and Freedoms*. Astonishingly, its adoption was opposed by a number of premiers, and as a trade-off a limited right of a government to opt out of certain of its specific provisions was added.

Since the *British North America Act, 1867* (a statute of the Parliament of Great Britain) was the principal source of the constitutional law of Canada, the patriation resolution had to be sent to Britain for approval. Subsequently, the new *Constitution Act* became a law of Canada when it was proclaimed by Queen Elizabeth II in Ottawa on April 17, 1982. Elizabeth continues to be the Queen of Canada, a status beloved by Canadian monarchists and one of the few remaining vestiges of Canada's former colonial subservience to the British Empire.

During negotiation of the terms of the new Constitution, consultations were held with representatives of various interest groups. Among them were delegates of the Indians, the Inuit and the Metis. The federal government wanted their support for patriation.

Harry Daniels participated in the meetings as President of the Native Council of Canada (now the Congress of Aboriginal Peoples), which at the time represented Metis and non-status Indians. The federal Minister of Justice Jean Chretien (who became Prime Minister over a decade later) asked Daniels to travel to Britain to support patriation - that is to bring the Constitution under Canadian jurisdiction rather than that of Great Britain.

According to Daniels, he said that he would only do so if the Metis were specifically included in the Constitution as an Aboriginal people. Chretien initially refused; Daniels erupted angrily and said that he and his people would not accept anything less. Chretien left the meeting to consult with Prime Minister Trudeau. He returned to the room and said that all of Daniels points would be agreed to.

Daniels stands tall alongside Louis Riel in having the Metis constitutionally recognized. Sadly, this dynamic Metis advocate (who is profiled in a later chapter) died in September 2004.

An item in the *Globe and Mail* newspaper of May 5, 1981 reported that Chretien rejected recognition of the rights of the Metis in the Constitution stating that "the claims of the Metis were general and largely undocumented". Duke Redbird, the President of the Ontario Metis and Non-Status Indians at that time, stated that "thousands of documents" had been included in a report on their claims.

Incidentally, Chretien was the Minister of Indian Affairs who introduced the drolly-named White Paper in 1969, proposing to repeal the *Indian Act.* Two years later the comically-named (under the circumstances) White Paper was effectively confined to the waste-basket.

The landmark recognition provision of the Metis, the Indians and the Inuit is found in s. 35 of the *Constitution Act, 1982.* It reads as follows:

> 35.(1) The existing aboriginal and treaty rights of the aboriginal peoples of Canada are hereby recognized and affirmed.
>
> (2) In this Act, "aboriginal peoples of Canada" includes the Indian, Inuit and Metis peoples of Canada.

This enshrined status was a glorious event for the Metis and assured their past, present, and future legal existence as a people of Canada. This acceptance was a culmination of the sterling contributions the Metis people made to the history and cultural mosaic of Canada, contributions which add to the luster of the fabric of this great nation.

However, s. 35 did not answer two key questions:

- Who are the Metis people(s) referred to in it?
- What are their "existing aboriginal and treaty rights"?

It should also be noted that s. 35 did not "create" aboriginal rights. It "recognized and affirmed" these rights. The full extent of these rights for the Metis people remains to be determined. However by the use of the word "includes" rather than "are" or "comprise" in s. 35(2), there is the possibility that the term "aboriginal peoples" may extend further than just Indian, Inuit and Metis.

Since 1982 several propositions have been advanced with a view to answering these questions. Section 37 of the new Constitution made provision for a First Ministers conference to determine these aboriginal rights.

After the 1982 patriation of the Constitution, the Prime Minister held follow-up conferences between 1983 and 1987 on constitutional reform affecting the Aboriginal peoples. These conferences were unsuccessful in defining either the Metis or Metis rights.

The three national organizations that were invited to the first of these conferences were the NCC, the Assembly of First Nations, and the Inuit Tapirisat of Canada. A group of western Metis, who had broken away from the NCC and formed the Metis National Council in 1983, requested inclusion and in due course participated in these meetings.

At the 1984 Conference the Metis National Council presented a definition of "Metis" for the purpose of S. 35(2) of the Constitution. Its proposal was that the Metis comprise the descendants of the Metis who received land grants or scrip pursuant to the *Manitoba Act, 1870* or the *Dominion Lands Act, 1879* (without any reference to a requirement by them for self-identification).

As well under their proposal, the Metis were to include others of aboriginal descent who self-identify as Metis and are accepted by the said Metis community. That community would be any Metis people as a group whose ancestry was traceable to the Metis legally identified as such under those two statutes.

This submission would have required a Constitutional amendment.

Over the subsequent years attempts were made to encourage Quebec to sign the 1982 Constitution. A major initiative was the 1987 Meech Lake Accord which collapsed due to provincial discord.

A further attempt to define "Metis" was the Metis Nation Accord. This document was settled in 1992 by representatives of the federal government, the provincial governments of Ontario and the four western provinces, and the Metis National Council in conjunction with the Charlottetown Accord of that year.

The Charlottetown Accord was an attempt to forestall a further Quebec referendum on sovereignty. Nevertheless, one of its key points was a commitment to an aboriginal right of self-government.

The Metis Nation Accord defined "Metis" in a manner similar to that of the 1984 Conference with respect to their being descendants of those Metis that received land grants and scrip. It did add to that definition those who had been "entitled" to land grants and scrip, and an additional requirement of self-identification. However, it omitted other persons of aboriginal descent except in the definition of "Metis Nation". Indian and Inuit were also excluded. "Metis Nation" was defined as the community of those Metis descendants referred to above as well as persons of aboriginal descent accepted by that community.

The Charlottetown Accord was seen by many Canadians as the making of a deal behind closed doors by a group of middle-aged white men in suits (the Prime Minister and the Premiers). The Canadian public soundly rejected that Accord in a referendum. With that rejection, the Metis Nation Accord also died.

The federal government established a Royal Commission on Aboriginal Peoples on August 26th 1991. The mandate of this Commission was to look into the evolution of the relationship between the Government of Canada, Aboriginal Peoples and the Canadian nation generally.

On April 22, 1992, two prominent Metis made a presentation to the Royal Commission on behalf of the Manitoba Metis Federation (MMF). One of the presenters for the MMF was W. Yvon Dumont who subsequently on March 5, 1993 became the Lieutenant-Governor of Manitoba (the first Metis in any province to serve in this capacity). The other presenter was David N. Chartrand, who is currently the President of the MMF.

The Report of this Royal Commission on Aboriginal Peoples was made in 1996. The Report took the position that the aboriginal peoples of Canada have, within limits, an inherent right of self-government and of self-definition.

An article in a 2004 issue of the *Saskatchewan Law Review* by Albert Peeling and Paul L. A. H. Chartrand explored the question of Metis self-government from a constitutional perspective. In it these legal authors concluded:

> The constitutional and common law of Canada can and should recognize that Metis societies must have been self-governing, and that the right of self-government, to the extent it has not been extinguished, is constitutionally protected by s. 35 of the Constitution Act, 1982.

At the annual general assembly of the Metis National Council (MNC) held in Edmonton, Alberta in September 2002, the members of the MNC adopted a National Definition of Metis. As noted above, Metis individuals registered with the provincial Metis associations are not themselves members of the MNC. Accordingly the Definition was approved by Metis officials, not by the general Metis membership.

The Definition and defined terms therein as adopted read as follows:

> National Definition of Metis
>
> 1.1 "Metis" means a person who self-identifies as Metis, is distinct from other Aboriginal peoples, is of Historic Metis Nation ancestry, and is accepted by the Metis Nation.
>
> 1.2 "Historic Metis Nation" means the Aboriginal people then known as Metis or Half-breeds who resided in the Historic Metis Nation Homeland.
>
> 1.3 "Historic Metis Nation Homeland" means the area of land in west central North America used and occupied as the traditional territory of the Metis or Half -breeds as they were then known.
>
> 1.4 "Metis Nation" means the Aboriginal people descended from the Historic Metis Nation which is now comprised of all Metis Nation citizens and is one of the 'aboriginal peoples of Canada' within the meaning of s.35 of the Constitution Act 1982.
>
> 1.5 "Distinct from other Aboriginal peoples" means distinct for cultural and nationhood purposes.

This Definition, while not specifically defining the borders of the Historic Metis Nation Homeland, changes the scope of who is a Metis from that of the Metis Nation Accord of 1992. This current Definition removes the qualification (previously provided for in the Metis Nation Accord) of being a descendant of a Metis who obtained or was entitled to obtain scrip or a land grant. However it clearly excludes the Maritimes, Quebec, Newfoundland and Labrador.

Although similar in many respects to a 2001 proposal, this revision varied from the 1984 and 1992 definitions. By its reference to 'central' North America, it appears designed to include members of the Metis Nation of Ontario (only formed in 1993) whose ancestors did not receive scrip or land grants.

Metis of the Upper Great Lakes area, such as the Powleys referred to in the following chapter, would fall within this definition. Many, if not most, of these Metis would not have received land grants or scrip under the *Manitoba Act, 1870* or the *Dominion Lands Act, 1879.*

The above definition is problematic in several respects. One example is that to be Metis one must be accepted by the Metis Nation. Acceptance by a provincial Metis organization does not meet the test. Also the use of the word "west" with "central" appears to geographically exclude lands to the east of the historic area occupied by the Metis of Red River and western Canada, and to exclude much of British Columbia, including historic Metis communities that existed in that province.

Since the MNC can determine for itself its own criteria for membership, it is open to them to expand their present definition to cover a much larger area. There is precedent for such a revision; in 2002 the MNC broadened their prior definition by removing the reference to scrip and land grants.

An area that appears to be included in the scope of the MNC definition of "Homeland" is the Northwest Territories, but Metis people there are not currently affiliated with the MNC. Apparently there is a movement in some quarters to have them included.

The definition of "Historic Metis Nation Homeland" is geographically broad enough to include northern areas of the United States, such as North Dakota, Minnesota and Montana. Consequently descendants from the Historic Metis Nation living in these areas of the United States would fall within the definition. However these American Metis would have to be "accepted by the Metis Nation", and they would not qualify under s. 35 of the *Constitution Act, 1982* since they are not a Canadian people.

The Metis Nation literally could grant this acceptance. However in doing so, it could cause problems under the *Constitution Act*.

The authors have had personal experiences with North Dakota and Montana Metis descended from those of the Red River area, which is part of the Historic Metis Nation Homeland. In the year 1999, the authors were en route to Altona, Manitoba to meet with Friesens, the printers of their book *The Trial of Louis Riel - Justice and Mercy Denied*.

When driving through northern North Dakota for this purpose they were stopped by a flag-man near Belcourt, due to road construction on a highway that passed through the Turtle Mountain Indian Reservation. They chatted with him and found that he was a member of that Reservation.

They asked him if he had ever heard of Louis Riel. He said he was quite familiar with Louis Riel, and that most of the people on the Reservation were descendants of the Red River Metis. However they lived on the Reservation because the United States Government did not recognize the Metis and only recognized Indians.

Only a few miles further east the authors were stopped near Rolla, North Dakota by a flag-woman. She belonged to the same Reservation and they had the same conversation with her about the Metis ancestry on the

Reservation, as they had with the flag-man in Belcourt.

In the year 2000, the authors were invited to give a talk on Louis Riel and the Metis people at the annual Montana Metis Days in Lewistown. They found that many Metis members they spoke to were descendants of the historic Red River Metis. One lady was a descendant of the Metis balladeer Pierre Falcon (who is referred to elsewhere in this book).

George discovered a Metis from North Dakota to whom he was indirectly related through the Red River Metis of old. The Metis in Montana go under the name of the Little Shell and for some time have been attempting to obtain recognition by the government of the United States.

For the purposes of s. 35 of the *Constitution Act, 1982* there must be an impersonal, objective identification process and valid proof of descent from an historic Metis community. The MNC definition is not legally decisive as to who are Metis for the purposes of s. 35. While the MNC and the Provincial Metis Associations have the right to lay down the qualifications for membership in their own organizations, they do not have the unilateral legal power to determine who, and who are not "the Metis peoples of Canada" within s. 35 of the Constitution.

As a result of the Powley judgment discussed in the next chapter, it may be expected that a number of groups in Canada self-identifying as Metis (but who do not fit within the MNC definition and whose ancestors never shared in the way of life, culture and traditions of the "Historic Metis Nation") will seek to be recognized and to assert constitutional rights under s. 35. If these other groups can meet the requirements and tests prescribed by the Supreme Court of Canada in the Powley Case, they will undoubtedly be entitled to constitutional status as a Metis people of Canada.

The question as to which of these groups can do so remains to be determined. It seems likely that, in the event of a dispute, the Supreme Court of Canada would have to decide on the status of the disputed group.

However it is clear that these groups, having emanated from an entirely different tradition, have little, if anything, in common with members of the historic Metis Nation.

While the federal and provincial governments have failed in the past to come to grips with precisely who the Metis are and what rights they are entitled to, there is a Federal Interlocutor for Metis and Non-Status Indians. He (no women have occupied this position to date) is a member of the Federal Cabinet, but also heads another Cabinet department. For example, in the 1990s Ralph Goodale combined appointments as Minister of Natural Resources, Minister responsible for the Canadian Wheat Board and Federal Interlocutor (a portfolio having little in common with the first two positions).

In July 2004 the then Prime Minister Paul Martin took the unusual step of appointing the same Cabinet Minister, Andy Scott, as the Minister of Indian Affairs, Federal Interlocutor for Metis and Non-Status Indians and Minister responsible for the Inuit. While some aboriginals do not perceive this as problematic, others are apprehensive that a pan-Aboriginal approach could pose a problem if the affairs of Status Indians, of Inuit and of the Metis come into conflict.

Some believe that this appointment may foreshadow an eventual Department of Aboriginal Affairs covering all of the aboriginal peoples of Canada under one umbrella. The MNC fears that this will take away from the Metis the right to determine their own priorities and processes.

It is interesting to note that in February, 2006 the new Federal Conservative Government appointed Jim Prentice to the same positions of Minister of Indian Affairs, Federal Interlocutor for Metis and Non-Status Indians and Minister responsible for the Inuit.

The federal government has frequently recognized the Metis encompassed by the provincial organizations comprising the MNC. It did so by virtue of its invitation to, and acceptance of participation by, representatives of the MNC at various conferences held to discuss matters affecting the Metis peoples of Canada. An example was a conference convened in 2004 by the Prime Minister. At that meeting with aboriginal leaders, the Prime Minister made specific reference to the "Metis Nation".

Another meeting was one with Prime Minister Martin and all of the Premiers of Canada in September 2004 to which Clement Chartier (President of the MNC) and the heads of the Inuit, First Nations, Congress of Aboriginal Peoples (CAP), and the Native Women's Association of Canada were invited to give their input on health matters. Representation by CAP gives a strong indication that Metis members of CAP are looked upon as Metis by the various governments of Canada.

The Federal Cabinet Committee on Aboriginal Affairs held a Policy Retreat with Aboriginal leaders on May 31, 2005 in Ottawa. Pursuant to this Meeting the federal government entered into a Framework Agreement with the Metis Nation, recognizing it and the national governance structure of the MNC.

Subsequently a First Ministers Meeting on Aboriginal issues was held in Kelowna on November 24-25, 2005. Clem Chartier, President of the MNC, was the representative of the Metis Nation at the table with the First Ministers. Various agreements were signed with the Aboriginal peoples with a view to closing the socio-economic gap between Aboriginals and other Canadians. The principal areas targeted in these Agreements were education, housing, health, economic opportunities and relationships. The estimated amount of funds allocated for these programs was $5.1 billion.

However before this Kelowna Accord could be implemented, a federal election was held on January 23, 2006 and the Conservative Party replaced the Liberal Party as the government of Canada. It is likely that the new Conservative Government will advance its own policies in lieu of this Accord.

Chapter Reference Sources

- *Constitution Act of Canada, 1982*, s. 35.

- *Globe and Mail* Newspaper of May 5, 1981.
- *Royal Commission on Aboriginal Peoples,* Vol. 4 ch. 5, Appendix 5A 1.
- "Sovereignty, Liberty, and the Legal Order of the 'Freemen' (Otipahemsu'uk): Towards a Constitutional Theory of Metis Self-Government" by Albert Peeling and Paul L. A. H. Chartrand, *Saskatchewan Law Review,* Vol. 67(1), 2004, p. 340-57.
- *Who are Canada's Aboriginal Peoples,* edited by Paul L A. H. Chartrand and Foreword by Harry W. Daniels, *passim.*

Chapter XVII

SUPREME COURT of CANADA RECOGNITION

In the history of Canada, the Powley judgment rendered by the Supreme Court of Canada on September 19, 2003 together with the *Manitoba Act, 1870* are the two most significant legal victories affecting the Metis. The Powley triumph is a tribute not only to the perseverance and fighting spirit of Steve and Roddy Powley of the Sault Ste. Marie Metis community, but also to their stalwart supporters, the Metis Nation of Ontario and the Metis National Council. Sadly, Steve Powley died less than six months after this memorable event.

With respect to the judgment, the prosaic style of judicial writing by the Supreme Court fails to capture (and in most cases even mention) the romantic and colorful aspects that are an intrinsic part of the culture, customs, traditions, and heritage associated with the historic Metis and their way of life.

Nonetheless, the Supreme Court's findings will have an explosive effect. As a matter of honor, the judgment should prod and compel the responsible Federal and Provincial Governments to refrain from stonewalling. It should also induce them to actively deal with the constitutional commitment to recognize the Metis and the obligation to enhance their survival as distinctive communities.

The following summary of salient points in the Powley judgment sets forth the authors' observations on that decision. However it is not advice and any person or group who wishes to have a legal assessment thereon, and its impact on them, should consult legal counsel. In addition a reader may wish to peruse the judgment itself. The citation for this case is R. v. Powley, [2003] 2 S.C.R. 207.

The facts of the Powley Case briefly are that the Powleys, father and son, were charged with unlawfully hunting moose and knowingly possessing game contrary to an Ontario statute. They argued that as Metis they had an aboriginal right to hunt for food under s. 35 of the *Constitution Act, 1982*. The Ontario government denied the existence of any such Metis right.

The Powleys were acquitted in the trial court, in the Superior Court, and by unanimous decision in the Court of Appeal of Ontario. The Ontario government chose to appeal every verdict it lost. It did so again in filing an appeal with the Supreme Court of Canada. A number of provinces intervened to support Ontario's position. However the Supreme Court of Canada, in a nine to nothing decision, unanimously dismissed the appeal by the Province of Ontario.

What is very significant in this judicial process is that four levels of courts and all 14 judges who presided over these legal proceedings unanimously agreed that the Metis possess "existing" aboriginal rights.

The focus of the Powley Case is s. 35 of the *Constitution Act, 1982* of Canada in relation to the Metis people and their aboriginal rights thereunder. The Supreme Court wrote that s. 35 "reflects a new promise" and it made clear that one of the purposes of this constitutional guarantee is "a commitment to recognizing the Metis and enhancing their survival as distinctive communities".

It also stated that this commitment recognizes and values the distinctive Metis cultures and the historically important and integral features relating thereto that endure today. The Court referred a number of times to Metis practices, customs and traditions.

This decision also stated that s. 35 requires recognition and protection to be extended to historically important customs and traditions of the Metis that existed before effective European control (and not the pre-contact test prescribed for Indians) since Metis ethnogenesis only occurred after European contact.

The Court discussed who the Metis and Metis peoples were and are for the purposes of s. 35. It indicated that it was not listing the various Metis peoples there may be in

Canada. It described, without providing an all-inclusive definition, the Metis and who they are. Mixed Indian and European heritage in itself does not make one a Metis. The Court added that "the recognition of Metis rights in s. 35 is not reducible to the Metis' Indian ancestry."

The historic Metis were distinctive peoples who not only had mixed ancestry from their European and Indian or Inuit forebears, but shared the common experience of developing their own customs, way of life, and recognizable group identity separate from these ancestors. They constituted a historic Metis community.

While the Supreme Court specifically refrained from formulating a comprehensive definition of "Metis" with respect to s. 35, it indicated that important components of a future definition for that purpose would require proof of three broad factors as indicia of Metis identity. These three are:

- self-identification;
- ancestral connection; and
- community acceptance.

Self-identification as a member of a Metis community should not be of recent occurrence, or belatedly made. Ancestral connection must be to a historic Metis community.

Over 125 years earlier in describing "Metis", Louis Riel said "Why should we care to what degree exactly of mixture we possess of European blood and Indian blood?" Riel's sentiments accurately foreshadowed the statement by the Supreme Court that it would not require a minimum 'blood quantum" for a Metis to be a beneficiary under s. 35. Ancestral connection must be objectively provable regardless of how a contemporary Metis community defines its own membership.

An historical Metis community is one that came into existence post European contact, but prior to the entrenchment of European control and the dominant influence of white settlers and political institutions. This is a variation of the pre-European contact test for First Nations formulated by the Supreme Court in the Van der Peet Case [1996] 2 S.C.R. 507. This case is the seminal decision with respect to the nature of aboriginal rights and some of the language in it is similar to that in the Powley Case.

The third indicia to establish that one is a Metis for purposes of s. 35 is acceptance by the modern Metis community that has continuity with the historic Metis community. Membership in a Metis political organization, while helpful and required, is insufficient in itself to determine community acceptance. One must have previously taken part and continue to do so in the traditions, cultures, and customs making up the distinguishing features of a Metis community.

Evidence of one's participatory relationship could include confirmation from other members of the community. However regardless of the definition of membership prescribed by the present-day Metis community, convincing and objective proof of a person's past and current association, recognition and historical ancestral connection is essential.

The Court on two occasions used the words "urgent priority" in its judgment. It so stated, with respect to establishing "appropriate membership tests" before disputes arise and again with respect to developing a "more systematic method of identifying Metis rights-holders". The Court added it was imperative that membership requirements in Metis communities become more standardized. However, difficulty in identifying Metis community members is not a basis for defeating their constitutional rights.

In respect to standardizing membership requirements the authors have one approach to suggest. A national registry should be established that would issue a uniform national rights-holder card to all members of the provincial Metis organizations that constitute the Metis National Council.

Another point that requires consideration as a result of the Powley Case is that the Court continually referred to a Metis "community". Accordingly it would seem appropriate that the term "local" presently used for identifying individual councils within a province should be changed to the term "community."

In the Powley Case, the Supreme Court issued a ten item "correct test" for the purposes of Metis entitlements under s. 35. This is sometimes called the Powley test. Without going into details, the following discussion abbreviates and sometimes paraphrases the Court's ten items:

- Characterization of the Right - The right that is being claimed must be characterized. These rights are contextual and site-specific. It is not simply the right to hunt for a specific species but the right to hunt for food.
- Identification of the Historic Rights-Bearing Community - To demonstrate the existence of an historic Metis community to support a site-specific aboriginal rights claim there must be not only demographic evidence, but also proof of shared customs, traditions, and a collective identity.
- Identification of the Contemporary Rights-Bearing Community - Aboriginal rights are communal rights; consequently a current Metis community must be ancestrally based on an historic Metis community. An individual who is not a member of such an ancestrally based present day community would not be entitled to s. 35 rights.
- Verification of the Claimant's Membership in the Relevant Contemporary Community - Over and above community self-definition, the process of identification must be objectively verifiable. The three indicia of self-identification, ancestral connection and community acceptance must be demonstrated.
- Identification of the Relevant Time Frame - This is the post-European contact but pre-control test discussed

earlier in this chapter.

- Determination of Whether the Practice is Integral to the Claimants' Distinctive Culture - In the Powley Case it was held that subsistence hunting for food was an important aspect of Metis life.
- Establishment of Continuity Between the Historic Practice and the Contemporary Right Asserted - This is to reflect the constitutional commitment to protect today historically important practices, such as a Metis aboriginal right to hunt for food.
- Determination of Whether or Not the Right was Extinguished - A determination must be made as to whether abolition of the aboriginal right has occurred.
- If There is a Right, Determination of Whether There is an Infringement - If the right is not being recognized or honored by a government, that government must be justified in failing to do so.
- Determination of Whether the Infringement is Justified - One justification would be conservation if exercising a right would be a threat to an animal population being hunted. In the case of food for subsistence needs even if there was such a threat, the Metis would nevertheless be entitled to a priority allocation similar to that of the First Nations in R. v. Sparrow, [1990] 1 S.C.R. 1075. The blanket denial in Ontario of any Metis right was not justified.

The Metis right to hunt for food is not species-specific but a claimant must belong to an identifiable Metis community with some degree of continuity and stability to support a site-specific aboriginal rights claim.

The result of the Powley decision is that the aboriginal rights of the Metis peoples under s. 35 have been constitutionally recognized. This includes a commitment to the Metis to enhance their survival as distinct communities and to value and protect their historically important cultures, customs and traditions. The Supreme Court has effectively said that governments in Canada must respect the Metis peoples and their aboriginal rights.

However in the Powley Case, the Supreme Court did not rule on or deal with a number of relevant matters, and left for future consideration significant issues. Some of these points are discussed below.

Scope of Recognition of Metis

The Court referred to the Metis on two occasions as having an identity separate from their Indian or Inuit and European forebears, and added a third reference to Inuit in quoting from the Report of the Royal Commission on Aboriginal Peoples. The Court also referred to Inuit in the Blais Case referred to later in this chapter.

It also stated the possibility that there may be Metis "peoples" under s. 35. This language leaves open the possibility that if there is a Metis group (in addition to those encompassed under the definition of the Metis National Council) that can meet the prescribed tests and requirements laid down by the Court, that group would be entitled under s. 35.

There are commentators who express the opinion that there are no such groups who can meet the tests and requirements. They would argue that some of these "supposed Metis groups", such as the Labrador Metis, only identified as such after the Metis were included in s. 35. The Labrador Metis take the view that it is the substance of their ancestry (European and Inuit) and identity that is determinative, not the designation used.

As well, in the Powley Case the Supreme Court of Canada quoted the Royal Commission on Aboriginal Peoples describing the evolution of Metis communities. The passage it quoted specifically referred, among other matters, to the "Labrador Metis (whose culture had early roots)". The Supreme Court in the Blais Case also stated "Other Metis emerged in eastern Canada", but did not specify or delimit the extent.

It has also been said that those who refer to themselves as Nova Scotia Metis have no historical connection to the concept of what a Metis is - the culture and traditions, the way of life, the rise of a New Nation and so on. It is argued by some that those in the Maritimes that call themselves Metis did not develop a distinct culture or political presence.

Whether or not other groups can qualify as Metis under s. 35, remains to be seen. It seems probable that this situation will result in future litigation by any such group to have its status determined and recognized by the courts.

Physical Extent of a Metis Community

The physical extent of any particular Metis community was left unsettled. The Supreme Court referred in part to a community as a group of Metis "living together in the same geographic area and sharing a common way of life." It did not decide whether the community of Sault Ste. Marie was also a Metis 'people' or whether it was "part of a larger Metis people extending over a wider area such as the Upper Great Lakes."

The Metis National Council (MNC) definition of Metis given in the prior chapter described the "Historic Metis Nation Homeland" as the area of land in west central North America used and occupied as the "traditional territory" of the Metis, but did not lay down the boundaries of this territory.

It seems most unlikely that the gigantic geographical area within the traditional territory of the Historic Metis Nation Homeland would be considered one Metis community, but rather a number of different communities.

While the Canadian Metis of "west central" North America may collectively be a Metis people under s. 35, it was only the classic historical Metis of Red River and Western Canada, and not other communities identifying themselves as Metis, that actively participated in the memorable events discussed in this book.

These events included the Battle of Seven Oaks, the Red River Expedition to the Oregon Territory, the Battle of the Grand Coteau, the Red River Resistance, and the North-

West Uprising. Consequently, it appears more probable they would constitute a Metis people and that qualified Metis from other areas would make up one or more other communities of Metis peoples. However if it is established that there is more than one Metis people in Canada, there is no doubt that the classic Metis descended from those of the traditional Metis Homeland are a unique people distinct from any other such people.

The Blais Case, reported at [2003] 2 S.C.R. 236, was a decision issued on the same date as the Powley judgment. In this decision, the Supreme Court of Canada ruled that a Metis was not an Indian under the *Natural Resources Transfer Agreement, 1930*, Schedule (1) to the *Constitution Act, 1930.* The Court specifically stated that "The Red River Metis distinguished themselves from the Indians." In this Case Blais did not claim a right to hunt for food under s. 35 of the *Constitution Act, 1982*.

In the Blais decision, the Supreme Court stated "members of Metis communities in the prairie provinces collectively refer to themselves as the "Metis Nation", and trace their roots to the western fur trade .... Other Metis communities emerged in eastern Canada."

Also in Blais, the Court made reference to the "Red River Metis" and to the "Manitoba Metis". In these statements, the Supreme Court appears to distinguish Metis communities in the Red River, in Manitoba, and in the Prairie Provinces from those in eastern Canada.

Perhaps a stronger case could have been made for Blais if he had proceeded under s. 91(24) of the Constitution relating to "Indians" and their lands. In the case re Eskimos [1939] S.C.R. 104, the Supreme Court ruled that Eskimos (Inuit) are Indians thereunder. It could have been argued that s. 35 together with the equality provision of s. 15 of the *Charter of Rights and Freedoms* entitled the Metis to equal treatment with the Indians and Inuit under s. 91(24).

Sharing a Common Way of Life

The Supreme Court left unanswered the question of the

extent to which there must be a "sharing [of] a common way of life" today to constitute a Metis community under s. 35. Many Metis reside in large urban centers. They convene on special occasions and from time to time. They get together for activities such as annual festivals, celebrations and flag raisings on Louis Riel Day, annual meetings, dinners and dances. These activities are usually accompanied by fiddling, jigging, singing, and sash-wearing amidst a genuine atmosphere of camaraderie.

However most Metis living in metropolitan areas, while sharing these common activities in their lives, live in various suburbs, have dissimilar lifestyles, practice a variety of faiths, and engage for most of their time in non-Metis pursuits.

Are such occasional Metis activities sufficient to constitute "sharing a common way of life"? If they do not but one meets the three indicia of self-identification, ancestral connection, and community acceptance, is that sufficient to constitute a person a Metis for purposes of s. 35 of the Constitution?

Another question may arise where one's parents were born in a Red River Metis community and the current descendent was born in an unrelated Metis community. Does that child not have any Metis rights under s. 35 because as stated by the Court there must be "ancestrally based membership in the present community"?

What is the situation of an individual who meets the Court's three indicia of Metis identity, and whose valid ancestrally based community is in one area of Canada, but he or she moves to another area?

In both cases it would seem preposterous that they lose their Metis identity, but past resistance and denial by various governments may witness similar tactics and obstruction in the future. In such event litigation may be necessary to establish status and in some instances a party may argue that by virtue of their "rights of mobility" under the *Canadian Charter of Rights and Freedoms*, their Metis rights are maintained under s. 35 of the Constitution.

Metis Determination in Law

The Metis National Council takes the position that the right to determine who its members are rests exclusively with their people. This is certainly true for membership in their organizations. However as earlier noted, in itself it is not the final arbiter of who qualifies as a Metis people for the purposes of s. 35. This is a constitutional question, not a question of unilateral determination.

It seems beyond doubt that the registered members of the Metis Nation, as defined, would qualify as a Metis people under that Section. That definition effectively includes the three Supreme Court indicia of Metis identity set forth in the Powley Case - self identification, ancestral connection to an historic Metis community, and acceptance by a contemporary Metis community. As well, representatives of the Metis Nation have frequently been invited to participate in governmental conferences, thereby effectively being given governmental recognition as a "Metis people".

Scope of Metis Aboriginal Rights

With respect to Metis aboriginal rights generally, the specific determination of the Supreme Court in the Powley Case is that the "relevant right is not to hunt moose but to hunt for 'food' in the designated territory".

The Court referred to the "practice of 'subsistence' hunting and fishing" in the Metis community. It also approvingly quoted authors of reports who wrote of the Metis obtaining "their livelihood off of the land" and "from hunting, fishing, gathering and cultivating". The *Canadian Oxford Dictionary* defined the term "livelihood' as "a way of earning a living; an occupation".

It is arguable that the right to hunt food extends to doing so for commercial purposes. The Supreme Court referred to not only subsistence hunting but to the Metis obtaining their livelihood off of the land.

In the days of the buffalo hunt the Metis, in pursuing

their way of life, were engaged on the prairies not only in hunting for subsistence but also as a commercial venture in order to make pemmican and other products available to the fur trading companies, the Red River Settlers, and others. These factors may be one of the reasons why the Court also stated that "the contours of the Metis right to hunt" will be more clearly defined in the longer term by a combination of negotiation and judicial settlement.

On the other hand, if a species was threatened by Metis hunting, the right may be justifiably infringed for conservation purposes, but the Metis would still be entitled to a priority allocation in accordance with the criteria for First Nations set forth in *R. v. Sparrow* [1990] 1 S.C. R. 1075.

In the Powley Case, the Court did make reference to fishing. Fishing has been recognized as an aboriginal right in the case of British Columbia First Nations. The Supreme Court has specifically included commercial fishing rights in *R. v. Gladstone* [1996] 2 S.C.R. 723.

One beneficial effect of the ruling in the Powley Case has already happened in Alberta where an Interim Metis Harvesting Agreement between the Government of Alberta and the Metis Nation of Alberta came into effect on October 1, 2004. This Agreement recognizes the Metis right to hunt, trap and fish for subsistence on harvesting lands within the Province of Alberta.

However a number of other provinces have denied the Metis hunting rights determined under the Powley decision. Since the ruling there have been a number of prosecutions against Metis hunters in Ontario, Manitoba, Saskatchewan and British Columbia. The provinces argue that there is no historical Metis community in the relevant area, or there were no Metis harvesters whose ancestors had continuously exercised the right.

From a practical point of view many Metis will not exercise the right to hunt, particularly those that reside in urban areas and even more so if the right is construed to be only for subsistence purposes. Consequently, the question of what other aboriginal rights the Metis are entitled to or should negotiate is a matter of great interest to the Metis peoples.

Obvious goals, which would bring significant and meaningful benefits to a much larger segment of the Metis people than hunting rights, include rights with respect to land grants, day care, early childhood learning, post-secondary education, health and non-insured medical benefits and coverage, housing, nutritional programs, employment programs, and others.

Some of these matters were negotiated and agreed upon at the First Ministers Conference in Kelowna in November 2005, but it is unknown to what extent the Kelowna Accord will be implemented under the new Conservative Government.

The Supreme Court left many questions and issues unanswered in the Powley Case and there is no doubt that unsympathetic governments will stonewall on a number of matters. The Court stated that:

> .... courts faced with Metis claims will have to ascertain Metis identity on a case by case basis.

If past governmental attitudes are any guide, the Metis will have to fight tooth and nail and by all legitimate means to realize rights over and above that of hunting for food.

Members of the First Nations already enjoy a number of benefits in addition to their hunting rights. These additional rights are derived through treaty rather than aboriginal rights. Some members of the Congress of Aboriginal Peoples assert that certain of their Metis ancestors participated in treaties.

It appears that the historic Metis did not sign specific treaties with the Crown and, while their descendants have aboriginal rights under s. 35, they may not have treaty rights and they do not now have the extended programs and benefits based on treaty rights. However, treaty rights were specifically mentioned in the "Metis Nation

Framework Agreement" of May 31, 2005 between the federal government and the Metis National Council.

A preamble to this Agreement states:

> AND WHEREAS the Metis National Council asserts it represents Metis that have Aboriginal and Treaty rights, including rights to lands and resources and to the exercise of self-government.

One of the objectives set forth in this Agreement was to:

> .... address any Aboriginal and Treaty rights of the Metis, including the inherent right of self-government.

Since some governments will likely disagree that the Metis have such rights (with a possible exception related to land), the Metis will undoubtedly have to undertake governmental negotiations and possibly litigation in an attempt to achieve such programs and benefits.

In the Powley Case the Supreme Court did not define or specify the scope of the aboriginal rights of the Metis people, or indicate whether they had any treaty rights under s. 35. On the latter point, there are some Metis who argue that the arrangements negotiated on behalf of the Metis to enter the Canadian Confederation, most of which were constitutionally enshrined in the *Manitoba Act, 1870*, amount to a treaty.

Section 31 of that Act, a Federal Statute, provided for land grants totaling 1,400,000 acres to be distributed among Metis children. It specifically stated that this land grant was for:

> .... the extinguishment of the Indian Title to the lands in the Province.

In so doing, the Canadian Parliament officially recognized in 1870 that the Metis people had an Aboriginal right in the land. Prime Minister John A. Macdonald, whose government was responsible for introducing this Act, confirmed in Parliament at that time that the land grant was for that purpose. He stated that the

> ..... half-breeds had a strong claim to the lands in consequence of their extraction, as well as from being

settlers.

In a speech in the House of Commons on July 6, 1885 (the year of the North-West Uprising) Macdonald attempted to backtrack on these statements.

In the years following the *Manitoba Act, 1870*, many Metis were done out of their entitlements by fraud, deception, and political chicanery. The bitterness and resentment over the manner in which these land claims were handled by the government and its officials continue to this day.

There is a long-standing lawsuit in Manitoba in respect to claims that many Metis were defrauded of their right to land after Manitoba came into Confederation. After more than 20 years of legal maneuvering, this case began hearings in the Court of Queen's Bench in Winnipeg on April 3, 2006.

Immediately prior to the commencement of the trial, a large group of Metis assembled around the statue of Louis Riel on the Manitoba Legislative grounds to express their support. At this gathering David Chartrand, President of the Manitoba Metis Federation, stated in an interview on Aboriginal Peoples Television news:

> We're putting Canada's history on trial today; we're forced to do it. We'd rather negotiate, but we're forced to litigate.

At the time of the writing of this book, the case is proceeding through the court system. With the probability of appeals to higher courts, it is likely that a final decision will not be forthcoming for six or eight years.

Chapter Reference Sources

- *Constitution Act of Canada, 1982*, s. 35.
- "Historic SCC ruling affirms aboriginal rights of Metis", by Cristin Schmitz, *The Lawyers Weekly* Newspaper, Oct. 3, 2003, p. 1; 24.
- *Manitoba Act, 1870*, S.C. 1870 c.3.
- "Powley Text Analysis", Congress of Aboriginal Peoples Pamphlet.
- "Powley vindicated one last time" by Tom Spaulding, *Metis Voyageur* Newspaper, Sept./Oct. 2003, p. 10.
- "Re Eskimos" [1939] 2 S.C.R. 104.
- "R. v. Blais" [2003] 2 S.C.R. 236.
- "R. v. Gladstone" [1996] 2 S.C.R. 723.

- "R. v. Powley" [2003] 2 S.C.R. 207.
- "R. v. Powley A case Summary and Frequently Asked Questions" Metis National Council pamphlet.
- "R. v. Sparrow" [1990] 1 S.C.R. 1075.
- "R. v. Van der Peet" [1996] 2 S.C.R. 507.
- *Riel and the Rebellion, 1885 Reconsidered*, by Thomas Flanagan, chapter three.
- "Steve Powley 1948-2004 Our Nation in his debt", *Metis Voyageur* Newspaper, April/May 2004, p. 11-18.

SECTION C

MEMORABLE PERSONALITIES

Provincial Archives of Manitoba No. N7580

Gabriel Dumont

Buffalo Hunter and Military Strategist

Provincial Archives of Man. No.16983 MacLeod, Margaret A.22

Pierre Falcon

Bard of the Metis

Provincial Archives of B.C. No. A-01741

James Sinclair

Activist and Adventurer

Provincial Archives of Manitoba N21685

Elzear Goulet

Metis Martyr

Provincial Archives of Man. Delorme, Pierre 1

Pierre Delorme

Politician and Rights Activist

Harry Daniels
Metis Crusader

Senator
Thelma Chalifoux

Social Activist and
Metis Matriarch

Tantoo Cardinal

Metis Actor
Extraordinaire

American Indian Film Institute

Chapter XVIII

CUTHBERT GRANT

Premier Metis Leader

The first notable leader in the history of the Metis people was Cuthbert Grant. He ingrained in their psyche the conviction that they were a "Metis Nation", a unique people with indigenous rights in the land, in its resources, in their own self-government, and in their own way of life. With the help of Alexander Greenfield Macdonell and other officials of the North West Company (NWC), Grant instilled in his kinsmen the belief in the Metis Nation.

This belief has had a pervading influence on the Metis for nearly two hundred years. It was a concept that played a prominent role in many events such the Red River Resistance and the North-West Uprising.

Grant's memorable legacy in this respect continues to this day. As recently as May 31, 2005, the Government of Canada entered into the "Metis Nation Framework Agreement" with the Metis National Council. One of the objectives of this Agreement is "to engage a new partnership between Canada and the Metis Nation", thereby confirming federal recognition of this Metis status.

The Metis Nation was forged in the crucible of the Battle of Seven Oaks (discussed in the chapter of this book dedicated to that Battle) and incidents preceding it. The guiding star was a young Cuthbert Grant, only twenty-three years old, whom the Metis recognized as a leader with pre-eminent capabilities.

He was a native-born son of the West, a son of the fur trade. To this was added his formal education, his fluency in languages, his daring and magnetism, and his surpassing self-confidence. The respect accorded his leadership was based on his being a Metis - one of them.

Grant was born in 1793 at Fort de la Rivière Tremblante (the NWC fort not far from what is now known as

Kamsack, Saskatchewan near the Manitoba border). His father, Cuthbert Grant Sr., was born in Scotland. When the young Cuthbert was born his father was a fur trader who later became a wintering partner (or bourgeois) of the NWC. Little is known of Grant's mother except that she was a Metis of Cree and French descent.

There is not much information on Grant's early years. He did have a brother born in 1791 and three sisters. One of his sister's Mary married the Metis minstrel Pierre Falcon who is highlighted in another chapter of this book.

Grant was orphaned when his father died in 1799. Young Cuthbert was taken to Montreal as an eight year old by his guardian William McGillivray, a prominent partner of the NWC who eventually became its Chief Director. In Montreal Cuthbert was baptized in the Scotch Presbyterian Church.

In his father's will, instruction was given that young Cuthbert was to receive an education. As a result he was educated in Montreal and later sent to Scotland to further his education. While there he met his Scottish relatives. Sometime after his return to Canada, Cuthbert became a clerk of the NWC in 1812 and placed in charge of a minor post on the Qu'Appelle River.

Not long after at Brandon House, a fort of the Hudson's Bay Company (HBC), Grant made the acquaintance of John R. McKay and, as an added attraction at that post, he met McKay's sister Elizabeth. In 1814 he married Elizabeth a la façon du pays (in the fashion of the country), that is without benefit of clergy. This was a common practice among the Metis in areas where there were no men of the cloth.

In 1814 the NWC, Grant, and the Metis had a common interest in opposing the proclamations (referred to herein under "The Battle of Seven Oaks") with respect to pemmican and running the buffalo issued by Governor Miles Macdonell (the cousin of the NWC's Alexander Greenfield Macdonell). In order to maintain the cooperation of the Metis in the struggles with the colonists and the HBC, Duncan Cameron (a wintering partner of the NWC) named Cuthbert Grant a captain of the Metis in the latter part of that year.

The Metis harassed the Selkirk Settlement and many colonists left. The Metis captains had Peter Fidler, then in charge of the Settlement, sign an agreement dated June 25, 1815. It contained terms requiring all settlers to immediately leave Red River; it also declared a number of Metis rights as well as serving the interests of the NWC. This document was signed on behalf of the Metis by Grant, Bostonais Pangman, William Shaw and Bonhomme Montour as "The four chiefs of the Half-breed." This may have been one of the first political acts by a group of Metis in asserting their rights.

However later that year Colin Robertson of the HBC arrived in the colony with a group of settlers, followed not long after by the new Governor Robert Semple.

Prior to the Battle of Seven Oaks, the NWC had realized the leadership and great influence which Cuthbert Grant exercised among his people and the high esteem in which they held him. Consequently in March 1816, the NWC promoted him and gave him an impressive title. An observer at the time, James Sutherland wrote:

> The flag was flying in honor of Cuthbert Grant having been appointed Captain-General of all the Half Breeds in the country.

Fort Douglas was surrendered to the NWC shortly after the Battle of Seven Oaks. Two months after receiving word of the Seven Oaks incident of June 19, 1816 Lord Selkirk, with about 100 mercenaries, seized the NWC's grand and pivotal Fort William. Since the Government would not accede to Selkirk's request for an army, he had hired his own mercenaries of mainly retired de Meuron soldiers (originally from Switzerland).

Fort William was the NWC's major transport depot and one where wintering partners and Montreal agents rendezvoused every summer for their annual general meeting. In January 1817, Selkirk's army recaptured Fort

Douglas and took prisoners in the Red River Settlement. At this time Cuthbert Grant was in the Qu'Appelle region.

Miles Macdonell wrote Grant in March of that year:

> Your people are assembled unlawfully. I order you in His Majesty's name to disperse them ..... [otherwise] you must take the consequences.

Grant had no intention of kowtowing to this upstart intruder in his native land. With disdain, he immediately and firmly replied as follows:

> Your threats you make use of we laught [sic] at them and you may come with your forces at any time you please .... I dare you to come out with your forces. Since you will not come to any reasonable terms you may do your worst and you may perhaps have cause to repent your expressions and folly.

Some time after these written exchanges Commissioner W. B, Coltman, who had been directed to investigate the disturbances in the North West and the violence at Seven Oaks, arrived on the scene. In 1818 he persuaded Grant to go to Montreal to face charges, one of which was that he had murdered Owen Keveny of the HBC.

Coltman considered the battle at Seven Oaks had been a "private war" and hinted to Grant that the offences could be pardoned. In fact, nothing ever came of the charges against Grant and in particular he was never convicted of anything related to the Battle of Seven Oaks or other incidents. Any thought of prosecuting Grant seems to have been pigeon-holed after François Fermin Boucher, the first Metis to confront Semple at Seven Oaks, was acquitted of Semple's murder.

The involvement of Grant with Alexander Greenfield Macdonell, Governor Robert Semple, the Selkirk Settlers, the NWC, and the HBC are further discussed elsewhere in this book.

In his 1818 last will and testament made while he was in Montreal awaiting trial, Grant referred to his wife Elizabeth as a "Maitiss [sic] woman." She was the mother of his son James. When he returned from Montreal to the North West in 1818, Grant was truly thunderstruck when he realized that in his absence his wife Elizabeth had deserted him. She disappeared without a trace, taking their infant son James with her. He never saw either of them again.

Not long after, Grant again married a Metis woman a la façon du pays. Her name was Madelaine Desmarais. Their daughter Maria was born in 1820, but the matrimonial union dissolved shortly thereafter.

About this time negotiations were underway in England to merge the NWC and the HBC. Andrew Colvile, Lord Selkirk's brother-in-law, represented the Selkirk interests (the Earl had died in 1820). Colvile was a member of the London Committee of the HBC and also represented that Company in the negotiations.

The amalgamation occurred in 1821 under the continuing name of the HBC. Many of the NWC personnel were not taken on by the merged company. Among the numerous Metis and other Nor'Westers suddenly out of work were two of their leaders who had resolutely opposed the HBC - Cuthbert Grant and Alexander Greenfield Macdonell.

However, Governor George Simpson of the HBC met Grant in 1822 and was quite impressed with him. Simpson wrote Andrew Colvile on May 20th of that year stating in part:

> There I met the celebrated Cuthbert Grant .... and had occasion to see a good deal of him .... he assured me that the melancholy catastrophe [of Seven Oaks] was entirely the result of the imprudent attack made upon them by Mr. Semple's party, and once the Indian blood was raised his utmost efforts could not arrest the Savage Revenge of his associates ....
>
> Grant is now about 25 Years of Age, an active clean made fellow, possessing strong natural parts and a great deal of cool determination; his manners are mild and rather pleasing than otherways ....
>
> The half-breeds and Indians of this part of the Country look up to him with great respect, indeed there is not a man in the Country possesses half the influence over them ....

> I am therefore of opinion that it might be policy to overlook the past and if you did not object to it he might be smuggled quietly into the Service again.

Simpson realized that with Grant's great influence over the Metis he would be a valuable asset to the HBC. Although it took over a year after that letter to Colvile was written, in the summer of 1823 Simpson offered to make Grant a clerk in the HBC at a salary of £120 per year for a three year period.

Grant was stationed at Fort Garry, a mystifying posting since many residents there were quite aware of his leading role at Seven Oaks and they were not inclined to forgive or forget. This hostile attitude of the settlers found vent in some of them assaulting Grant without provocation. Grant decided to resign his position in 1824.

In 1823 Grant had wed Marie, a Metis and the oldest daughter of Angus McGillis, at St. Boniface Cathedral and converted to Roman Catholicism. It has been said that he actually wished to marry Marie's sister Marguerite and that he had an illegitimate son Charles with her. Cuthbert and Marie eventually had nine children and some of their descendants still live in that area.

There is some thought that Governor Simpson may have precipitated Grant's departure from the HBC in 1824 because he saw a more useful role that Grant could play in assisting the HBC. In 1823 when the western dispute over the international border to the Rocky Mountains was settled at the 49th parallel, Pembina ended up in American territory.

Pembina was a trading community with a large Metis population. Simpson was concerned that if the Metis remained there they would be beyond HBC jurisdiction and a threat to the HBC trade monopoly.

Simpson arranged for Cuthbert Grant to receive a large tract of land on the Assiniboine River at a location on the White Horse Plain approximately 30 kilometers west of Fort Garry. This grant of land was six miles adjacent to and six miles back from the Assiniboine River. Grant was asked to travel to Pembina and persuade the Metis families to migrate from there and resettle on large river lots at White Horse Plain.

One of Simpson's aims for this settlement was in keeping with the HBC's policy to encourage agriculture in an attempt to make their communities self-sufficient. In addition Simpson well knew that this new community would also provide a buffer zone and a source of protection to other nearby communities against the potential of attack by hostile Sioux braves.

The clergy was very supportive of this human transplantation since they wanted the Metis to follow agricultural pursuits rather than their semi-nomadic way of life. With their encouragement, Grant was successful in getting about 100 Pembina families to pull up stakes and migrate to White Horse Plain.

A colony was established there and became known as Grantown after its founder. In addition to those from Pembina, a number of other Metis and their families also followed Grant to Grantown. Among them were his three married sisters, his father-in-law Angus McGillis, and his brother-in-law Pierre Falcon.

Grant was considered the Seigneur of this new community of mostly French Roman Catholic Metis. He built a roomy log house in the Red River style. It was used for several years for religious services and as a schoolhouse.

Many of the new settlers took up farming, but this did not stop them from going on the buffalo hunts in the spring and in the fall, or from acting as voyageurs in boat brigades and transporters by Red River carts. The food obtained from the buffalo hunt was still essential for the people of Red River.

Grant, the born leader, was elected Captain of the Hunt for a number of years. He also farmed his land and built a water mill (which proved unsuccessful) and successfully built a wind mill. He also became a private freighter conveying goods, including those of the HBC, from York

Factory and Norway House to the Red River Settlement. In addition he was licensed as a private fur trader by the HBC which wanted to use his talents to forestall American competitors from coming into the HBC bailiwick.

In the 1827 Red River Census the information shown for Grant indicated that he was living in the village of Grantown and had 34 acres of cultivated land. He was described as a 31 year old Roman Catholic, which if correct would mean he was born in 1796 (not 1793 the generally accepted year), that he was married and had two daughters under the age of 15 years.

The 1835 Census disclosed that Grant and his wife Marie McGillis then had six children. As well as cultivated land he owned 24 cattle, six horses and 10 carts. The number of carts indicates his extensive involvement in freighting.

In furtherance of its objective to prevent trading in furs in contravention of its monopoly, the HBC created a new position for Cuthbert Grant. In July 1828 the HBC named him Warden of the Plains of Red River with his duties to include "the prevention of illicit trade in Furs within that District". His salary was fixed at £200 per annum, a relatively large sum for that time.

Grant's prestigious title (which he held until after the Sayer Trial of 1849) was a mantle of authority empowering and enjoining him to police the fur trade and to enforce the HBC monopoly. However Governor Simpson in his *Character Book No. 31* described Sinclair's appointment as:

> .... a sinecure offered him entirely from political motives ....
>
> This appointment prevents him from interfering with the Trade on his own account which he would otherwise do in all probability; it moreover affords us the benefit of his great influence over the half breeds and Indians of the neighbourhood.
>
> .... [he] is always ready to obey our commands and is very effective when employed as a Constable among the half breeds or Indians ...

Simpson also referred to Grant as "A very stout

powerful fellow of great nerve & resolution." This is very similar to a comment made by John Siveright (originally with the NWC and later a Chief Factor of the HBC under Simpson). Siveright observed:

> Grant is a good fellow. I have met with none who possessed more personal bravery and determined resolution in time of danger ....

After the HBC reacquired the District of Assiniboia from the Selkirk estate in 1834, other positions for Grant followed. Between 1835 and 1839 he was appointed Justice of the Peace for the White Horse Plain District, a magistrate, a sheriff, and a member of the Council of Assiniboia.

In 1837 a colorful character, the self-styled General James Dickson, arrived in Red River and befriended Grant. Dickson had a dream of liberating the "Indian Nations" and came to Red River to recruit a Metis army for this purpose.

The no-nonsense Governor Simpson, fearing that a loss of a large number of Metis would be detrimental to the community, put a quick end to Dickson's quixotic campaign. He did so by a simple stratagem - the HBC was ordered not to accept Dickson's money drafts.

Dickson spent that winter in Red River and Grant helped him out. Before he left the area after the failure of his droll escapade, Dickson bestowed his epaulettes and gold inlaid sword on Cuthbert Grant. The epaulettes were subsequently burned in a fire at St. Francois-Xavier Convent where they were being held in safekeeping. The sword is now in the possession of the Manitoba Museum in Winnipeg.

Governor Simpson thought in later days that Grant drank too much liquor from time to time. In his Character Book No. 31, Simpson refers to Grant being then about 38 years old. He writes that Grant is:

> A generous Warm hearted man .... but now getting unwieldy and inactive. Drinks ardent spirits in large quantities .... but is so well Seasoned that he is seldom intoxicated altho [sic] it undermines his constitution rapidly. A sensible clear headed man of good conduct except in reference to the unfortunate

habits of intemperance he has fallen into.

However MacLeod and Morton in their book *Cuthbert Grant of Grantown* refer to an incident involving Grant and the Sioux in 1834. Simpson wrote that an alarming aspect with the Sioux almost occurred due to "a fit of inebriety" on Grant's part.

MacLeod and Morton said of this event that if Grant had been drinking that it wasn't to such an extent as to affect his judgment when the situation became clear. They added that "in later years there was little further comment on his private habits." It is quite possible that Simpson's views may have been colored by HBC people who still resented Grant over the Battle of Seven Oaks.

With the advent of the 1840s more Metis became involved in what the HBC considered illicit trafficking in furs with the Americans. They did so because United States traders offered significantly higher prices for furs and other products than did the HBC.

Grant's role as Warden of the Plains was to stop illicit trafficking in furs. In this position he was beholden to and acting on the side of the HBC, not that of his Metis kinsmen. As a result his rapport with them started to decline.

Younger Metis, such as James Sinclair and Jean Louis Riel, emerged as leaders. They were not happy with the control and other measures taken by the HBC with a view to enforcing its monopoly.

The Metis agitated for greater rights, but the outcome of their unrest was that in 1849 the HBC pressed charges against Pierre Guillaume Sayer and other Metis for illegal trading. At the trial Grant sat on the bench as a member of the Council of Assiniboia and a Magistrate next to the disliked Recorder Adam Thom.

The Metis saw that Grant was in effect opposing their interests. Consequently the Sayer Trial challenged not only the HBC monopoly but the influence of Grant over the Metis. Both the HBC and Grant lost.

After the trial Grant, whose authority over his Metis people had been receding, no longer had any effective control over them. Reference is made to the chapter in this book titled "The Sayer Trial and Free Trade" for a detailed discussion of this landmark legal case.

The result of the Sayer Trial was that the HBC monopoly was effectively broken. The HBC almost immediately realized that Grant no longer had a dominating influence over his people.

This meant that Grant, holding a "sinecure offered him entirely from political motives", was no longer of any use to the HBC. The HBC did not renew his office of Warden of the Plains. From that time until his death Grant no longer played a pre-eminent role among his kinsmen.

During his lifetime Grant had many careers. He was a superb buffalo hunter, a fur trader, a freighter, a farmer, a politician and a magistrate.

Cuthbert Grant had another great talent – his knowledge of European medicine that he likely acquired when he was in Scotland. He had sufficient familiarity in the field to request medications from the HBC medical doctors by their scientific names.

He had at least two medicine chests, one of which accompanied him on the buffalo hunt. One of his chests made in England about 1825 is now in the possession of the Manitoba Museum. It is an oak box measuring about 18 inches by 11 inches by 10 inches. Glass medicine bottles are stored in its drawers.

In 1854, now in his sixties, he had a fall from his horse and died on July 15 of that year. He was buried in the parish church at Grantown. Not long after Grantown was renamed St. François-Xavier, its current name.

A stone cairn built at St. François-Xavier by the Historic Sites and Monuments Board of Canada stands today in the town site and reads as follows:

CUTHBERT GRANT 1793-1854

Son of a Scots trader and an Indian mother, Grant became a

> clerk in the North West Company and leader of the Metis in their struggle against the Selkirk Settlement and the Hudson's Bay Company. In 1816 he led the party which killed Governor Semple and his followers at Seven Oaks and captured Fort Douglas; but after 1821 he became reconciled with the colony. The Company named him 'Warden of the Plains', and charged him with keeping order on the southern prairies. In 1839 [sic] he became a Councillor of Assiniboia and magistrate capping a life dedicated to the native people of the West.

Although Grant lost favor with many of his Metis kinsmen during his later years due to his close association with the HBC and his role in protecting its monopoly, he nevertheless ranks as one of the most pre-eminent Metis in history.

He made many contributions on behalf of his people during his lifetime, but his consummate achievement was in inspiring these native-born children of the fur trade to view themselves with pride, to view themselves as a nation - the Metis Nation. Grant's legacy lives stronger than ever today.

Chapter Reference Sources

- *Canadian Prairies, a History, The,* by Gerald Friesen, p. 69; 76-7; 80; 90.
- *Cuthbert Grant of Grantown, Warden of the Plains of Red River,* by Margaret A. Macleod and W. L. Morton, *passim.*
- *Cuthbert Grant,* by The Manitoba Historic Resources Branch (1985), pamphlet.
- "Cuthbert, Grant: Captain-General of all the Half-Breeds", by Cherie Dimaline, *Metis Voyageur* Newspaper June/July 1999, p. 11.
- "Cuthbert Grant the Metis Leader, 1793-1854" by Mary McCarthy Ferguson - Hudson's Bay Company Archives, Winnipeg - Files on Cuthbert Grant.
- "Cuthbert Grant - The Warden of the Plains", by Margaret Complin, *The Winnipeg Tribune* June 19, 1937, 3; 7.
- "Grant, Cuthbert", by Emma Larocque, *The Canadian Encyclopedia,* p. 1003.
- "Grant, Cuthbert", by George Woodcock, *Dictionary of Canadian Biography* Vol. VIII, p. 341-44.
- *Metis Canada's Forgotten People, The,* by D. Bruce Sealey and Antoine S. Lussier, p. 37-42.
- *Pioneers and Early Citizens of Manitoba,* editor Manitoba Library Association, p. 88-89.
- Provincial Archives of Manitoba - "Cuthbert Grant File" p. 073-075.

- "Red River Gossip, A" by Elaine Allan Mitchell p. 6.
- "Simpson's Character Book", by Sir George Simpson, p. 88-89 - *Hudson's Bay Record Society*, Vol. XXX (1975), Winnipeg, p. 209-211.
- "Warden of the Plains' Oak Medicine Chest", *The Globe and Mail*, Sept. 21, 1944.

Chapter XIX

PIERRE FALCON

Bard of the Metis

Pierre Falcon continues to this day to be the unsurpassed bard of the Metis. He often wrote songs spontaneously. His ballads were sung by buffalo hunters around campfires, by voyageurs to the rhythm of their paddles, by the Red River cart brigades, by the Metis at parties. His songs echoed across the North-West from the Assiniboine to the Mackenzie Rivers, up to Hudson Bay, and across the Great Lakes.

Falcon was born on June 4, 1793, the same year as Cuthbert Grant. They were contemporaries, neighbors, close friends and brothers-in-law from early adulthood until Grant's death in 1854.

Pierre, the Metis minstrel, was born at Elbow Fort in the Swan River District. This Fort owned by the North West Company (NWC) was in an area of what is now eastern Saskatchewan. His father was Pierre Falcon Sr., a Quebecker born at the village of L' Acadie. Young Pierre's mother was a Cree of who little is known. Some writers believe that she was actually from the Missouri River Country. Pierre Sr. was a clerk with the NWC in the District in which his son was born.

In 1798 the five-year old future Metis bard was taken to Quebec to be christened and afterwards to be educated. He was baptized at L'Acadie on September 18, 1798. Young Pierre returned to his native-born land in 1808 and like his father became an NWC clerk. He was initially stationed in the Swan River-Qu'Appelle area of what is now Saskatchewan.

Pierre was a lively, spirited and sparkling individual whose qualities are reflected in his songs. As for his appearance, he let his hair grow to the nape of his neck and sported a wispy beard. He felt deeply the concept of a Metis Nation and strongly identified with his own kinsmen.

A prime example is his marriage in 1812 to the Metis woman Mary Grant of Fort de la Rivière Tremblante. Mary was the sister of Cuthbert Grant, resulting in Pierre and Cuthbert becoming brothers-in-law. In due course Pierre and Mary had seven children - three sons and four daughters.

One of Pierre's sons, Jean Baptiste, eventually became a leader of the White Horse Plain Metis. Jean Baptiste was the leader of their buffalo hunt in 1851. About 25 years ago a writer incorrectly identified the 58 year old Pierre, rather than his son Jean Baptiste, as the leader of that hunt. As commander of the 1851 hunt, Jean Baptiste played a pivotal and life-saving role in the momentous Battle of the Grand Coteau (the subject of another chapter of this book).

Pierre's son Jean Baptiste married Marie Nolin, the Metis granddaughter of Duncan Cameron. Cameron was a wintering partner of the NWC who is mentioned in the chapter of this book titled "The Battle of Seven Oaks".

It was as a direct result of the Battle of Seven Oaks that Pierre Falcon wrote his most notable composition *La Chanson de la Grenouillère* (The Song of Frog Plain) and earned a memorable place in Metis history. He also composed the music for this battle hymn that has been called by some a Metis National Anthem.

Falcon was present but did not directly participate in the fireworks on June 19, 1816 at Seven Oaks near Frog Plain (la Grenouillère). Cuthbert Grant had ordered Pierre and other Metis to accompany and protect the supplies of pemmican which the Metis of the NWC were taking to NWC traders at Lake Winnipeg.

As a result Falcon was at Seven Oaks with the other Metis brigades when Governor Robert Semple made his foolhardy and ill-advised venture to intercept them on Frog Plain. Falcon was an eye-witness to the warfare that broke out. As mentioned previously W. B. Coltman, the Royal Commissioner subsequently designated to investigate the confrontation, wrote that this armed conflict was "next to certainty" initiated by Governor Semple's party.

Falcon saw Semple and his men routed and gunned down by the Metis. Shortly after the Battle, he composed his celebrated chanson. It quickly spread across the Metis homeland. It galvanized them even further in their belief that they were indeed a unique people, a Metis Nation that would not hesitate to fight for their rights when they were threatened.

As he was riding on horseback away from the scene of this confrontation, he started writing *La Chanson de la Grenouillère* in French. It gives a rhythmical and stirring narrative of that event as seen through the eyes of a balladeer. It tells of the English coming to attack and of the bois-brûlés sending "an ambassador" to Governor Semple to parley. Instead of doing so the Governor ordered his men to fire on the Metis, leading to their retaliation and to most of his "Grenadiers" being killed.

It was a complete triumph for the Metis in repulsing an attack, and it gave them immense pride in their military ability. Loosely translated, the last two stanzas of this song are:

> If you had seen those Englishmen
> And all the Bois-brûlés after them
> From mound to mound the Englishmen we did destroy
> While all the Bois-brûlés uttered cries of joy.
>
> Who is the one who composed this song?
> It is the poet of this area, Pierre Falcon
> The song was composed and sung
> As a result of the victory we had won,
> It was written on that day
> To sing the glory of the Bois-brûlés.

When sung, the first two lines of each stanza were repeated.

In his book *Red River* written in 1871, Joseph James Hargrave wrote the following:

> I have been fortunate enough to secure from the lips of its author a metrical account of this battle [of Seven Oaks] composed on horseback while on his way home from the

> scene of its occurrence, by Monsieur Pierre Falcon, who is now a petty magistrate in the colony, aged about 76 years.

This passage illustrates the quick, agile, gifted mind of Pierre. He was capable of creating a striking song more or less off-the-cuff while riding on a horse. Hargrave added that Falcon's composition was:

> .... caught up by friendly ears and conveyed from mouth to mouth that it might be heard throughout the country wherever the axe of the woodcutter fell or the paddle of the canoe kept time to the cadence adapted to its measure.

When the Hudson's Bay Company (HBC) and the NWC merged in 1821, Falcon was kept on by the HBC. Presumably this was because unlike Cuthbert Grant, who was let go, Pierre had not been front and center at Seven Oaks and did not incur the continuing enmity of the HBC personnel. He remained with the HBC until Grant persuaded him and his family to move to Grantown on the White Horse Plain shortly after that community was established in 1824.

In an article in the *Winnipeg Tribune* of July 9, 1938, Margaret Complin tells of speaking to Francois-Xavier Falcon, the grandson of Pierre. When she spoke to Francois he was 90 years old. He had been born in his grandfather's house and Pierre was still alive when Francois was a teenager. Francois told Complin that he had "many interesting memories of him and of Maria [sic] Grant [Falcon], his grandmother."

According to this article Cuthbert Grant never went anywhere without Pierre Falcon, who was like his aide-de-camp. His grandchildren described their grandfather Pierre as a "saintly, tender, noble old man."

More than one writer, including Hargrave in *Red River*, has written that Pierre could neither read nor write. This is highly improbable. As a lad Pierre was sent to Quebec to be educated and was there ten years; as well on his return to the west he was hired as a clerk by the NWC. In addition he was appointed a magistrate in 1855.

Falcon composed many other songs during his lifetime

besides *La Chanson de la Grenouillère*, but they were never published and only a few have survived to this date. However *Songs of Old Manitoba* (1960) by Margaret A. MacLeod contains some songs composed by Falcon that were not lost.

One of his songs that survived is *Lord Selkirk at Fort William, or the Dance of the Bois-brûlés*. The lyrics to *Lord Selkirk at Fort William* tell of the seizure in 1816 of the NWC's Fort William by Lord Selkirk and the private army he personally hired.

It was not unusual in the days when a rival fur trade company usurped a competitor's fort to attempt to hold on to the subordinate staff of the vanquished post. Falcon's song embodies this theme. It depicts Lord Selkirk throwing a victory party at Fort William.

The NWC personnel, particularly the bois-brûlés, were all urged to attend where they would sing, dance, eat, drink and enjoy to their hearts content. One of the other purposes of the regale was to ply the party-goers with sufficient drink so as to make it easier to pry information from them on the plans of the NWC.

Another of Falcon's surviving songs is *The Ballad of General Dickson*. The profile in this book on Cuthbert Grant contains brief words on the quixotic General James Dickson and his whimsical dream of freeing the "Indian Nations".

Falcon composed a song about this strange man's efforts to recruit an army of bois-brûlés for this purpose and of Dickson's departure from Red River. The lyrics also tell the story of Dickson presenting his silver epaulettes to Cuthbert Grant.

With the passing years Falcon slowed up physically, but his Metis nationalistic spirit remained vigorous. As mentioned in another chapter of this book, in late 1869 the Metis learned that Prime Minister John A. Macdonald had named the xenophobic William McDougall as Lieutenant-Governor designate for the North-West Territories, of which the future Province of Manitoba was a part.

McDougall decided to enter this area and assert his authority notwithstanding the fact that at that time neither he nor Canada had any jurisdiction there whatsoever. This action by McDougall was contrary to the determination of the Metis that he not be allowed entry into the country.

When the 76 year old Falcon learned that a Metis group intended to forcefully evict McDougall from their territory, Falcon wanted to be part of the Metis contingent sent to do so. Falcon passionately declared that while the enemy would be occupied in killing him, his friends could strike hard and give many well-directed blows to the enemy.

However Ambroise Lepine (the Metis in charge of the group sent to expel McDougall) would not accept Falcon's offer to participate because of Falcon's advanced age. The Metis expelled McDougall from their territory on November 2, 1869.

While still living in Grantown, Falcon was nearing the end of his life. More than 50 years after he had first settled in Grantown on the White Horse Plain he died there at the ripe old age of 83. The date was October 21, 1876.

The impact of his life as the Bard of the Metis continues to shine and inspire the Metis Nation today. In eastern Manitoba close to the Ontario border there is a lake and summer resort named after him that are frequented today by the citizens of Winnipeg. This beautiful holiday area now known as Falcon Lake commemorates and honors the memorable Metis Minstrel Pierre Falcon.

Chapter Reference Sources

- "Bard of the Prairies" by Margaret A. MacLeod, *The Beaver*, p. 20-25.
- *Cuthbert Grant of Grantown, Warden of the Plains of Red River*, by Margaret A. Macleod and W. L. Morton, *passim*.
- "Falcon, Pierre", by Margaret Chartrand, *The Canadian Encyclopedia*, p. 812.
- "Falcon, Pierre", by Bruce Peel, *Dictionary of Canadian Biography* Vol. X, p. 276-277.
- "Pierre Falcon - The Singer of the Plains", by Margaret Complin, *The Winnipeg Tribune*, p. 3.
- *Pioneers and Early Citizens of Manitoba*, editor Manitoba Library

Association, p. 74.

- *Red River,* by Joseph James Hargrave, p. 75.
- *Remarkable History of the Hudson's Bay Company, The* , by George Bryce, p. 266-267.

Chapter XX

JAMES SINCLAIR

Activist and Adventurer

James Sinclair is without a doubt the most unsung man of action in Metis history. In his exceptional life he:

- fought energetically for the rights of the Metis;
- was instrumental in breaking the monopoly of the Hudson's Bay Company (HBC) and bringing free trade to the Metis and to the West;
- was a bold adventurer, a pathfinder, and an explorer;
- fearlessly spearheaded a trek of Red River Metis men, women and children half-way across a continent to the Oregon Country during which they traversed awesome mountainous terrain and uncharted lands.

James Sinclair was a Scottish Metis born in 1806 in Rupert's Land probably at Oxford House, an HBC post. His father William Sinclair was born in the Orkney Islands of Scotland and came to the North West in the late 18th century as a servant of the HBC. The senior Sinclair rose quickly in the HBC service and became a Chief Factor in 1810.

The mother of James Sinclair was a Cree or Metis Cree woman named Nahoway (or Nahovway) whom William Sinclair had married according to the custom of the country. William Sinclair and Nahoway became the parents of 11 children of whom James was the seventh. William stayed with Nahoway until the day he died in April 1818.

In his will he gave directions that his son James (not yet a teenager) should be sent to Britain to be educated. Not long thereafter, James along with one of his brothers embarked for their father's ancestral home in the Orkney Islands.

James stayed with his father's siblings in an Orcadian

village. He attended school there for several years prior to being enrolled in 1822 in the University of Edinburgh, the capital city of Scotland. Over the ensuing four years, he received an advanced Arts education with some law at this University. During this time he also learned a great deal about life in the cosmopolitan atmosphere of Edinburgh.

On completion of his education, James Sinclair returned to Rupert's Land arriving at Moose Factory in 1826. He initially worked for the HBC at Fort Albany and at Chickney Goose Tent (both in present day Ontario). Goose tents were in more than one area. At these tents wild geese acquired from the fall hunts were salted and sent as provisions to nearby posts. Sinclair was not enamored of transporting supplies from this wild goose chase and quit the HBC in 1827.

Now 21 years-old, Sinclair departed on July 6, 1827 from Fort Albany for the Red River Settlement. His widowed mother Nahoway had moved there the year before. In Red River James met up with Thomas Bunn, an older man who had been one of his father's best friends and who, notwithstanding his age, had married James' sister Phoebe.

Bunn introduced James to a number of important men in the community. These included author Alexander Ross, Chief Factor James Curtis Bird, and Governor George Simpson. Bunn also arranged an immediate meeting with the Irish immigrant Andrew McDermot, a prominent and charming Red River merchant and free trader who had known James' father. Bunn made these introductions with a view to assisting his young brother-in-law in finding a suitable job in the community.

In 1824 McDermot had received a rare private license from the HBC authorizing him to trade in furs. The HBC granted it to him so as to dampen American competition. He acquired furs privately and resold them to the HBC. McDermot was also planning to expand into construction and into freighting by land and by water.

He soon became the young Sinclair's mentor. Sinclair

became his associate and eventually his partner in the free trade business. This gave him an opportunity to travel to various forts and communities and may have fueled his wanderlust for regions much farther away.

Sinclair's introduction to HBC Chief Factor Bird led to invitations to the latter's home. There he met Bird's daughter Elizabeth. The young couple fell in love and on December 3, 1829 they were married by banns at the Red River Protestant Church by the Reverend David T. Jones. They eventually had a number of children, many of whom died early.

A census was taken in the Red River Settlement on May 31, 1832. In it, Sinclair is shown as a 26 year-old native of Rupert's Land. He is described as a married Protestant with one daughter.

During the 1830s Sinclair successfully carried on his entrepreneurial activities. He built a comfortable family home in the Red River Community. In his business, he and McDermot had dealings with, among others, Sinclair's Metis kinsmen.

Using their own York boat brigades Sinclair and McDermot shipped, among other items, tallow from Red River to York Factory for shipment to Great Britain on HBC ships. Tallow was one of the by-products obtained by the Metis from the buffalo hunt. It was used by the English for making candles and soap.

During this time many of the Metis were engaged in some fur trading in contravention of the HBC's monopoly. Through his dealings with them, Sinclair became aware that the Metis were becoming increasingly agitated with the HBC and the methods it was employing to counter the illicit trafficking.

Sinclair developed a rapport with his aboriginal kinsmen, both those who were free traders and those who were employed by the HBC. He found that the Metis employed by the HBC were at the bottom rung of the ladder. They rarely became officers of the Company. Officers were usually brought in from outside the community.

As noted in the Chapter of this book titled "Red River Expedition to the Oregon Country", Governor Simpson found one method of reducing private trading in furs. In 1841 he selected James Sinclair, who was one of the more prolific free traders, to lead that phenomenal trans-mountain venture.

Sinclair's illustrious leadership role in safely guiding a group of Metis men, women and children on an overland mission through undeveloped and uncharted lands is all the more remarkable considering the austere conditions that prevailed en route. There were no modern amenities to alleviate the hard slogging - no motels, no stores, no restaurants, no paved highways, no motorized vehicles, and no medical facilities.

It took a man with steely determination, great nerve and resolution, a crusading spirit, sound physical agility, and intuitive abilities to successfully shepherd the families entrusted to him on their long arduous journey. James Sinclair accomplished this momentous project with flying colors.

The repudiation by the HBC of its promises to the overland emigrants when they arrived at Fort Vancouver (in what is now Vancouver, Washington) angered Sinclair. He attempted to re-cross the mountains to return to Red River in December 1841 but ran into snow so deep that he was obliged to spend the winter at Fort Colvile. He arrived back at Red River in 1842 and resumed private trading with McDermot.

When he returned Sinclair found that a number of Metis were privately trapping and trading in various areas of the Metis Homeland, contrary to the HBC policies.

In 1844 Norman Kittson established a trading post for John Jacob Astor's American Fur Company at Pembina. Pembina was in Dakota Territory just outside the jurisdiction of the HBC. The Americans offered much better prices than the HBC did.

With Kittson's Pembina trading post close by and convenient, many more young Metis hurried to get in on the profitable opportunity to trade furs there. What was ironical about this situation was that this American town had once been the location of a principal fort for the thoroughly British HBC. This was prior to the Company establishing its headquarters at Fort Garry.

To avoid the HBC learning of the extent of their trading activities, the Metis hid their catch in their homes, in their barns, in the woods and in other places. In pursuit of this clandestine fur trading the Metis transported their furs to Pembina, St. Peter's and eventually to St. Paul in the United States. Sinclair became a proponent of their activities and one of their leaders in the push for free trade in opposition to the HBC monopoly.

Sinclair's impetus in this direction was precipitated by the actions of Chief Factor Duncan Finlayson of Fort Garry in 1843. In that year Finlayson ordered that York Factory should not accept tallow from Sinclair and McDermot for shipment to Britain. Finlayson also declined to extend their contracts as freighters. They interpreted these actions as blows aimed at their fur trading and their other activities as retail merchants.

Finlayson must have rued the day he tried to play hard ball with Sinclair and McDermot who, in large part, had sold the furs they acquired to the HBC. Undoubtedly however they also did some non-HBC deals as well.

The Metis free trading activities were flourishing to the extent that the HBC felt a threat to its monopoly. The Company determined it would not tolerate what it considered a breach of its rules and regulations. As a result, coercive measures were taken by the HBC authorities. The Metis homes and Red River carts were searched for contraband furs and when found were confiscated.

Shortly thereafter Alexander Christie, the new HBC Governor of Assiniboia:

- imposed a duty on imported products;
- authorized an inspection by the HBC of Metis mails;
- brought in licensing of traders generally conditional on their declaring that they had not engaged in the fur trade; and
- attempted to deprive any illicit fur-traders of title to their lands.

The various measures by the HBC placed the prominent Metis Cuthbert Grant (profiled in another Chapter of this book) in a most awkward position. As Warden of the Plains he was obliged to prevent illicit Metis trading, but if he did so he would alienate his own kinsmen.

Governor Simpson, who only a few years earlier had given Sinclair authority over the Red River Expedition to Oregon, wrote the following to the HBC's London Office on June 20, 1845 about Sinclair and Andrew McDermot:

> Over and above the direct results of their own operations, the example of these two persons have proved to be peculiarly pernicious, inasmuch as their superior standing and comparative intelligence gave considerable weight to their opinions.

Simpson's attitude towards Sinclair seemed to change with the circumstances. Simpson at one point had Sinclair's sister Betsy as his lover and fathered a child by her.

The Metis and Sinclair were incensed at Governor Christie's imposition of oppressive conditions on the free traders. As a consequence James Sinclair drafted a letter to Governor Christie containing a series of questions. It bore his name and that of 18 others (including Alexis Goulet another prominent Metis trader). They delivered this letter to Governor Christie on August 29, 1845.

The letter declared:

> .... a very strong belief that we as natives of this country, and as half-breeds, have the right to hunt .... whenever we think proper and again to sell those furs to the highest bidder.

The questions in this letter dealt with particulars of

their "aboriginal rights". Christie quickly and totally rejected the Metis claims. He asserted that they had only the same rights as other British subjects and they must obey the HBC's Charter rights. This response helped to inflame the confrontation and led to a demand for representative government in Assiniboia.

The reply of Governor Christie to the letter resulted in petitions being drafted in February 1846 by the Metis traders and settlers to present their case to the British Government. The emerging new chief of the Metis, the articulate James Sinclair, was designated by them to travel to London, England to have the petitions presented to the British authorities.

In London Sinclair sought the assistance of Alexander Kennedy Isbister, a Metis born at Cumberland House in Rupert's Land. Isbister had immigrated to London after attending university in Scotland. He was an educator in London in 1846 and later became a lawyer there. Although the petitions were submitted to the British authorities, nothing came of them.

In 1846, ostensibly because the Oregon Country boundary dispute might erupt into a British-American war in the area, several hundred British soldiers were sent to Red River upon the urging of Governor Simpson. Since the troops were stationed many hundreds of miles from the Oregon, Simpson's request for them was a pretext for wanting them in Red River to control the by now extensive unlicensed free traders. As noted in *The Fur Trade and the Northwest to 1867* by E. E. Rich, Simpson made this clear when he wrote:

> If we succeed in getting a garrison at Red River we shall be able to put down the illicit trade and keep the settlers in order.

The HBC even paid part of the costs for the 300 soldiers. The presence of the troops had the desired effect. Free trade decreased significantly until 1848 when the soldiers departed and were replaced by the ineffective Chelsea Pensioners.

Free trade then returned with a vengeance, as did heightened animosity towards the HBC monopoly. The young turks in the Metis free trade movement, led by their young new leaders James Sinclair and Louis Riel Sr., displayed their might when in 1849 Pierre Guillaume Sayer and three other Metis were charged with illegal trafficking in furs.

Reference is made to the chapter in this book titled "The Sayer Trial and Free Trade". That chapter deals with the prominent roles that James Sinclair and Louis Riel Sr. took in matters relating to that trial, in the destruction of the monopoly of the HBC, and in bringing free trade to their countrymen.

In 1848 Sinclair escorted his daughters Maria and Harriet to Knox College in Galesboro, Illinois in order that they could advance their education. After leaving Galesboro, he traveled to St. Louis then considered the fur capital of America. From there he continued on to the California gold rush. It is said that he made a profitable gold strike there, and then returned to Red River for the winter.

The exact date of the death of Sinclair's wife Elizabeth in uncertain but it may have been in 1847, the year before he took his daughters to school in Illinois. He remarried on April 20, 1848. The bride was Mary Campbell whose father was Colin Campbell, the Chief Trader of the HBC in the Athabaska District. Mary's brother was John Campbell mentioned hereafter in relation to the 1854 journey led by Sinclair to the Oregon. Sinclair had four children by his wife Mary.

After the Sayer Trial, Sinclair decided that he wished to move to the Oregon area with his family. He started to make plans for this purpose. He took out United States citizenship at St. Paul in 1849 and passed the winter in St. Louis. While there he contracted to ship his furniture and family belongings to Oregon via Cape Horn. Unfortunately the ship went down at sea and his property on board, including his daughter's prized piano, went down with it.

Floods in Red River prevented Sinclair from taking another group of Red River residents including his family across the mountains to Oregon in 1850. However that year he did cross the mountains without them after his return from St. Louis.

He likely made this journey through a mountain pass that he had referred to in an 1848 conversation with John Palliser, an explorer. Palliser later led an Expedition named after him which explored the west to and through the Rocky Mountains. The route Sinclair took through the mountains is attributed to Palliser but in his Papers, written a number of years after Sinclair's premature death, Palliser noted:

> And to myself I reserved the exploration of a pass, the existence of which I had heard of when in the American Indian country in the year 1848, from Mr. James Sinclair, a very intelligent half-breed, well known and deeply regretted.

After his 1850 crossing Sinclair remained west of the Rocky Mountains for two years, first in the Oregon Country and subsequently in California and the California gold fields. His nomadic tendencies saw him leave California and travel by land through the Isthmus of Panama and then by boat to Cuba. He stayed in Havana for a short time after which he made his way to New York. He eventually returned to his family in the Red River Settlement in June of 1852.

In 1853, Governor Simpson of the HBC again approached Sinclair about leading another group of Red River residents to the Oregon Country, although this land had already been ceded to the United States by Great Britain. Simpson offered Sinclair a position with the HBC which included responsibility for reinvigorating Fort Walla Walla. This arrangement indicates the continued business activities of the HBC in the United States after American acquisition of the Oregon Country.

Sinclair entered the HBC service with a five year contract. He was appointed an HBC clerk, but asked for and was granted the same allowance as that of a

Commissioned Officer.

Sinclair intended to establish a stock farm at Walla Walla and the HBC agreed to assist him in this venture. Simpson indicated that Sinclair would receive 200 head of cattle at a reasonable price. Sinclair wrote in a letter to Simpson of August 28, 1853 that he intended to leave the following spring and that he would bring his family with him.

On May 5, 1854 one hundred emigrants, mostly Metis, left Red River for their new American homeland. Details of this trip across the mountains were given by John V. Campbell whose sister Mary was the second wife of Sinclair. Campbell's account appears in The Washington Historical Quarterly of July 1916.

Much of the route and other aspects of this trans-mountain journey were similar to that of the 1841 Expedition led by Sinclair, including the same Indian guide Crooked Arm (Mackipictoon). His guide told Sinclair that he knew of a better pass through the mountains than that which they used in the 1841 trip. However the opposite proved to be the case. According to Campbell, it took "the whole of September in getting through the mountains" much to Sinclair's annoyance.

In a letter of January 3, 1855 to his son-in-law in Red River Dr. William Cowan (husband of Harriet), Sinclair mentioned a number of reasons why the journey took so long. One reason he gave was that en route "Mrs. Brown had a son" causing a 15 day delay; another was that their guide took a new route through the mountains that took 30 days rather than the 10 days that it took "by my old route."

The route that they took through the mountains is believed to be the south Kananaskis Pass. This was the first time in history that this more difficult Pass had been traversed by non-natives. The pass that John Palliser took four years later was the easier north Kananaskis Pass.

The Sinclair party did not reach its destination until December 1854. Sinclair arrived at Fort Vancouver on December 30, 1854 and left for Walla Walla about two weeks later. He and his family then settled there.

However Indian troubles were brewing in the area. In October 1855 the United States Government Indian Agent Nathan Olney ordered Sinclair, his family, the employees and others to leave Walla Walla immediately. Olney believed "that a War with the Tribes of Indians in your immediate vicinity is unavoidable."

In November Sinclair returned to Walla Walla under the protection of volunteers dispatched by Governor Currie of the Oregon Territory. There was a battle between the natives and this volunteer force. The natives retreated but Sinclair found that they had damaged the Fort and seized all its property.

On February 5, 1856 Sinclair returned from Walla Walla to Fort Vancouver and remained there for about seven weeks. He headed east again on March 24, 1856 intending to go to The Dalles on the Columbia River to attend to business matters.

En route he stopped at the settlement at the Cascades. He was there two days later when an armed group of hostile Indians attacked the settlement. They killed 18 men, women and children. They also shot and killed the 50 year old James Sinclair as he helped in bringing a woman to safety, thus bringing to a tragic end the life of this distinguished and well regarded Metis leader.

It is notable that two of Sinclair's daughters and a granddaughter told of his remarkable exploits.

- In *Women of Red River* Harriet (Sinclair) Cowan recalled, among other matters, how Governor Simpson induced her father to make the 1850 trek to the Oregon to bring "order to the confusion into which the business at some of the Company's posts at the coast had fallen."
- In the early 1900s a daughter (described as Mrs. Copeley of Portland, Oregon) narrated an unpublished account of her father's career from 1840 to 1856 titled The Career of James Sinclair. Mrs. Copeley believed that her father's 1850 trip was made via the Sinclair Pass,

although she may have mistaken this for the Sinclair Canyon near Radium Hot Springs.

- Anna M. Cowan, in a handwritten unpublished manuscript entitled James Sinclair, an early colonizer of Oregon wrote, among other things, that Sinclair:

> was a most genial and affable man, generous to a degree .... he made warm and lifelong friends wherever he went.

A note to this manuscript (in a different handwriting) identified Anna as James Sinclair's 'daughter', but in fact she was the daughter of Harriet Cowan.

Anna Cowan also wrote of her grandfather's earlier acquaintance in St. Louis with a young Lieutenant Ulysses S. Grant. He later became President of the United States. Cowan stated that Sinclair "entertained a warm friendship" with Grant.

Some years after his death, this friendship eventually resulted in President Grant backing a Government Bill to bestow land in the Walla Walla Valley on Sinclair's widow Mary for the losses they incurred during the Indian Wars.

Today there is a plaque dedicated to James Sinclair overlooking the Columbia Valley a short distance south of Radium Hot Springs (formerly Sinclair Hot Springs) in British Columbia. It reads as follows:

> JAMES SINCLAIR
>
> In 1841, Sinclair guided 200 [sic] Red River settlers from Fort Garry through the Rockies to Oregon in an attempt to hold the territory for Great Britain. By 1854 he had recrossed the mountains several times by routes which were later followed by trails and highways - - a tribute to this great pathfinder, traveller, free trader, and colonizer.
>
> Province of British Columbia
>
> 1966

It should be noted that the number of settlers that actually started on this journey was 121, not 200.

Today a landmark passageway in British Columbia honors the bold-spirited chief of the Red River Expedition in its name - Sinclair Canyon. Sinclair was also commemorated in the rushing mountain stream nearby, in a mountain, and in the springs on the west side of the Canyon. They are respectively named the Sinclair River, Mount Sinclair and Sinclair Hot Springs, although the latter is now called Radium Hot Springs. All are adjacent or close by to the modern-day Banff-Windermere highway.

While his life was snuffed out at a relatively early age James Sinclair left a memorable legacy, albeit one that has too frequently been overlooked by historians. Rather astonishingly, The Canadian Encyclopedia fails to profile James Sinclair, and Douglas MacKay's book on the HBC titled The Honourable Company does not mention James Sinclair by name. As well the three-volume series on the HBC by the noted journalist/historian Peter C. Newman makes no mention at all of Sinclair leading the momentous 1841 Red River Expedition.

James Sinclair was a great Metis leader, explorer, trailblazer, advocate, adventurer, and pioneer. He was a stellar champion of free trade and Metis rights. He is one of the most remarkable and memorable Metis personalities in history.

Chapter Reference Sources

- *Birth of Western Canada, The,* by George F. G. Stanley, p. 45.
- *Canadian Prairies, a History, The,* by Gerald Friesen, p. 99-100.
- *Canadian Rockies Early Travel and Exploration, The,* by Esther Fraser, p. 2; 8; 69.
- "Career of James Sinclair, The", told by his daughter Mrs. Copeley to L. J. Doupe (unpublished) Provincial Archives of Manitoba No. MG 9-A69, P. 1-15.
- *Fur and Gold in the Kootenays,* by Clara Graham, Ch. VI and IX.
- *Fur Trade and the Northwest to 1857,* by E. E. Rich, p. 260-265.
- Hudson's Bay Company Archives, Winnipeg, "James Sinclair Files".
- *Hudson's Bay Record Society* - Vol. XIX, p. lx-lxiii; lxxviii- lxxix; and Vol. XXIX p. xxxiv-xxxvii.
- "James Sinclair, an early colonizer of Oregon", by Anna M. Cowan (unpublished) British Columbia Archives A/C/30/Sin 6C.
- "McLoughlin and the Settlers", *Hudson's Bay Record Society* - Vol. XXII p. 35; 723-24.
- *New Peoples , Being and Becoming Metis in North America, The,* edited by Jacqueline Peterson and Jennifer S. H. Brown, p. 108-112.
- *Papers of the Palliser Expedition 1857-1860,* by John Palliser, p. xlix-l; lxxxii-lxxxiii; 124-125; 260; 268.

- "Routes Through the Rockies" by Irene M. Spry, *The Beaver* Winter, 1960, p. 26-39.
- "Sinclair, James", by Irene M. Spry, *Dictionary of Canadian Biography* Vol. VIII, p. 819-820
- "Sinclair Party - an Emigration Overland Along the Old Hudson Bay Company Route from Manitoba to the Spokane Country in 1854", by John V. Campbell, *The Washington Historical Quarterly* of July 1916, Vol. VII, No. 3 p. 187-201.
- *Trials and Tribulations,* by J. M. Bumsted, p. 82-82; 97-100.
- *West of the Mountains - James Sinclair and the Hudson's Bay Company*, by D. Geneva Lent, *passim*.
- *Women of Red River,* by W. J. Healy, *passim*.

Chapter XXI

LOUIS RIEL

A Metis Icon

Louis Riel is the consummate Metis icon, the embodiment of Metis symbolism to the nth degree. He is also considered to be the most controversial individual in Canadian history. His very name conjures up visions in stark contrast to one another: martyred hero – murderous renegade; rational leader – mindless lunatic; cultured gentleman – irate rabble-rouser; selfless advocate – grasping self-seeker; inspired leader – faithless heretic; unjust victim – guilty traitor.

No one who is familiar with the Riel saga is indifferent to the man. He is either revered or reviled, often on the basis of raw emotions rather than bare facts. A French Catholic Quebecer would likely have a more benign interpretation of Riel's conduct and motives in the last year and a half of his life than a militant Protestant Orangeman from Ontario.

Regardless of one's feelings or perspective, Louis Riel was a remarkable personality whose life profoundly influenced Canadian society, politics, the founding of Manitoba and the rights of Western Canadians. His impact continues to this day and will continue into the future. Riel was a wunderkind, a *rara avis*, a natural-born charismatic leader, highly intelligent, handsome and educated. He was elected to the Parliament of Canada on three separate occasions while he was still in his twenties, but due to politics was never able to take his seat.

His fascinating life combined the acme of success and the nadir of defeat, the sacred and the profane. To some he conjoined fame and infamy; to others he was an iconoclast who became an icon. To Riel himself he had a prophetic mission – to lead and champion his people, the Metis, in having their grievances remedied, their rights obtained, and their lives uplifted.

Riel has been called the first prairie populist politician. Some consider him to be the precursor of Thomas Crerar of the Progressive Party in the 1920s; of William Aberhart of the Social Credit Party in the 1930s and 40s; of Peter Lougheed of the Alberta Conservative Party in the 1970s and 80s; and of Preston Manning of the Reform Party in the 1990s. Riel is a symbol of the alienation that many Western Canadians frequently feel as a result of the disregard or meddlesome policies towards the West of the Eastern-dominated federal government.

There is a plaque accompanying the monumental statue of Louis Riel which stands between the banks of the Assiniboine River and the magnificent Manitoba legislative buildings in Winnipeg. This plaque briefly recites highlights of his life and concludes with the statement:

> In 1992, the Parliament of Canada and the Legislative Assembly of Manitoba formally recognized Riel's contribution to the development of the Canadian Confederation and his role, and that of the Metis, as founders of Manitoba.

On January 7, 1998 the government of Canada issued a Statement of Reconciliation relating to past treatment of the aboriginal peoples of Canada. The Statement referred to "the sad events culminating in the death of the Metis leader Louis Riel." It added that it would look for ways of "reflecting Louis Riel's proper place in Canada's history." To date nothing has been done by the Government in this respect.

On Canada Day in 1998, *Maclean's* (Canada's Weekly Newsmagazine) published its list of "The 100 Most Important Canadians in History". Louis Riel was one of the select few and appeared under the category of "Activists". The writer of the Riel profile in *Maclean's* ventured the view (repudiated by many including the authors of this text) that Riel was likely insane at the time of the North-West Uprising.

Louis Riel was born in the Red River Settlement, Rupert's Land on October 22, 1844. His parents were Jean Louis Riel and Julie Lagimodière, both born in what is now

Western Canada. Jean Baptiste Lagimodière and Marie-Anne Gaboury, both born in Lower Canada (Quebec), were the maternal grandparents of Louis Riel. Marie-Anne was the first white woman to live in Western Canada, traveling there with her husband in 1806.

On his paternal side Louis Riel's grandfather was Jean Baptiste Riel, a Quebec French Canadian. In 1812 Jean Baptiste married Marguerite Boucher, a Metis, at Ile-à-la-Crosse in what is now Northern Saskatchewan. Marguerite Boucher's mother was a Chipewyan, and it is through her that Louis Riel inherited his only source of Indian blood.

As a child Louis was brought up on his parents' farm in the parish of St. Vital. The farmhouse was on the banks of the Seine River. A settlement, the Red River Settlement, had grown up in the area centered near the forks of the Red and Assiniboine Rivers. These forks are today the background setting for an up-scale shopping complex (called "The Forks") with trendy boutiques, restaurants and shops in the heart of Winnipeg, the capital of Manitoba, which has a current population in excess of 650,000 people.

In the 1840s the Red River Settlement area consisted of a mixed population of perhaps 10,000 people. There were several distinct groups living in the settlement primarily the French Metis, the English and Scottish mixed bloods (then called "half-breeds" but today called English speaking Metis), and the offspring of the Selkirk settlers. By the time Louis Riel was born in 1844 there was a distinctive self-conscious Metis group - a western people united by ethnic, religious, social and cultural ties and shared experiences.

Louis Riel received his pre-adolescent education from Roman Catholic priests and nuns in the Red River Settlement. His intellectual talents and religious devotion attracted the attention of Bishop Alexandre A. Taché of St. Boniface. In 1858 Taché selected Riel to receive a scholarship from Sophie Masson, a wealthy Quebec chatelaine, to attend a prestigious college in Montreal run by the Sulpician Order of Roman Catholic priests. Bishop

Taché's intent was that Louis would study for the priesthood and return home to minister to the faithful in Red River.

On his arrival in Montreal, Louis was a strapping 13 year-old, soon to grow to about five feet ten inches tall, handsome with piercing brown eyes and dark brown naturally wavy hair. At the Sulpician College, in a hieratic atmosphere, Riel was educated in the classics, as well as in science, French, English, history, philosophy, mathematics and oratory. He was brought up and educated in a highly religious Roman Catholic atmosphere imbued with saints, sacraments, prayers and priests.

He was a fine student, but often somber and reserved, although he became less so as his studies progressed. He could also be headstrong and short-tempered in discussions and debates. He had a consuming interest in politics, and was kept up-to-date on matters in the Red River Settlement by letters from his father.

Young Louis also took to writing poetry. An example of the poignant poem he wrote after his father's death appears elsewhere in this book. During his lifetime Riel was a prolific writer. Besides his verses, he left diaries, letters, and other documents.

During a part of each summer, Louis stayed at Terrebonne, the home of his patron Sophie Masson. There he became familiar with the lifestyle of a prominent and wealthy family and their conservative politics, and grew in self-confidence. He also witnessed how the rights of the French-Canadian minority were protected by constitutional guarantees, an observation that would play a significant part in his future actions.

When his father died in Red River in February 1864, Louis, 19 years old, and thousands of miles from home, was grief stricken. His father had been his hero. Louis soon lost interest in his education and in a priestly vocation. Although he was only a few months short of obtaining a degree, in March 1865 Louis left the college.

He had received an intensive education over a seven-year period in Montreal and was a highly intelligent, intellectual and erudite young man, much better schooled than many of his contemporaries. He wrote and spoke English well and French fluently, was learned in Greek and Latin.

After leaving college, Louis worked as a law clerk in a Montreal law office for a brief time, but soon he decided to leave Montreal. While influenced in part by the untimely death of his father the previous year, this decision was undoubtedly precipitated by his being rebuffed by the parents of Marie Julie Guernon. Marie was a young lady with whom he had fallen in love. He wished to marry her but her parents would not countenance the marriage, and their daughter Marie abided by their wishes.

Although Louis Riel intended to return home, he first worked in St. Paul, Minnesota as a clerk in a general store in 1867. Here he met Red River Metis transporters, friends and relatives who came to St. Paul and who told him of the growing apprehension back home. A group of newcomers from Ontario, primarily Anglo-Saxon Protestants, had arrived in the Red River area after young Riel's departure for Montreal. They styled themselves the "Canadian Party" and wanted Rupert's Land to be annexed to Canada. They also detested the HBC's control of government.

Louis then determined that it was time for him to return home. After an absence of 10 years the 23 year old Riel arrived at Red River in the summer of 1868. Little did he realize that he would shortly become a *deus ex machina*, (an intervener who was to unexpectedly change the course of events in the Red River Settlement). For a discussion of Riel's pivotal role in the "Red River Resistance" refer to the Chapter in this book bearing that title.

As a result of his involvement in the Red River Resistance, Riel had to flee the Red River area in August 1870 to escape violence at the hands of Colonel Wolseley's troops. Riel spent most of the next nine months in Dakota Territory in the United States, primarily at St. Joseph. He lived in constant fear that Schultz's cohorts would attempt to assassinate him. He returned to St. Vital in May 1871 but Riel lay low publicly.

In October 1871 there was a Fenian scare in Manitoba. The Fenians were members of the Irish Republican Brotherhood, a militant nationalist organization founded by the Irish in the United States. The term "Fenian" is most likely derived from fiann, warriors reputed to have fought for the defense of Ireland in the time of Finn and other legendary Irish kings.

The Fenians were responsible for isolated revolutionary acts against the British and were abhorred by the Orangemen. William B. O'Donoghue (who had been in Riel's provisional government but had subsequently had a falling out with Riel) wanted to have the United States involved in Manitoba.

O'Donoghue had assembled a group of Fenians in Dakota Territory and on October 5, 1871 they crossed into Manitoba and occupied a trading post of the HBC not far from the border. The day before Lieutenant Governor Archibald had issued a proclamation calling upon all loyal men "to rally around the flag of our country." Riel and the Metis did so. O'Donoghue was arrested and this small Fenian uprising dissipated.

Archibald's approval of Metis participation backed by Riel did not go down well in Ontario. There was Orange outrage. After winning the election of 1872, the Premier of Ontario Edward Blake offered a $5,000 reward for the capture and conviction of the "murderers" of Thomas Scott, notwithstanding that Ontario had no jurisdiction whatsoever in this matter. Scott was the obnoxious hothead whom Riel, as President of the Provisional Government, ordered to be tried by a court martial. After Scott was found guilty, he was shot by a firing squad.

To avoid hostility between Quebec and Ontario in the 1872 federal election, John A. Macdonald offered what amounted to a bribe of $1,000 (through Archbishop Taché) to have Riel leave the country for a period of time. Donald Smith contributed £600 in this respect. Riel, realizing his life was in danger, accepted the money and left for St.

Paul.

However his St. Boniface friend Joseph Dubuc talked Riel into running in the constituency of Provencher in the September 1872 federal election. This was the seat that had been held by the prominent Metis Pierre Delorme, who is profiled in another chapter of this book.

Riel had the nomination all but locked-up when word came that Macdonald's Quebec lieutenant George Étienne Cartier had lost his seat. Riel agreed to step aside so that Cartier could win the safe Provencher seat.

Riel stated that his only condition would be the pledge by Cartier to fulfill the promise of the land grant to the Metis. Riel was willing to trust Cartier's conscience as to the question of his amnesty. An amnesty for all who were involved in the Red River Resistance had been verbally promised by Ottawa to the Metis negotiators in 1870 and to Archbishop Taché.

When Cartier died in May 1873, Riel decided to run in the by-election and was nominated by Pierre Delorme in whose home the nominating meeting was held. Riel won the Provencher seat in October 1873. Afraid for his life he did not take his seat.

In any event the corruption in John A. Macdonald's government, known as the Pacific Scandal, caused its resignation. In the general election of February 1874 the Liberal Party under Alexander Mackenzie won, as did Riel for a second time in Provencher.

Riel went east and with the aid of his old Montreal school chum Romuald Fiset (the member from Rimouski) crossed the river to Ottawa where, without naming Riel, Fiset asked the Clerk of the House to administer the oath to his old friend. Riel then signed the members' role and scurried out.

Riel did not appear at the opening of Parliament. Mackenzie Bowell (who was to become the Conservative Prime Minister in 1894), a high officer of the Orange Order, moved that Riel appear in the House on April 9, 1874 or be expelled. Fearing for his life, Riel did not appear and was expelled from the House of Commons.

At that time he was in Keesville, New York near the Canadian border, staying with Father Fabien Barnabé in his parish rectory. However Riel ran in the by-election in Provencher created by his expulsion and was elected for a third time in September 1874. He was not yet thirty years old.

When Parliament convened in February 1875 Prime Minister Alexander Mackenzie proposed a resolution granting a full amnesty to Riel and Ambroise Lépine with respect to all acts committed by them during

> .... the North West troubles .... conditional on five years banishment from Her Majesty's Dominions.

Lépine chose to serve a two-year prison term rather than accept exile. Meanwhile Riel went into exile in the United States, a political refugee. His adversities, constant fear of assassination, the $5,000 bounty hanging over his head, forced exclusion from his family and friends in the Red River Settlement, and no future prospects, led to his emotional breakdown.

He spent some time in the eastern United States. While there his emotional distress and vulnerability led him to believe he had a mission to lead the Metis to greater things. His thought that Divine Providence was with him was bolstered by a letter of July 14, 1875 from Bishop Ignace Bourget of Montreal in reply to a letter from Riel. In his letter Bourget told Riel that God "has given you a mission which you must fulfill in all respects."

Riel spent some time in Washington D.C. in the fall of 1875 with Edmond Mallet, an expatriate Quebecer, and even had a meeting with President Ulysses S. Grant. While at Mass in Washington in December 1875, Riel suddenly became ecstatic and wept uncontrollably for a short time. Mallet then made plans to send Riel to Father Primeau in Worcester, Massachusetts. Father Primeau tried to help but felt Riel was not normal. Father Richer at

Suncook fared no better.

Father Barnabé came back into the picture but at his rectory Riel was agitated, frequently weeping and bellowing like a bull. Barnabé arranged for John Lee, Riel's uncle in Montreal, to come for him because he felt that Riel was not in his right mind. After a number of days at his home, Lee had Riel placed in an asylum in Longue-Pointe, Quebec on March 6, 1876 under an assumed name.

Dr. Henry Howard, the supervising doctor, was uncertain whether Riel was acting. When Riel was addressed by his pseudonym, he showed a nun his prayer book in which his beloved sister Sara had written his name. The nun immediately tore out the page and Riel justifiably became berserk.

In May 1876, fearful that Riel's presence at Longue-Pointe would be discovered, the nuns wanted him out. He was transferred to Beauport Asylum near Quebec City where he stayed until January 1878. The Superintendent of Beauport was Dr. François Roy who would later testify at Riel's 1885 trial for high treason.

On his release from Beauport Riel returned to Father Barnabé's rectory at Keeseville in New York where he and Father Barnabé's sister, Evelina, soon fell in love. Towards the end of 1878 Riel decided to go to St. Paul, Minnesota. He met many Metis who could not accept that he had ever been deranged. Riel told some that he had feigned mental sickness.

Over the next few years Riel moved a couple of times in the mid-western United States; he was an interpreter, wood-chopper, supplies purchaser, and trader.

In 1881 while working in the Carroll, Montana area he met and married a young Métisse, Marguerite Monet *dit* Bellehumeur. They had a common-law marriage since there were no priests in the area. A priest later solemnized the marriage in March 1882. Riel then had the delicate task of writing Evelina Barnabé in Keeseville to let her know she had been jilted. She was not amused.

Riel became involved in Montana politics on behalf of the Republican Party, and he denounced the whisky trade with Indians and Metis. In 1882 Riel helped get out the Metis vote in the Congressional elections. In 1883 he was charged with urging Metis who were not United States citizens to vote, but the charge was dismissed.

Louis Riel's banishment from Canada, imposed by the Alexander Mackenzie administration, had expired while Riel was in the western United States. However, Riel had decided to apply for American citizenship, which was granted to him on March 16, 1883 at Fort Benton, Montana.

Shortly after, he accepted a position as a schoolteacher at St. Peter's Mission, Montana. At that time he and his wife had a son Jean who had been born in May 1882. Their daughter Marie was born in September 1883. His life as a schoolteacher was pedestrian and unemotional, but secure.

This secure, placid life was soon to be displaced by one much more hectic. While at Sunday Mass on June 4, 1884 Riel found out that a delegation of French and English Metis from the North-West (Saskatchewan), over eleven hundred kilometers distant, had arrived on horseback at St. Peter's Mission to see him.

The four men (Gabriel Dumont, James Isbister, Michel Dumas and Moïse Ouellette) had come at the behest of the North-West Settlers. They came to plead with Riel to come to the North-West and help them to obtain their rights and to seek remedy for their grievances against the Canadian government. Their petitions and complaints had been completely ignored and they were being treated as second class citizens.

The settlers had no right of election to or representatives in the Canadian Parliament and needed an effective voice to speak for them and to get their message through to Ottawa. They also knew from past experience in Manitoba that immigration from the east would threaten their way of life and their land.

Riel told the delegation he would think on it overnight, but there was no doubt in his mind that he would agree to go with them. In a sense this highly religious man thought it was a Heaven-sent opportunity to help his Metis people. He would, in a sense, be their prophetic messiah.

The next day Riel accepted their invitation, putting his acceptance in writing, adding at the same time that the Canadian government owed him his Manitoba land grant and "something else" not specified. He stated he would return from the North-West to Montana in September.

Several days later Riel, his wife and children left with the delegation on the long journey to the South Saskatchewan; a fateful journey that would cost Louis Riel his life in less than eighteen months and revolutionize Canadian politics for generations. The Chapter entitled "The North-West Uprising" in this book describes the circumstances of the Uprising and Riel's activities after he arrived in Saskatchewan.

After the Metis were crushed at Batoche on May 12, 1885 by an overpowering Federal army, Riel voluntarily surrendered. He expected to have the equivalent of a state trial where he could air the grievances of the Metis and be defended on the merits of his actions. He was badly mistaken on both counts.

Riel was unceremoniously clapped in jail with a ball and chain clamped around his leg. He was charged with high treason under the ancient *1351 Statute of Treasons* of Great Britain. He could have been charged under an 1868 Canadian treason-felony statute passed by the federal government led by Prime Minister John A. Macdonald.

However, Macdonald realized that under his own made-in-Canada law, if Riel was convicted he could only be imprisoned. Macdonald wanted Riel executed. Consequently the Prime Minister dredged up an archaic English Statute (passed over 500 years earlier) under which a person convicted of high treason would suffer the death penalty.

The authors of this book collaborated on a book dealing

with Riel's trial. It is titled *The Trial of Louis Riel - Justice and Mercy Denied*. The web site for the third edition of this book is www.fabjob.com/riel.htm. The subtitle of this book reflects the judgments and opinions that the authors arrived at after extensive documented research.

The lack of justice and mercy relating to Riel's trial included, but was not limited to:

- Riel's unlawful conviction and execution under an inapplicable 534 year old statute of Great Britain.
- The mistreatment and defiance of Riel by his own lawyers. This was most evident in their failing to provide him with a full answer and defense that the law entitled him to.
- The doomed strategy employed by Riel's own lawyers in defending him and in failing to give him a defense on the merits of his actions as he had specifically instructed them.
- No defense was presented to the jury except an insanity plea, which both Riel and the jury unanimously rejected.
- The flagrant conflicts of interest of Riel's lawyers, one of whom, Charles Fitzpatrick, was the law partner and brother-in-law of Adolphe Caron, the Minister of Defence in Macdonald's government. It was the Minister of Defence who had sent the troops to Batoche to suppress the Metis.
- The statements in open court by Riel's lawyers that they were acting on the instructions of "others" and "parties ... who were really our clients in this case."
- The errors and omissions of Riel's lawyers and their unprofessional shabby treatment of him.
- The trial magistrate's bias and lack of independence.
- The political, judicial and legal improprieties at the highest level.

The result of the trial was that Riel was convicted of

high treason and, notwithstanding the unanimous recommendation of the jury for mercy, the Macdonald government had Riel executed on November 16, 1885. The stately Riel went to the gallows and to his death in a dignified and quiet manner. His body was returned to St. Boniface for burial in the Cathedral Cemetery, where he lies at rest today.

Many of the demands in the Bill of Rights he championed for the Metis and for Westerners in 1885 came to pass after his death. Here are some of the end results that his life contributed to:

- Manitoba became a Province of Canada in 1870, and today he is widely recognized as the Father of Manitoba.
- In 1886 the people of the Northwest Territories (which then embraced what is now Saskatchewan and Alberta) finally won the right to vote for and elect Members of Parliament.
- In 1887 responsible government was obtained for the Northwest Territories.
- In 1905 Saskatchewan and Alberta became Provinces of Canada.

Other notable outcomes inspired by Riel's life include:

- The Metis people being specifically recognized in 1982, in the *Constitution of Canada*, the highest law of the land.
- Riel being looked upon by the Metis as a hero and their greatest symbol.

Another legacy of Riel's life was the creation of a booming cottage industry in Canadian literature and the arts. More books and biographies have been written about this charismatic Metis icon than any other Canadian in history.

Harry Somers, a leading Canadian composer who died in 1999, wrote an opera entitled *Louis Riel*. It was his masterpiece and was premiered by the Canadian Opera Company in 1967. It was also the first Canadian opera to be performed at the Kennedy Center in Washington, D.C. and was staged as recently as 2005 in Montreal.

Riel's life has been the subject of stage, radio, film and television productions and documentaries, as well as historical fiction including a musical and a play. A postage stamp bearing his likeness was issued a generation ago, when Canadian stamps sold for six cents each.

The city of Saskatoon celebrates "Louis Riel Days" every summer. In June 2001 a main highway in Saskatchewan was renamed the "Louis Riel Trail". A pedestrian bridge, built between Winnipeg and St. Boniface, was named Esplanade Riel in 2004 in honor of Riel. The home of the Riel family in St. Vital (a suburb of Winnipeg, Manitoba) has been designated a National Historic Park by Parks Canada.

Statues of Riel have been erected on the legislative grounds of Winnipeg and Regina, the capital cities of Manitoba and Saskatchewan where the Red River Resistance and the North-West Uprising respectively occurred. The statue of Riel in Regina was subsequently removed because of its controversial depiction of Riel, a fate similar to that which befell an earlier sculpture of Riel in Winnipeg, which was replaced by a more traditional one.

On November 16, the anniversary date of his execution, Riel is honored every year in a number of Canadian cities, large and small, with flag raising ceremonies. These are usually held at city halls and other public places including his grave site in St. Boniface.

On November 16, 1999 the Governor-General of Canada spoke at Confederation Park in Ottawa at the Celebration of Louis Riel Day. She was escorted by members of the Royal Canadian Mounted Police wearing Metis sashes. The Governor-General stated that Riel's "role in building this country was not recognized during his lifetime .... we all have a responsibility to remember the legacy of Louis Riel."

One frequently hears laments from historians and

others with respect to the sorry state of the study of history in our schools. These are often accompanied by complaints bemoaning the fact that Canadian heroes are not being recognized.

Some years ago, the well-known Ontario historian J. L. Granatstein labeled Riel a "bastardized hero". He added that Riel lacked credentials as a hero to all Canadians and that his life should not be taught in schools as if he was such a hero. Using that credentials test, no one in Canada or in the world would qualify as a hero.

Others have a different view of Riel. Another historian, Professor Gerald Friesen, doesn't apply this insurmountable test. In Professor Friesen's view, Louis Riel is "paramount" among "multicultural heroes". Professor J. M. Bumsted has called Riel "one of our few mythic heroes". The prominent Canadian journalist and author Peter C. Newman pithily stated that Riel "was one of our genuine frontier heroes."

On June 30, 1999, the results of a national survey to nominate Canada's top 10 "heroes" were published in the *National Post* newspaper. The Dominion Institute and the Council for Canadian Unity conducted the survey. Louis Riel was among the top ten heroes selected.

Professor George F. G. Stanley, an eminent historian (and incidentally the designer of the Canadian flag in the 1960s) referred to Riel as "A Canadian legend" and "our Hamlet, the personification of the great themes of our human history."

Is Riel a hero? If a hero is one who forfeits his life as a result of fighting for the rights of his people in a just cause, then Louis Riel is a hero. Over the years Riel has transcended from being a Metis hero to that of being a Canadian hero.

Chapter Reference Sources

- *Birth of Western Canada, The,* by George F. G. Stanley, *passim.*
- *Debates of House of Commons,* Sessions 1885-1886.
- Hudson's Bay Company Archives, Winnipeg, "Riel Files".
- *Last War Drum, The,* by Desmond Morton, *passim.*

- *Life of Louis Riel, The,* by Peter Charlebois, *passim.*
- *Louis 'David' Riel Prophet of the New World,* by Thomas Flanagan, *passim.*
- *Louis Riel,* by George F. G. Stanley, *passim.*
- *Louis Riel and the Metis,* editor A. S. Lussier, *passim.*
- *Louis Riel 1844-1885,* by William McCartney Davidson, *passim.*
- *Prairie Fire, The 1885 North-West Rebellion,* by Bob Beal and Rod MacLeod *passim.*
- Provincial Archives of Manitoba, "Riel Files".
- *Queen v. Louis Riel, The* [Trial Transcript] introduction by Desmond Morton *passim.*
- *Riel, a Life of Revolution,* by Maggie Siggins, *passim.*
- *Riel and the Rebellion 1885 Reconsidered,* by Thomas Flanagan, *passim.*
- "Riel, Louis", by George F. G. Stanley, *Canadian Encyclopedia,* p. 2019.
- "Riel, Louis", by Lewis H. Thomas, *Dictionary of Canadian Biography* Vol. XI, p. 736-752.
- *Strange Empire, Louis Riel and the Metis People,* by Joseph Howard, *passim.*
- *Trial of Louis Riel, Justice and Mercy Denied, The,* by George R. D. Goulet, *passim.*

Chapter XXII

ELZEAR GOULET

Metis Martyr

In the 1860s Elzear Goulet was a prominent, intelligent, educated and well-respected Metis in the Red River Settlement and in Pembina, Dakota Territory. His relatively short life came to a tragic end in 1870 when he was pursued and assassinated by several of Colonel Garnet Wolseley's "peace-keeping" soldiers sent to Manitoba by Prime Minister John A. Macdonald.

Elzear was a descendant of the voyageurs who came west to trade in furs. His French Canadian ancestry actually pre-dates the voyageurs and can be traced directly back to Louis Hebert, a Parisian apothecary. Hebert was the first permanent colonial settler in Canada's history. He and his family settled in what is now Quebec City in 1617 at the request of Samuel Champlain. Previous to that date, he had been one of the members of Pierre de Monts' expedition that made several attempts to settle in Acadia starting in 1604.

Louis Hebert's great granddaughter married Antoine Goulet in Quebec in 1692. Their descendant Jacques Goulet, born in 1779 in Quebec, came to Athabaska in the early 1800s as a voyageur with the North West Company (NWC). In the west Jacques married Genevieve Beignet, a Metis from Lac Vert in what is now Saskatchewan. Alexis Goulet, born about 1811, was one of their children and Elzear was a son of Alexis.

Alexis Goulet was a very interesting individual in his own right. He was a Metis hunter and a guide for sportsmen. He also became a very successful private trader and was quite influential in the Red River Settlement.

He was one of those who participated in the letter of August 29, 1845 to Governor Alexander Christie declaring the rights of the Metis to hunt and sell furs to the highest bidder. This letter is referred to in the Chapter titled "James Sinclair - Metis Activist and Adventurer". Alexis was also a witness in the Sayer Trial of 1849 which resulted in free trade for the Metis (this trial is the subject of another chapter in this book).

Alexis married a Metis woman Josephte Siveright (Elzear's mother) at St. Boniface on October 1, 1833. Josephte had been born in Pembina 16 years earlier. Her father was John Siveright, a Scotsman born in the Parish of Cairnie by Huntley in the Grampian Highlands not far from Aberdeen, Scotland.

When it merged with the Hudson's Bay Company (HBC) in 1821, Siveright was a fur trader with the NWC. Notwithstanding that he was a loyal NWC man and had been implicated in supporting the Metis during the Battle of Seven Oaks in 1816, the HBC hired him.

John Siveright married a Metis woman Josephte (or perhaps Louise) Roussin according to the custom of the country. When the HBC assigned him to Sault Ste. Marie, Siveright left his children (including his daughter Josephte) with a Metis family in the Red River Settlement.

Siveright later became a Chief Factor of the HBC and on his retirement he returned to Scotland without his family and settled in Edinburgh where he died and is buried. A brief biography of Siveright appears in Volume VIII of the *Dictionary of Canadian Biography*.

Alexis Goulet and Josephte Siveright had eight children born between 1834 and 1855. Among their children was Elzear born in 1836 in St. Boniface and Leonide (the grandfather of the author George Goulet) born in 1852. In the English scrip record of July 6, 1875 of Leonide Goulet applying for his Manitoba Metis land grant, he is described as a "half-breed" and "a voyageur" of the Parish of St. Boniface.

Elzear Goulet was educated in St. Boniface. He married the teen-aged Helene Jerome *dit* St. Matte at Pembina on August 3, 1859. Her grandfather was St. Matte Jerome. Elzear's granddaughter, the author Marie Therese

Courchaine indicated that St. Matte Jerome was from a Louisiana family whose relatives included Jennie Jerome, the mother of Winston Churchill.

Helene Jerome had been brought up in Pembina by her uncle Joseph Rolette and her aunt Angelique Jerome. Joseph Rolette was a freighter, trader and politician and is the same person who hosted a dance at his Pembina home that is mentioned in the chapter of this book titled "Good Times and other Topics".

Pembina was very close to the international border, but it lay on the American side. At the time, Metis families who were related to each other lived on the river lots on both sides of the boundary. Many of them moved back and forth and did not concern themselves with the international boundary line.

After their marriage, Elzear and Helene established a home at Pembina and all their children were born there. Elzear became an American citizen. His primary occupation during the 1860s was that of postal courier between Pembina and Upper Fort Garry, a distance of some 65 miles. He assumed this position when his older brother Roger, who had the mail delivery contract, was appointed the collector of customs in 1861.

The round trip between these locations took three or four days, for which he received 25 shillings. Elzear provided this "pony express" delivery of mail in the summer and traveled by dogsled in the winter. Since he performed this task for almost a decade, Elzear obviously knew how to mush dogs and ride horses superbly.

On March 12, 1966, Marie Therese Courchaine (who wrote under the pen name Manie Tobie) presented a paper to the St. Boniface Historical Society titled "Discourse on the Goulet Family". She told of her father Roger Goulet (Elzear's son) being contacted by a "Mrs. McLeod", a Manitoba writer. This was undoubtedly Margaret Arnett MacLeod (referred to elsewhere herein) who wrote a book titled *The Frozen Priest of Pembina*. MacLeod consulted her father to verify certain historical facts relating to Father

R. P. Goiffon, the parish priest of Pembina.

In her presentation Manie Tobie stated that when Elzear Goulet was traveling on his mail route he came across an Oblate priest Father Goiffon lying next to his horse in the snow. The priest's legs were frost-bitten. Elzear brought him to safety where the priest's legs had to be amputated. Apparently Mrs. MacLeod's version of this rescue differs in some details from that of Manie Tobie.

The Goulet Family of Red River was also profiled by Judge L. A. Prud'homme in an article in *Memoires de la Societe Royal du Canada*. In this article Judge Prud'homme discussed the life of Elzear Goulet as well as those of Elzear's siblings, parents and other family members. There is also an informative article on Elzear Goulet by Todd Lamirande (currently a reporter with the Aboriginal Peoples Television Network) in chapter 4 of *Metis Legacy*.

In October 1869 the Metis learned that the xenophobic William McDougall, who was the Lieutenant-Governor designate for Rupert's Land, was en route to Pembina. He and his entourage were bringing hundreds of rifles with them.

The Metis set up a barricade on the La Salle River. They did so to prevent armed foreigners with no jurisdiction in the Red River Settlement, including McDougall, from entering their homeland without their approval. Mail passing through this blockade was made subject to inspection by the Metis for subversive content.

Elzear, of course, was aware that Canada had not consulted the Metis in its determination to take over Rupert's Land. A committed Metis, he threw in his lot with the militants and with Louis Riel. By doing so, Elzear's mail courier role came to an end in the fall of 1869. He was named a captain of the Metis 'military' that had been formed under the command of Ambroise-Didyme Lepine. Lepine was the adjutant-general of this group.

A prominent member of the Provisional Government formed soon after by the Metis was Louis Schmidt. He later stated in his Memoirs:

> Poor Elzear Goulet, who had so sad an end, very much resembled Lepine. He had all his qualities and all his defects. He was superior to him in his pleasant manner and was the idol of the soldiers.

At the end of January the Convention of Forty (20 French and 20 English representatives) met and resulted in the establishment of a second Provisional Government in early February 1870 with Louis Riel as President. Subsequent to that date Major Charles Boulton, Thomas Scott and others were imprisoned by this Provisional Government for fear that they would lead an insurrection in the Settlement.

The sequence of events at this time is discussed in the chapter of this book titled "The Red River Resistance". That chapter deals with details surrounding the execution of the odious, bigoted Orangeman Thomas Scott as a result of his court martial that was ordered by the Provisional Government.

Elzear Goulet was among the members of the Court Martial that sentenced Scott to death by a majority vote and Scott was executed in early March 1870. On the following July 15th, Manitoba became a Province. At this time Canada sent out a so called "peace-keeping" force under Colonel Garnet Wolseley that arrived in Fort Garry on August 24, 1870.

Some of these troops were intent on revenging the execution of Thomas Scott, whom they considered to be one of their own. In fact there were a number of retaliatory incidents against members of the Settlement after Wolseley's troops arrived at Red River.

The thirst for blood of Wolseley's extremist troops led directly to the assassination of Elzéar Goulet. One day when Goulet was seen in Winnipeg he was pursued by a number of men, among them Ontario soldiers who had arrived with Colonel Wolseley.

Goulet ran to the Red River and was swimming to the other side when his pursuers threw rocks and stones at him. He was hit on the head and the result was that he drowned, stoned to death. Although this happened in broad daylight, his body was not recovered until the next day; the malefactors simply returned to their activities rather than attempting to retrieve his body. The culprits were never prosecuted. The historian Alexander Begg wrote that "a large number took part in the disturbance."

Several historians have related that when Elzear Goulet's body was recovered from the river, it was brought to his home. There his widow Helene had their children kneel before the body of their dead father and pray not only for their father's soul but also for the souls of his murderers.

Lieutenant-Governor Adams G. Archibald ordered an investigation into this murder. It was carried out by a Montreal lawyer H. J. G. McConville. He reported that the Magistrate's met "in the rooms of the Government of Manitoba in the house formerly known as the establishment of the 'New Nation'." McConville stated in his report (reproduced in the Canada Sessional Papers) that:

> .... all the testimony of witnesses previously adduced before them having been read and examined carefully, I asked that warrants be issued against three parties - that is to say, against two for having feloniously caused the death of the deceased [Elzear Goulet] and another warrant against a third party as having incited others, etc.

After receiving the Report of the investigator dated September 27, 1870, the Lieutenant Governor sent it to the federal Secretary of State for the Provinces. However, the Lieutenant Governor ignored the Report's recommendations and instead sent it to Judge Francis G. Johnson to review.

The Anglo-Saxon Judge Johnson advised the Lieutenant Governor that the evidence was "not sufficiently strong" to issue warrants and none were issued. As a result no one was ever charged, although it was believed within the community that Goulet's murder had been carried out by the soldiers of Colonel Wolseley's regiment. The formal

Report made by Judge Johnson is apparently lost and the authors were not able to review it.

It is interesting to note that the Prime Minister's son, Hugh John Macdonald, was involved in both the Red River Resistance and the Uprising in the North-West Territories. Hugh John was a member of Colonel Wolseley's troops that arrived in Red River after the Provisional Government of Riel was disbanded.

Many years after the incident on July 18, 1911 in a newspaper interview, Hugh John Macdonald recalled the killing of Elzéar Goulet. Hugh John said that he witnessed "a crowd of our men running ... towards the river." He later referred to Goulet doing a "record run" pursued by "a large party of soldiers." He added that Goulet could not swim sufficiently well and drowned "while the infuriated soldiers were struggling to rescue him that he might be brought to justice." Hugh John made no mention of Goulet being stoned by Hugh John's fellow soldiers, or of Goulet's body being left in the river overnight.

In an August 2, 1911 open letter to Hugh John Macdonald that was published in part in the *Winnipeg Free Press*, the son of Elzéar Goulet replied in detail to the Hugh John Macdonald interview. In this letter Roger Goulet (who was then the Provincial Inspector of French Public Schools in Manitoba) stated:

> After reading your statement, sir, I am convinced that you could not make it without having been one of the "crowd" that pursued my father in that race to death.

Hugh John Macdonald replied in a letter of August 3, 1911 in the *Winnipeg Free Press* that he had no hand or part in Goulet's death.

Most sources believe that Elzéar Goulet's participation in the court martial of Thomas Scott was probably the cause of Goulet's murder. Goulet was a close friend of Riel and although Riel was not in Winnipeg when Goulet was murdered, he was well aware of the circumstances.

The death of Elzéar Goulet was not the only penalty inflicted on the Metis in the Red River Settlement for their support of the Provisional Government. A number of biographers of Riel, including George F. G. Stanley, cite the killing of Elzéar Goulet as one of many of the reprisals against the settlers in retaliation for Scott's execution.

Since no action was taken on the recommendations in the Report investigating Goulet's murder, his assassins were allowed to walk the streets of Winnipeg scot-free. Meanwhile Elzear's grieving widow was left to bring up their now fatherless six children. The children's ages at the time of their father's murder ranged from the age of ten to a baby born in the year of his death.

In relation to Elzear Goulet's murder, Dr. Peter Charlebois wrote in his book *The Life of Louis Riel*:

> No meetings were convened, no lodge members importuned, no pressure applied to politicians, no writers inspired to fill columns of newspapers, to clamour for justice and punishment for the murderers of Elzear Goulet. He was a Metis. He spoke French. He was dead.

In his *Memoir* on the Red River Resistance, Louis Riel wrote in 1874 of the assassination of Elzear Goulet and called him a 'noble spirit'.

Elzear was buried in St. Boniface Cemetery. The tombstone contains an inscription for him and for his parents Alexis and Josephte Goulet.

The memory of Elzear Goulet is still alive today. In 2004 Andrea Currie (the daughter of Elzear's great granddaughter Claudette Ek) wrote and recorded a song titled "Elzear Goulet" to honor his spirit.

Some years ago a group in St. Boniface formed a Metis organization and named it the Elzear Goulet Council. This Council is a member of the Manitoba Metis Federation.

There is a Crow Wing Trail Association in Winnipeg that states that the Trail:

> is a historical route between the forks of the Assiniboine and Red Rivers in Manitoba and the Mississippi in Minnesota. In the 1840s fur traders used the route. Today part of it has become a segment of the Trans Canada Trail.

On October 13, 2002 this Association issued a Trail Certificate dedicating one meter of the Trail to the memory of Elzear Goulet.

It is most fitting that this martyred Metis should be memorialized in these and other ways. He was a Metis leader who stood up for the rights of his Metis people. Although his life was brutally ended while he was still a young man, Elzear Goulet is memorable as a symbol of the valiant Metis who suffered and died in the fight for Metis rights.

Chapter Reference Sources

- *Alexander Begg's Red River Journal*, p. 466.
- *Canada Sessional Papers* (No. 20) 34 Victoria, 1871, p. 15; 51-55.
- *Discourse on the Goulet Family,* (unpublished) by Marie Therese Courchene (March, 1966).
- *Elzear Goulet (1863-1870) and The Goulets of Manitoba,* (unpublished thesis) by Louise Delisle (1986).
- "Goulet, Elzear", by J. A. Jackson, *Dictionary of Canadian Biography* Vol. IX, p. 329-30.
- *Hold High Your Heads (History of the Metis Nation in Western Canada)*, by Auguste Henri de Tremaudan, p. 104.
- Hudson's Bay Company Archives, Winnipeg (Ref. F.4/32 p. 397; B.239/g/ p. 61-64).
- *La Famille Goulet*, by Judge L. A. Prudhomme, p. 23-41.
- *Life of Louis Riel, The,* by Peter Charlebois, p.89.
- *Louis Riel*, by George F. G. Stanley, p. 160-61.
- *Louis Riel 1844-1885,* by William McCartney Davidson, p. 68; 95.
- *Resistance Activist Elzear Goulet,* by Todd Lamirande, p. 79-91.
- *Riel, a Life of Revolution*, by Maggie Siggins, p. 193-94.
- St. Boniface Historical Society Archives, St. Boniface, Manitoba, "Elzear Goulet and Goulet Family Files".
- *Strange Empire, Louis Riel and the Metis People*, by Joseph Howard, p. 209.
- *Vanishing Spaces, Memoirs of a Prairie Metis*, by Louis Goulet, p. 74.
- *Winnipeg Free Press*, "Letters to the Editor" August 2 and 3, 1911.
- *Winnipeg Telegram*, "Letter to the Editor", July 18, 1911.

Chapter XXIII

PIERRE DELORME

Politician and Metis Rights Advocate

Pierre Delorme was a Metis leader who championed Metis rights throughout his varied career. He was a freighter, a farmer, and a trader. He was also a politician. He was a member of Louis Riel's Provisional Government in the Red River Resistance of 1869-70.

A number of months after Manitoba entered the Canadian Confederation as a Province Pierre Delorme was elected to be the first Member of Parliament for the Constituency of Provencher. Prior to that, in December 1870 he was also elected as the first Member of the Legislative Assembly of Manitoba for the Constituency of St. Norbert South. In those days, politicians were allowed to sit both federally and provincially and for a time Pierre Delorme simultaneously represented his constituents both nationally and provincially.

He was a close friend and confidant of Louis Riel. Delorme was a refined, intelligent, well-educated gentleman, and a family patriarch. The authors have an extra special interest in Pierre Delorme. George Goulet is his great grandson and the authors' children are his great-great grandchildren.

Fred Shore, a prominent Metis professor at the University of Manitoba, wrote a brief profile of Delorme in the *Dictionary of Canadian Biography.* In it he stated that Delorme "played an important role in the early development of Manitoba."

Pierre's father was Joseph Amable Fafard *dit* Delorme, a French-Canadian Roman Catholic. The senior Delorme was born in Quebec but emigrated to the west as a young man. Joseph Delorme married a Metis woman Josephte Belley who was born in 1799 to Antoine Belley and a Cree mother. Pierre Delorme was born to Joseph and Josephte Delorme at St. Boniface in the Red River Settlement (now part of Manitoba) on October 1, 1832

Young Pierre received his education in St. Boniface. While the extent of his studies is not documented, it is evident that it was more extensive than that of most of the other youths in the Red River Settlement. He could read and write both French and English fluently. His correspondence in both languages reveals a fine vocabulary and well-structured sentences. Contrary to most Metis applicants who signed for scrip certificates with an "X", Delorme's scrip application is personally signed by him.

In the 1850s a young Delorme signed on with the Swan River District of the Hudson's Bay Company (HBC) as a "Midman" (middleman). A middleman was one of several persons who, sitting in the middle between the bowsman and the steersman, paddled a canoe that transported goods and sometimes passengers between trading posts in the North West. The middleman was normally a Metis voyageur. Delorme's contract with the HBC expired in 1856 and he returned to the Red River Settlement.

In October 1856 Pierre wed Adelaide Beauchemin in St. Boniface Cathedral. The marriage ceremony was performed by Father Louis Laflêche, the same priest who encouraged the Metis at the Battle of the Grand Coteau (referred to in another chapter of this book).

Adelaide was the Metis daughter of a Quebecker Andre Millet Beauchemin and a Metis woman Madeleine Ducharme (who was born in Riviere Qu'Appelle in what is now Saskatchewan). Madeleine Ducharme's mother is shown in genealogy records as "C. (Ojibwa) Chippewa". Pierre's father-in-law Andre had been a member of Alexander Henry the Younger's Red River Brigade and arrived in the region in 1800.

Pierre Delorme and Adelaide had five sons and two daughters. One of the daughters was Veronique J. Delorme (the author George Goulet's grandmother) who later married a Metis, Joseph Albert McDougall.

Not long after his wedding to Adelaide, Pierre Delorme

acquired a river lot at Pointe Coupée (today the town of St. Adolphe, not far from Winnipeg). He built a family home on that land.

A pamphlet issued by the Government of Manitoba Department of Natural Resources-Parks describes this home and is titled "Delorme House, St. Norbert Heritage Park". This pamphlet states that Delorme's home was of log construction and covered with clapboard. The one and a half storey house was relatively large for the times measuring 31'8" by 23'8". It consisted of a dining room, parlor, sitting room, bedrooms and a reception area.

The Delorme home also served as a meeting place and eventually, while still Pierre's residence, a station stop along the Pembina Trail. In 1982 Delorme's unrestored home was conveyed to the St. Norbert Provincial Heritage Park on the outskirts of Winnipeg where it currently sits.

This Government pamphlet also states that Delorme's "education, wealth and family connections made him a natural leader among the Metis of St. Norbert."

Pierre had an entrepreneurial spirit. He not only farmed but carried on small business enterprises. He transported merchandise, produced beef, and was involved in the Metis buffalo hunts.

A census taken in 1868 when he was 36 years old, disclosed that in 1867 he had produced 100 bushels of potatoes and 400 bushels of wheat. The census stated that he owned 17 head of cattle, 10 horses, and 11 oxen. The 1870 Manitoba census described Delorme as aged 40 (rather than 38). It also stated that he was a Catholic, French Metis at St. Norbert, born at Red River, married to Adelaide Beauchemin, and then had five children.

During the mid 1860s, Pierre became aware of the Canadian annexation movement to take over the Red River Settlement and Rupert's Land. This movement is discussed in the chapter of this book titled "The Red River Resistance". Like many others in the Settlement, Pierre would have been unhappy at being kept in the dark about the plans of Canada, the HBC, and the British Government.

The rumors about Canada's prospective takeover and the lack of consultation with the inhabitants of Red River fueled their concerns about how they would be treated on any acquisition of Rupert's Land by Canada. Their anxieties were heightened by the fact that the local proponents of annexation were primarily transplanted Anglo-Saxon Protestant Orangemen from Ontario. Two of them were John Christian Schultz and Charles Mair, both of whom vigorously disdained the Metis.

Not willing to stand by while his and his fellow kinsmen's lands were being bartered away by foreigners, Delorme determined to actively participate with his Metis brethren in bringing their demands to the forefront prior to any transfer of Rupert's Land to Canada. In 1868 he allied himself with Louis Riel, the young forceful advocate for Red River rights who is profiled in another chapter of this book.

Delorme advocated for:

- Metis title to the lands they occupied;
- 200 acres of land for each Metis child (this foreshadowed the 240 acres per Metis child that the 1870 *Manitoba Act* provided for at a later date);
- Indian status for the wives of the Metis, which would qualify them to share in any Indian land settlement for the Metis (such a spousal right would not have been dissimilar to today's situation where a white woman gains Indian status on marriage to a status Indian);
- A tax-free trade zone to be established south of the Assiniboine River, a request that would benefit many of the Metis businessman.

In January 1870 Delorme represented Pointe Coupée in the Convention of Forty which was convened in Red River to discuss a Bill of Rights respecting the admission of Red River into Canada. As mentioned he became a member of the Provisional Government organized during the Red

River Resistance.

The photograph of the Provisional Government shows Delorme standing second from the left in the back row. He was well dressed in shirt, bow tie, and stylish suit with a vest. He appears to be of average height, and with a confident bearing. He had a thick head of black hair and a full beard of the same color.

While Delorme zealously pursued Metis rights, it is evident he was not a blind follower of Louis Riel. He drew the line at what he considered needless bloodshed. In February 1870 the Metis, including Delorme, captured and imprisoned the Portage La Prairie party which was apparently intent on overthrowing the Provisional Government.

The leader of this Party, Major Charles A. Boulton, was condemned to death. When Riel, as President of the Provisional Government, refused to commute Boulton's sentence Delorme departed for home saying he would "not return to the Fort in a hurry". In the end, Riel did accept pleas for Boulton's life and spared him.

A few weeks later Riel did not intervene to prevent the execution of the insurrectionist Thomas Scott, an obnoxious Orangeman. Although it is the opinion of the authors that this execution was legally sustainable, it was a serious political mistake on Riel's part that soon had grave implications for Riel and the Metis. However, Delorme had no hand in any matters relating to the court martial or to the execution of Scott.

As seen in subsequent contacts and correspondence between them, any falling out that may have occurred with Riel as a consequence of Delorme refusing to be part of the Boulton and Scott affairs soon dissipated.

Two and one-half months after Manitoba entered the Canadian Confederation as a Province on July 15, 1870, Delorme was appointed a Justice of the Peace by the Lieutenant-Governor of Manitoba.

In the first vote ever held to elect members to the

Manitoba Legislative Assembly, Pierre Delorme was elected to represent St. Norbert South in December 1870. He easily defeated William Dease, a Scottish Metis and large land owner at Pointe Coupée. In the Journals of the Legislative Assembly, the List of Members returned shows "St. Norbert South - Pierre de Lorme [sic.]"

His victory provincially did not stop Delorme from letting his name stand for nomination as a federal Conservative candidate. In March 1871 he was successful and became the first federal member ever elected for the constituency of Provencher.

He was then simultaneously a provincial member of the Manitoba Legislature in Winnipeg and a federal member of the House of Commons in Ottawa. This dual status indicates the great trust placed in him by his people.

In Ottawa Delorme pursued, among other matters, Metis land rights and an amnesty for Louis Riel. However a furor soon developed in Ottawa questioning what Delorme's role had been in the Red River Resistance, particularly relating to the execution of Thomas Scott. The flare-up quickly subsided when it was realized that it was Joseph Delorme, not Pierre, that had sat on the court martial of Scott and who had voted to have Scott shot by a firing squad.

In October 1871 there was a Fenian scare in Manitoba led by William B. O'Donoghue. He had been in Riel's Provisional Government but subsequently had a falling-out with Riel. On October 5, 1871 O'Donoghue led a group of Fenians from Dakota Territory into Manitoba. Lieutenant-Governor Adams Archibald asked for Metis help to put down this invasion.

Among the numerous Metis who responded to this request was Pierre Delorme and their leader was Louis Riel. Delorme was elected Captain of the Metis detachment from Pointe Coupée. This was a rather unique activity for the then sitting Member of Parliament and Member of the Manitoba Legislature. The uprising was a minor one and was easily squelched.

On April 10, 1872 Delorme wrote a letter in English

from the House of Commons to Louis Riel and stated he had met with a number of members about "... what we have spoken. They are all in your favour." This was undoubtedly a reference to an amnesty for Riel.

In a letter of April 26, 1872 Delorme advised Riel that he had been invited to dinner by:

> ... Sir Geo. Cartier. I would not go to see him but he came to me twice at the House; invitations are plentiful and tiresome.

It appears that Delorme was not enamored with life in Ottawa. It involved long absences from his home and family. He decided not to run in the federal election of September 1872. On September 14th, Delorme refused the nomination and in his place nominated Louis Riel as the candidate for the Provencher seat.

At the request of Archbishop Alexandre Taché, Riel turned down the nomination in favor of Sir Georges Etienne Cartier. Cartier had earlier been defeated in his own seat of Montreal East and Prime Minister John A. Macdonald asked Taché to find a safe seat for his Quebec lieutenant.

At the nomination meeting Cartier's name was put forward by Pierre Delorme. The Metis anticipated that Cartier would work for their unfulfilled land claims and for the amnesty previously promised for Riel. They were disappointed. Cartier was deathly ill and died the following May. Subsequently in the federal elections of October 1873 and the February and September elections of 1874, Delorme nominated Riel as the candidate for Provencher. The nomination meetings were held in Delorme's own large home. Riel won all of these elections.

Besides having been a federal and a provincial politician, Pierre Delorme was also a member of the North-West Territories Council. He held this position from 1873 to 1875. During this time, Delorme continued to strive for the land rights to which the Metis were entitled.

On May 19, 1873 Thornton Urquhart reported the following to Justice J. C. McKeagney:

> At a meeting held at the church door on Monday May 11th ....
> Pierre Denorme [sic] .... made a violent speech, calling upon the people to resist any attempt to interfere with their lands.

He added that Delorme proclaimed that ".... it is not sense but strength which gives us a right to these lands."

In the provincial election of 1874 Delorme was opposed by the transplanted Quebecer, Joseph Dubuc, a protege of Archbishop Taché. The Archbishop was a strong proponent of French Quebec immigration to the west. Many Metis felt that Taché favored these Quebec imports over them.

The Metis also strongly believed that Taché had been duped in 1870 by Prime Minister John A. Macdonald and his government into believing an amnesty for Riel and others would be forthcoming with the entrance of Manitoba into Confederation. At that time Taché had assured the Metis that the Macdonald Government would honor this obligation. Macdonald later denied ever having made such a commitment.

In the 1874 election, the Quebecer Dubuc beat the Red River Metis Delorme and assumed the seat as the member for St. Norbert South. Five years later on January 24, 1879 Delorme was re-elected as the member for St. Norbert in the Manitoba Legislature. Premier John Norquay then appointed Delorme as the Minister of Agriculture and President of the Executive Council of his Government.

Only four months later Delorme resigned from these positions over fundamental differences with Norquay. Shortly after his resignation a Bill entitled "To provide an equitable distribution of the Electoral Divisions for the Province of Manitoba" was introduced by the Norquay administration.

Delorme opposed this Bill along with a French-speaking member Joseph Royal. They realized the Bill would have the effect of reducing the number of French-speaking members in the Legislature. At this time many of the Metis spoke French. On June 18, 1879 Royal moved and Delorme seconded a resolution in the Legislative Assembly to shelve the Bill as it was:

> .... entirely destitute of justice and fairness toward the population of this Province speaking the French language.

Their motion was defeated by a vote of 12 to 8. The very next day the two men introduced another resolution that a Bill Respecting Public Printing be not now read. They stated that it would annihilate the French language from public records. They argued that both French and English were a part of Manitoba's Constitution, obtained by a grant of the Dominion of Canada and the sanction of an Imperial Act. The vote was 12 to 6 against them.

Official status for the French language in Manitoba was subsequently "annihilated" by the government of Thomas Greenway. It took 100 years, but Delorme's fight for the status of French in Manitoba was eventually successful. In 1979 the Supreme Court of Canada issued a decision requiring the reinstatement of institutional bilingualism in Manitoba.

After 1879 his career as a politician was over. Delorme continued to reside in St. Adolphe and carried on with his farming and business activities. However, he never abandoned his pride in his Metis roots. Many Metis dispersed from Red River in the 1870s and they were also ostracized socially, politically and economically after the North-West Uprising.

This prompted Delorme and other prominent Metis to start a movement to have their people recover their pride in themselves. As noted in the chapter of this book titled "The Metis - Post North-West Uprising to Date", Pierre Delorme and 14 others formed the Union Nationale Metisse St. Joseph du Manitoba in 1887, two years after the Metis were crushed at Batoche.

Prior to this, in September 1884 Louis Riel had initiated the formation of a Metis association in Saskatchewan of which St. Joseph was selected as the patron saint. This latter association did not survive the North-West Uprising.

The purpose of the Union Nationale Metisse St. Joseph

du Manitoba was to provide educational and other means to preserve and advance Metis traditions, history, and self-esteem. This organization exists and is active to this day, another fitting memorial to Pierre Delorme and the Metis of Manitoba.

An article in the *Winnipeg Free Press* dated October 20, 1906 had a write-up of the Golden Wedding Anniversary of Pierre and Adelaide Delorme. It stated that over 350 friends from all areas of Manitoba thronged to the ceremony at St. Adolphe.

There was a grand High Mass celebrated by a number of priests. All of the honored couple's children and grandchildren to the number of 33 were present at the breakfast which followed. That evening a banquet feast was held. Among many congratulatory speeches by politicians and others was one by the Treasurer of the "Union St. Joseph, a National Society". Many gifts were given to the couple and a dance followed "far into the next day's light".

Other memorials to Pierre Delorme are a street and a bridge in St. Adolphe named after him, and the presence of the unrestored Delorme House in St. Norbert Heritage Park. In his book *Hold High Your Heads* the author A. H. de Tremaudan wrote:

> .... the Honourable Pierre Delorme and many others whose names are known from one end of the North-West to the other. By their wisdom and determination they helped in the good organization and sound administration of the Metis Nation during its difficult debut.

While incorrect in equating Delorme with the "debut" of the Metis Nation (Cuthbert Grant over many decades earlier deserves that accolade), de Tremaudan nevertheless conveys the impact Delorme had with his people. Pierre Delorme contributed in no small way to the survival, self-esteem, and heritage of the Metis people when their fortunes were at their lowest ebb.

In his latter years Pierre Delorme lived a quiet life at his St. Adolphe home. He died there on November 10, 1912 shortly after his 80th birthday.

The headings of two newspaper obituaries were "Western Pioneer Dies" and "Was Noted Pioneer". One obituary stated that he was known to a large circle of friends in Manitoba and that he would be mourned by them and associates of both earlier and later days. He was buried in the cemetery of St. Adolphe Church where his grave site is marked by a prominent tombstone.

Delorme led a remarkable life. In addition to being a devoted family man he was a successful farmer, an entrepreneur, a provincial and federal politician, and a cabinet minister. Above all, he was a strong advocate of Metis rights and a champion of his people. In addition he was one of the few advocates who specifically pleaded for rights of the Metis' wives.

This memorable personality and his noteworthy contributions to his Metis people and to the Metis Nation deserve to be enshrined in Canadian history.

Delorme refused to let Metis culture, heritage and traditions die. To adopt St. Paul's words in his epistle to Timothy, Pierre Delorme "fought the good fight .... stayed the course .... kept the faith" on behalf of his Metis people.

Chapter Reference Sources

- *Canada Sessional Papers* (No. 20) 34 Victoria, 1871, p. 21.
- "Correspondence of Pierre Delorme to Louis Riel" (unpublished) Provincial Archives of Manitoba, Winnipeg (Ref. MG 3. D. 1 No. 141; 142; 144; 149; and MG 12-B1 #165).
- "Delorme House, St. Norbert Heritage Park" pamphlet issued by Manitoba Natural Resources Parks.
- "Delorme, Pierre", by Fred J. Shore, *Dictionary of Canadian Biography* Vol. XIV, p. 280-81.
- *Hold High Your Heads (History of the Metis Nation in Western Canada)* by Auguste Henri de Tremaudan, p. 12-13.
- *Holy Bible*, Second Epistle of St. Paul, c.4, v.7.
- "Hon. P. Delorme's Golden Wedding", *Winnipeg Free Press*, October 10, 1906.
- *Journals of the Legislative Assembly of Manitoba*, 1871,p. 6; 1879 p. 61-62; and 64-66; 1890, p. 23.
- *Louis Riel*, by George F. G. Stanley, p. 108-109; 167; 173; 186; 194; 208; and 263.

- *Louis Riel and the Metis*, editor A. S. Lussier, p. 71.
- *Pioneers and Early Citizens of Manitoba,* Manitoba Library Association, p. 66.
- *Snug Little Flock - The Social Origins of the Riel Resistance 1869-70, A,* by Frits Pannekoek, p. 192-193.
- St. Boniface Historical Society Archives, St. Boniface, Manitoba, "Pierre Delorme Files".
- "Western Pioneer Dies", *Winnipeg Telegram*, November 12, 1912.

Chapter XXIV

GABRIEL DUMONT

Buffalo Hunter and Military Strategist

Gabriel Dumont is in the first rank of memorable Metis leaders. His prowess as a captain of the buffalo hunt, as a sharpshooter, and as a master guerilla tactician, was unsurpassed. He was a Metis chief who pressed for and fought for the rights of his Metis people in what is now Saskatchewan. He has deservedly gone down in history as the pre-eminent Metis buffalo hunter and military strategist.

Gabriel's paternal grandfather was a Quebecer, Jean Baptiste Dumont, who came to the west from Montreal around the end of the 18th century as a voyageur. Jean Baptiste married a Sarcee woman. Isidore, Gabriel's father, was one of the children born to this couple.

Isidore frequently led a semi-nomadic life as an accomplished hunter and guide and spent his early years in the Saskatchewan Country. In 1833, he married Louise Laframboise who was the daughter of a Metis hunter from the White Horse Plain.

A few years later Isidore and Louise moved to the Red River area and took up farming on a river lot. In December 1837 Louise gave birth to their son Gabriel at St. Boniface in the Red River Settlement.

In addition to farming, Isidore also participated in the annual buffalo hunts. It was a common practice for the Metis to take their entire family on the hunt. Three year old Gabriel was part of the entourage that went on the great 1840 hunt.

Gabriel's father soon tired of the mundane aspects related to farming. Isidore's rambling spirit soon saw him pull up stakes. Traveling by Red River cart, he moved with his family back to the North Saskatchewan River area settling near Fort Pitt. On his return, he resumed his old lifestyle of hunting and guiding, and also continued to participate in the annual buffalo hunts from that area.

Because of their nomadic lifestyle, Gabriel did not receive a formal education. While he was illiterate, he was highly intelligent and in addition to French and Michif he could speak five or six native languages. In his milieu the opportunity to learn English was minimal, and he never acquired more than a few words in that tongue.

However, Gabriel's upbringing was more than suited to the world in which he grew up. Several years before he became a teenager, he was already proficient with a bow and arrow and could tame a bucking pony. He eventually became an expert horseman and a sharpshooter. He was also a fine swimmer.

The story of how young Gabriel received his first rifle illustrates the courage he was later to display during his memorable life. One night while his family was camped near the Carlton Trail, ten year old Gabriel heard the thump of pounding hoofs fast approaching them.

He was sure it was Sioux warriors coming to lay siege to their camp. He ran to alert his father and pleaded for a firearm to aid in fighting off the impending danger. By placing his ear to the ground, Isidore checked out Gabriel's warning. By doing so, he ascertained that it was a herd of buffalo that was heading their way, not the fierce Sioux braves.

Gabriel's uncle, Alexis Fisher, was so proud of the bravery that his young nephew exhibited in the face of a perceived threat that he gave Gabriel a musket. Gabriel named it "Le Petit"; this is the name he bestowed on all of the select rifles he subsequently owned.

In 1851 Gabriel's bravery in an actual battle was first put to the test. In that year his family joined the buffalo hunt at White Horse Plain. Isidore was one of the captains while the chief of the hunt was Jean Baptiste Falcon, the son of the bard Pierre Falcon.

At this hunt the thirteen year old Gabriel soon received

his baptism of fire at the Battle of the Grand Coteau in Dakota Territory. The courageous victory of the Metis over the overwhelming numbers of marauding Sioux warriors at that site is discussed in the chapter of this book titled "Battle of the Grand Coteau".

As noted in that chapter, the 13 year old Gabriel was one of the Metis riflemen who repulsed the Sioux and saved not only their own lives but the lives of the women and children who had accompanied them. The lessons he learned in this battle, particularly the use of rifle pits, formed part of his military tactics in the 1885 North-West Uprising.

During the 1850s, Gabriel continued to hone his skills as a rifleman and a buffalo hunter. His talents were becoming recognized and admired by the nearby Metis communities.

The year 1858 brought both sadness and joy to Gabriel's life. In that year his mother died; as well he married a Scottish Metis Madeleine Wilkie, the Pembina born daughter of Jean Baptiste Wilkie. Jean Baptiste was the chief of the 1840 buffalo hunt, probably the largest in Metis history. Three year old Gabriel was with his family on this hunt and it is likely that the infant Madeleine also accompanied her family.

Gabriel and Madeleine were married at St. Joseph in the Dakota Territory by Father Goiffon. Although they were very happy together, they never had any children from this marriage. Since they were both fond of children, they adopted a girl named Annie, and it is believed that they cared for and possibly adopted at least one other child.

Photographs of Gabriel portray him as powerfully built, but relatively short (perhaps five feet seven inches). His complexion reflected his bois-brûlé heritage. He had a strong broad face encased in a mane of abundant ruffled hair and a full beard and moustache.

A photo of Gabriel in his later years shows his flowing beard but his once shaggy hair had been replaced by a noticeably-receding hairline. His eyes were narrow and penetrating and he had bushy eyebrows. Gabriel had broad shoulders, was barrel-chested and presented a rugged, forceful and imposing appearance to one and all. He was a confident, straight-shooting (in both senses of that expression), courageous and unaffected individual.

His many talents soon led him to the leadership role of the Metis in the nearby areas. In 1863, at the age of 25 years, Gabriel was elected leader of the buffalo hunt involving approximately 200 hunters from the Fort Carlton area. He remained as chief of the Saskatchewan hunt continuously until 1881 by which time the buffalo had all but disappeared. In addition to the hunt Gabriel trapped, fished, and frequently went to the Red River Settlement to trade. In the 1860s Dumont exhibited another skill. Although his father and uncle were the main Metis peace brokers, Gabriel took part in negotiating peace accords between the Metis and the Sioux and subsequently with the Blackfoot tribes.

When the Red River Resistance broke out in 1869, Gabriel apparently traveled to Red River to meet with Louis Riel. It is said that he offered to send a large number of Metis from the Saskatchewan for support, but Riel did not take him up on the offer. However, some historians contend that Dumont never did make this trip or meet with Riel during the Red River Resistance.

In the early 1870s Gabriel decided to plant firmer roots in the Batoche area of Saskatchewan. One of his reasons for doing so was that he foresaw the day when there would be no more buffalo to hunt.

An Oblate priest, Father Alexis André, founded the Catholic parish of St. Laurent in 1871 on the South Saskatchewan River. This was the same priest who later testified so prejudicially against Louis Riel at Riel's 1885 trial for high treason.

In addition to St. Laurent, other Metis settlements came into existence along the South Saskatchewan River south of Prince Albert. These various communities became the heart and soul of the Plains Metis whose lifestyle was somewhat different from their Metis brethren in Red River.

The year after St. Laurent was established Gabriel commenced a ferry service not many kilometers away. The site became known as Gabriel's Crossing and still bears that name today. The Government of Saskatchewan erected a plaque in 1970, the English inscription on which reads as follows:

> GABRIEL'S CROSSING
>
> Gabriel Dumont operated a ferry on the South Saskatchewan River near this site from the early 1870s to 1883. According to the 1878 licence, the ferry was a scow measuring 7.6 m (23 feet) by 4 m (12 feet).
>
> Ferry service continued near Gabriel's Crossing until the completion of Gabriel's bridge on Highway 312 in 1969.

This ferry operation competed with that established in 1873 by Xavier Letendre, whose nickname was Batoche. Letendre established the village of Batoche in 1872, and that is the name by which the later nearby parish of St. Antoine de Padoue was commonly called.

The Batoche ferry was about 16 kilometers downstream from Gabriel's Crossing and was on the east bank where the Carlton Trail crossed the South Saskatchewan River. Gabriel claimed that his ferry service to Battleford was 25 miles shorter.

Dumont built his home at Gabriel's Crossing in 1873 and at a later date he constructed a store. One of the features of the store was a billiard table around which the Metis in the area would congregate to play, chat and have a few drinks.

Actuated by Father André, a group of Metis met at St. Laurent to discuss setting up a type of home-grown community government to maintain a degree of law and order in the area. Dumont played a leading role in the deliberations. The result was an organization similar to that of the buffalo hunt.

The high esteem in which Dumont was held by his confreres witnessed his election as President of this

Council, which consisted of eight elected members. This incipient democratic movement proclaimed its loyalty to Canada and that it would disband as soon as Canada established a system of law and order in their community. The group adopted a number of basic laws including administrative, criminal, buffalo hunt regulations, fines and others.

To approve land-holding regulations, the Council referred the matter to a special assembly. The assembly provided for river-lot frontage for each family head with the lot to extend two miles back from the river to common hay privilege lands.

At this time there were a number of American policies and other factors that were contributing to the near extinction of the buffalo herds on the northern Great Plains. This resulted in fewer animals being available for the Metis buffalo hunts.

Realizing that the buffalo were becoming scarce and with a view to conservation, regulations for the buffalo hunt were toughened. A renegade group, who actually worked for the Hudson's Bay Company (HBC), breached the rules in June 1875. Dumont warned them to obey the regulations or they would be punished. When they refused to do so, Dumont and several dozen armed Metis hunters attached some of their goods and imposed fines on a number of them.

A complaint was made to Lawrence Clarke by several of those who were fined. Clarke was a Justice of the Peace and a Chief Factor of the HBC. He wrote a highly prejudicial and misleading letter to Lieutenant-Governor Alexander Morris. In it Clarke alleged that Dumont and other used violence and robbery to collect large sums of money and, in effect, that they were rebels against the authorities.

A large detachment of North West Mounted Police (NWMP) under the command of George Arthur French was sent to the area to investigate the matter. Major General Edward Selby-Smythe, a commander of the Canadian

Militia, was also sent to the area as an observer. French reported that the Metis activities were inconsequential and that Clarke caused needless agitation with his alarming reports.

Superintendent Leif Crozier met with Gabriel and considered that neither Dumont nor the Metis had acted improperly, but had conducted themselves in conformity with the customs of the Prairies. However, the encounter with the NWMP brought an end to this early example of democratic government that was self-formed by the Metis in the South Saskatchewan River region.

The rapid decline of the buffalo in the 1870s led the Metis inhabitants in Saskatchewan to think about their future. The onset of the virtual extinction of the buffalo was nigh. Matters became more critical with the influx of Metis from Red River caused by the unfulfilled promises by the Canadian Government to them in the aftermath of the Red River Resistance.

As well, the Canadian Expansionist Movement into the west was at its height and non-aboriginal settlers were streaming in. The realization was setting in among the Metis that their semi-nomadic life was passing. Their concerns turned to land rights, the need for agricultural equipment, their lack of electoral rights and government representation, and other matters.

In the late 1870s and early 1880s Gabriel Dumont took the lead in petitioning on behalf of the Metis for redress of their concerns. The Metis wanted representation on the North-West Territories Council, a school, land patents, assistance to acquire farm equipment, and other support.

For the most part the federal government led by Prime Minister John A. Macdonald (well nicknamed "Old Tomorrow") ignored the Metis petitions. Over the years the government also ignored dozens of petitions from other Saskatchewan communities who equally wanted their rights and interests dealt with.

Canadian surveyors soon appeared in the area doing surveys on the square section block system, not that of the river lots of the Metis. Many of the Metis thought that their lands were being usurped.

They did not hold title to the property on which they had long been settled. They experienced great apprehension due to a number of factors including:

- no legal documented title to their land;
- no democratic representation and status in government;
- their lack of the fundamental right of voting;
- the influx of eastern newcomers looking for land;
- the unwanted type of surveys;
- the sudden presence of land speculators; and
- the do-nothing policy of the federal government.

The Metis were fed-up with the distant government in Ottawa that seemed to act in a despotic manner and to have little concern for their rights or welfare. On March 22, 1884, Gabriel convened a meeting of a few dozen Metis to discuss these grievances at the St. Laurent home of Abraham Montour.

Louis Goulet attended this meeting. In his Memoirs Goulet stated about Dumont that "his was a first-class mind and he spoke with extraordinary ease." Goulet also said that Dumont "could grip the attention of any audience"; hold people "in the palm of his hand"; and "had complete command of the meeting."

At the meeting it was suggested that Louis Riel, then a school teacher at St. Peter's Mission in Montana, should be invited to come to the Saskatchewan to help them. However, it was decided to first summon an assembly of as many Saskatchewan Metis as possible.

As a result, hundreds of Metis met on April 28, 1884. The upshot of the meeting was the election of a six-man committee (of whom Gabriel was one) to prepare a bill of rights and to put it forward at a combined meeting of the Metis and English settlers.

A large joint meeting of these groups was held on May 6th at the Lindsay schoolhouse, at which a decision was made to send a delegation to Louis Riel in Montana. The delegation was empowered to entreat him to come and help them to put their concerns before the Canadian Government in a proper shape and form "so that our just demands be granted".

Many of the Metis also saw this as an opportunity to have Riel lead their rights movement. The four delegates led by Gabriel Dumont included James Isbister, Michel Dumas and Moise Ouelette.

The delegation traveled to St. Peter's Mission by horseback some 1,100 kilometers in somewhat primitive conditions and with no modern amenities. They, of course, did not know what Riel's response would be to their request. Bearing in mind that whatever the response they would then have to travel another 1,100 kilometers in order to return home, one may appreciate how deeply they felt their concerns.

On June 5, 1884 Louis Riel did accept their invitation but stated his intention to resume his teaching position at St. Peter's Mission the following September. With the delegation, Riel traveled in a Red River cart to the Saskatchewan area accompanied by his Metis wife Marguerite and their two small children.

The Catholic clergy were not overly pleased that the Metis had brought Riel to Saskatchewan. Amedee Forget, secretary to Lieutenant-Governor Edgar Dewdney, had traveled with Bishop Vital Grandin for a meeting on September 5, 1884 with some Metis in the South Saskatchewan River area.

Grandin was unsympathetic to the Metis methods of handling their concerns. The next day Dumont met with Forget. Gabriel made clear that the Metis needed Riel "as our political leader", adding "In other matters I am the chief here."

Events in the year and a half after Riel's arrival are discussed in more detail in this book in the chapter titled

"The North-West Uprising". However the following provides a further description of some of the occurrences related to this Uprising.

After consultations and meetings with the white settlers and the Metis, Riel drafted a petition that was sent to the government on December 16, 1884. The government acknowledged receipt of this petition, but promptly ignored it. As a result Dumont and the Metis became more militant. The clergy and most of the English-speaking settlers wanted no part in military activism and would not continue their support of the Metis position.

On March 5, 1885 Riel, Dumont and other Metis activists swore that if required they would resort to force in order to have the government deal with their grievances. Riel and Dumont thought that a bellicose approach could lead the federal government to negotiate with them, as it had done in Manitoba 15 years earlier. They formed a Provisional Government on March 19, 1885. It was called the Exovedate. Gabriel was named Adjutant-General.

A week later in snowy conditions the NWMP came upon a group of Metis and some natives at Duck Lake. The NWMP under the command of Superintendent Leif Crozier had brought their cannon with them.

During a parley in an open field between Superintendent Crozier and the two representatives of the Metis, Gabriel Dumont's brother Isidore and a native Assywin were killed by Crozier's interpreter (Gentleman Joe McKay) on the direct orders of Crozier.

Prior to this occurrence, Riel and Dumont had no desire to engage in violent hostilities. However immediately after the Metis representatives at the parley were executed, general shooting broke out between the two groups and the North-West Uprising had lethally erupted.

The Metis were led by their great military tactician Gabriel Dumont. Meanwhile they were urged on by Louis Riel who was on horseback waving a large crucifix (from the Batoche Church) in the air.

Dumont had no intention of opposing the Mounties head-on. Prior to the parley Dumont had advised some of his followers to dismount, take cover in low-lying land and in the nearby woods and stealthily crawl ahead to a concealed shallow vantage point. Others had moved into a log cabin that was close by. The objective was to almost encircle the approaching Mounties, but not to shoot except in self defense.

At this confrontation a number of Mounties and several Metis were killed and the Mounties were ignominiously put to flight. Dumont wanted to pursue the Mounties with his men and do more of them in. Riel ordered him not to do so, stating that enough blood had been shed. This command by Riel at Duck Lake saved the lives of many Mounties and volunteers who, in fleeing for their lives, were virtually defenseless.

During this battle Gabriel himself had suffered a slight head wound. He had shrugged it off and wittily told Joseph Delorme (who thought Gabriel was dead);

> Courage. As long as you haven't lost your head you're not dead.

After the victory at Duck Lake, Riel proclaimed to the Metis:

> Give three cheers, Hurrah for Gabriel Dumont. Thank God who gave you so valiant a leader.

The Mounties and volunteers fled to Fort Carlton. Later the Metis allowed the NWMP to retrieve their fallen comrades from the battlefield.

Knowing that the Fort was vulnerable to attack, the Mounties made plans to abandon it in the middle of the night in order to head to the less risky community of Prince Albert some 65 kilometers away. As it happened a fire broke out before their departure and they left hurriedly as most of the Fort was burned to the ground.

The Metis did not follow up on their overwhelming victory at Duck Lake with an assault on Prince Albert which they could have taken without much difficulty. If they had they would have acquired guns, ammunition, provisions, goods and other articles to reinforce their own supplies. This lack of action may have discouraged some Indian tribes from joining the Metis; also such action if pursued may have put more pressure on the Canadian government to negotiate with the Metis.

The rout at Duck Lake galvanized the federal government into action. The austere and somewhat corpulent British career soldier Major General Frederick D. Middleton was placed in charge of the Canadian Militia. Several thousand soldiers and volunteers were promptly dispatched west with cannons and two Gatling guns (an early kind of machine gun) to crush the upstart Metis.

The Canadian Pacific Railway (CPR) offered to assist the Canadian government in transporting the troops west on the still unfinished railway. Only a few weeks earlier the cabinet had stopped government handouts to the CPR and it was in a serious financial situation. Nevertheless the government took the CPR up on their offer and troops were transported west on the incomplete railway system, thereby rescuing the CPR from imminent bankruptcy.

When Dumont learned that a large number of Middleton's army was in an encampment not far from Fish Creek, he planned to take them by surprise. This was so notwithstanding that there were four or five militia men for every Metis fighter. He intended to trap them when they entered a nearby ravine. He had his men hide their horses in the woods, take cover in the trees and conceal themselves in the coulee.

On April 24, 1885 firing broke out. The militia's cannons were brought into action but, due to Dumont's strategy, were ineffective and simply lobbed cannon balls over the heads of the Metis concealed in the ravine.

Although there were some defections, Dumont roused his fellow Metis to continuous action even when they appeared to be surrounded. Unexpectedly Middleton, who was unaware of the precarious Metis condition, had his troops retreat as night was falling. Fish Creek was a victory of sorts for the Metis, but they had not vanquished their enemy as they had at Duck Lake.

One thing the Battle of Fish Creek did was to make Middleton more cautious than he already was. He waited two weeks before again mobilizing his troops. Meanwhile the Metis organized to make a stand at Batoche. This was Riel's decision, one that Dumont was not too happy with. Dumont wanted to harass and ambush the enemy. Riel thought that, with God's help, negotiations with the Canadian government were still possible.

Putting into practice what he had learned as a teenager at the 1851 Battle of the Grand Coteau, Dumont instructed the Metis to dig rifle pits and trenches for concealment during any attack on Batoche. The remains of the pits and trenches can be seen there to this day.

On May 8, 1885 the Middleton troops were close to Batoche. They set up their cannons and Gatling guns. The next day on May 9th they commenced firing but, as at Fish Creek, their guns proved to be ineffective against the concealed Metis. They did damage to buildings in Batoche where some bullet holes are still visible today. However the Metis were hopelessly outnumbered; they had inferior arms and little ammunition; they had no allies except for a few Indians.

Middleton had previously given instructions for the steamer Northcote to come down the river loaded with soldiers. It would provide a diversionary tactic so that a direct assault by the ground forces could be made. The Metis countered this ploy by lowering the ferry cable as the Northcote was passing by. The cable knocked down the steamer's smokestacks and the boat futilely floated away.

Notwithstanding Middleton's overwhelming numbers and firepower, the Metis held the troops off for three days. However by then their ammunition was all but depleted; the women even melted nails and buckles to make bullets, but the doom of the Metis was imminent.

On May 12th Lieutenant Colonel Arthur Williams,

impatient with General Middleton's timid tactics, disobeyed his instructions and with a group of troops swarmed the Metis rifle pits. There they overpowered the Metis and bayoneted and killed a number of them. They showed no mercy, killing two old-timers Joseph Ouellette aged 93 and Joseph Vandal aged 75. Some Metis escaped including Riel and Dumont.

Dumont decided to flee to the United States with some of his comrades and wanted Riel to come with him. As noted elsewhere in this book, Riel did not do so and voluntarily surrendered, mistakenly expecting the equivalent of a state trial.

Dumont and his party successfully made their way hundreds of kilometers to Montana. They were immediately arrested but the President of the United States Grover Cleveland quickly ordered them released, probably because he considered them to be political refugees. They were never charged or brought to trial by the American government.

In Montana Dumont made plans to rescue Riel. Fearing this possibility, the Mounties took extra precautions in guarding their stately prisoner, and Dumont had to abandon this mission. Meanwhile Riel was charged with high treason by the Canadian government, was put on trial and was executed on November 16, 1885.

In the United States Gabriel originally spent time at the Metis community of Spring Creek (now Lewistown) Montana. Soon his wife Madeleine joined him, bringing news of his father's death. A few months later in early 1886 Madeleine died.

With his love and life companion no longer alive, Gabriel finally accepted an offer to join "Buffalo Bill" Cody's Wild West Show as a performer. His first appearance was in Philadelphia on July 7, 1886. The theatrical bills advertising the show prominently featured Dumont immediately below Buffalo Bill and above all the other members of the troupe including the renowned Annie Oakley. One poster stated:

> Gabriel Dumont, the Exiled Chieftian [sic] of the Riel Rebellion.

Another bill read:

> Gabriel Dumont, The Hero of the half breed Rebellion.

Astride his dashing horse, Gabriel rode into the arena holding his trusty rifle Le Petit. As he did so a cowboy threw four glass balls into the air. With uncanny accuracy Gabriel shot these balls into smithereens, electrifying the onlookers with his sharp-shooting skills.

In that same year of 1886, the Canadian government declared an amnesty with respect to the North-West Uprising. Dumont did not trust Prime Minister John A. Macdonald whom he knew had blatantly reneged on the amnesty promised for Riel and others, after the Red River Resistance of 1869-70. Consequently he did not immediately return to Canada.

However Gabriel quickly tired of being a showman on display. He eventually made his way to Quebec where the French-Canadian nationalists wanted to use him in their cause. This association ended abruptly as his interests and those of the nationalists had little in common.

Still not ready to return to the Saskatchewan and able to use the money, he rejoined the Wild West Show during the 1887 and 1888 seasons. However he was no longer a featured star, likely because the 1885 events had faded from view. He was now 50 years old. During these years he traveled extensively across the United States and it is believed that he also visited Paris, France with the Show.

After leaving the Wild West Show he spent the next few years in Montana and the adjoining states. It wasn't until 1893 that Gabriel returned to Saskatchewan to settle at Batoche close to his nephew Alexis. He led a much quieter life on these lands that he knew and loved. He fished, hunted, and chatted with old comrades.

In 1905 Saskatchewan and Alberta became provinces of Canada. This was one of the conditions that Dumont, Riel and other Metis had demanded in their Bill of Rights of

March 8, 1885.

At the age of 68, Gabriel died suddenly on May 19, 1906 while at the home of his nephew Alexis. He was buried in the cemetery at Batoche where his remains are today. The cemetery is part of a National Park that also contains a museum operated by Parks Canada.

During the 1870s and 1880s Francis J. Dickens, son of the English novelist Charles Dickens, was an inspector with the NWMP. Many years after his death, Francis' letters home to England were published in the book *Dickens of the Mounted.* In his letter of August 21, 1876, Dickens wrote of an encounter he had with Gabriel Dumont.

Among other matters he said that Gabriel:

> .... had a mien that inspired deference in the beholder .... [that he wore] a fringed hide jacket, handsomely decorated with needlework floral designs in the Metis style .... [in his face] blazed two eyes that would have daunted the panther, however famished ..... even Sam Steele had spoken the name [Gabriel Dumont] with something approaching reverence.

He also said:

> .... the most awesome legend belonged to this prodigious Nimrod [skilled hunter].

John Andrew Kerr wrote an article in a 1935 issue of the *Dalhousie Review* entitled "Gabriel Dumont: a Personal Memory". This article tells of Kerr's acquaintance with and first-hand observances of Dumont in the 1870s. Kerr stated that Gabriel had a "thickset appearance" and that:

> He was of medium height, square of shoulder, with a homely but kind face .... He had a remarkable memory .... he was kindly to a degree and thoughtful for others of his Metis friends not overburdened with this world's goods .... a man of unquestioned courage .... he was a 'crack shot' .... to show an ear or a finger would mean being hit.

Kerr indicated that Gabriel was very ingenious and possessed of a strong intelligence, that he was a first class hunter with a complete knowledge of plains lore and the habits of the buffalo, that ".... he was a remarkable Metis." Kerr stated that Gabriel had faults; he was to be avoided when he was in his cups, violent when double-crossed, and an inveterate gambler.

It was said that Gabriel could gamble and drink with the best of them. Apparently he once gambled for three straight days. His stamina was awesome not only in these activities but also when hunting.

Superintendent Sam Steele of the NWMP in his book *Forty Years in Canada* wrote of Gabriel Dumont: "He knew the plains as well as a housewife knows her kitchen." Gabriel could also be a very kind and considerate person as noted in this further extract from Steele's book:

> One might travel the plains from one end to the other and talk to the Metis hunters and never hear an unkind word said about Dumont. He would kill bisons by the score and give them to those who were either unable to kill or had no buffalo. Not until every poor member of the hunting party had his cart filled with meat would he begin to fill his own.

An interview with the then Prime Minister John G. Diefenbaker titled "Backstage with the PMs Western Hero" appeared in a 1958 issue of *Maclean's Magazine*. Diefenbaker (who was born in 1895 and whose father was a Saskatchewan homesteader) stated that as a boy he met Gabriel Dumont several times in 1903.

Diefenbaker said that Dumont "is the most romantic figure of the west in the last century" and indicated that Buffalo Bill didn't compare with Gabriel.

In June 1961 Diefenbaker declared the rectory and Roman Catholic Church at Batoche as historic sites. At the dedication Diefenbaker said that Dumont had a reputation "for generosity and integrity". Diefenbaker also stated of Dumont that:

> He deserves to rank with Tecumseh as one of the greatest strategists of Indian origin in both the United States and Canada.

On May 6, 1985 (100 years after the Battle of Batoche) a 32 cent postage stamp honoring Gabriel Dumont was issued by the Canadian Post Office. It depicts a likeness of Dumont superimposed on the Canadian soldiers attacking the Metis on the battlefield at Batoche.

His name has been commemorated by an institute, geographical locations, educational facilities and other memorials.

Gabriel Dumont was a famed buffalo hunter, warrior and chief of his people, a leader who fought so valiantly for their rights. The memory of this larger-than-life Metis legend lives on to this day.

Chapter Reference Sources

- "Backstage with the PM's Western Hero", by Klaus Neumann, *Maclean's,* Magazine, December 6, 1958.
- *Dickens of the Mounted,* editor Eric Nicol, p. 70-72.
- "Dumont, Gabriel", by Roderick C. Macleod, *Dictionary of Canadian Biography* Vol. XIII, p. 302-307.
- "Dumont, Gabriel", by George Woodcock, *Canadian Encyclopedia,* p. 702-703.
- *Gabriel Dumont, the Metis Chief and his Lost World,* by George Woodcock, *passim.*
- "Gabriel Dumont: a Personal Memory", by John Andrew Kerr, *Dalhousie Review,* p. 21-24.
- *Gabriel Dumont, Jerry Potts - Canadian Plainsmen,* editor Sandra Lynn McKee, *passim.*
- "Gabriel Dumont; the forgotten hero", by George Woodcock, *Saturday Night Magazine,* July, 1973, p. 21-24.
- *Forty Years in Canada, by* Sam B. Steele, p. 92-94.
- "Gabriel Dumont's Account of the North West Rebellion, 1885", translated by George F. G. Stanley, *Canadian Historical Review,* p. 249-269.
- *Last War Drum, The,* by Desmond Morton, *passim.*
- *Lord of the Plains,* by Alfred Silver, *passim.*
- *Louis Riel,* by George F. G. Stanley, *passim.*
- *Louis Riel v. Canada, The Making of a Rebel,* by J. M. Bumsted, *passim.*
- National Archives of Canada, Ottawa, Ref. Canadian Postal Archives.
- *Prairie Fire, The 1885 North-West Rebellion,* by Bob Beal and Rod Macleod *passim.*
- "Premier Pleads Case for Metis", *Calgary Herald,* June 29, 1961.
- *Riel, a Life of Revolution,* by Maggie Siggins, *passim.*
- *Strange Empire, Louis Riel and the Metis People,* by Joseph Howard, *passim.*
- *Trial of Louis Riel, Justice and Mercy Denied, The,* by George R. D. Goulet, *passim.*
- *Vanishing Spaces - Memoirs of Louis Goulet,* by Guillaume Charette, p. 109-110

Chapter XXV

THELMA CHALIFOUX

Social Activist and Metis Matriarch

Thelma Chalifoux follows in the activist tradition of memorable historic Metis personalities who so resolutely strived to advance the rights of their people. In promoting Metis causes, she is a modern-day leader who follows in the footsteps of such notables as Cuthbert Grant, James Sinclair, Louis Riel, Pierre Delorme and Gabriel Dumont.

Among her many distinctions, Thelma Chalifoux is the first aboriginal woman and the first Metis ever appointed to the Senate of Canada. This honor was bestowed on her in 1997.

The authors interviewed Senator Chalifoux on several occasions and their discussions invariably covered a wide range of topics. These related not only to her life but also included such diverse subjects as eagles being messengers of God; brief descriptions of some prominent Metis such as the "wild and wooly" Harry Daniels; spirituality; Metis politics; and on and on always in a convivial manner interspersed with humorous anecdotes.

The authors found this feisty living Metis legend to have a number of fascinating qualities. In addition to being a warm, caring person with a dynamic and strong will, Thelma is a highly entertaining raconteur with an ample fund of stories and a flair for humor. She has an infectious smile and wears colorful hats in keeping with her vivid personality. During interviews with her, the authors frequently found themselves laughing out loud at her anecdotes.

One incident that she recounted was about driving down a country road on Metis business with three of her associates, one of whom was the dynamic Harry Daniels (profiled in another chapter of this book). During this trip the men with her shot a duck in a slough. Thelma referred to this duck as "a poor little critter". In order to retrieve the bird, Joe Blyan took off his pants and jumped into the water. However the slough was icy-cold and when Joe came out of it he was frigid. The Senator quipped to the authors: "Have you ever seen a brown guy go purple?"

Thelma Chalifoux was born during a blizzard on February 8, 1929 in Calgary. Her father Paul Villeneuve wanted a boy, but he later said he was so thankful that he got her for she was a challenge to the family. Although she was very shy, she was protective of her brothers and sisters and, so to speak, defended them to the death.

Her Metis roots, inherited through her father, run deep. Her father, her grandfather, her great grandfather and her paternal grandmother were all Metis.

Thelma's great-grandfather Francois Villeneuve was born in St. Albert, Alberta in 1804. The town of Villeneuve, Alberta was named after her grandfather Severe Villeneuve. Severe became a Vice-President of the St. Albert Metis Association when it was formed in October 1896. He was married to Julia Boucher who was born in Lac Ste. Anne, Alberta. Thelma's mother Helene Ingwersen was born in Iowa of Danish ancestry.

Thelma was brought up in Calgary until she was nine years old. If the house in which she was raised was still there today it would be in the middle of the Saddledome, home arena of the Calgary Flames Hockey team. Before she was five years old she learned to do the waltz quadrille, a square dance that is often performed at Metis gatherings.

In 1938 her family moved to a small Metis community on the outskirts of Calgary where a number of her relatives lived. As a youngster, her role was to look after the elders in the family unit. As she herself has stated "We were a very, very proud extended family".

Thelma attended Victoria and King Edward Schools and Western Canada High School in Calgary but did not complete high school. She subsequently worked at a number of jobs. These were in a dry cleaning plant, in a bakery, in a packing plant, in a coffee shop, as a banquet waitress at the Palliser Hotel in Calgary, and she even set pins in a bowling alley.

It was while she was working at the coffee shop that she first met Normie Kwong who later became a star football player for the Edmonton Eskimos and the Calgary Stampeders. He was later named Lieutenant-Governor of Alberta in 2005.

As a teenager during World War II Thelma tried to enlist but was too young and ended up working as a volunteer in the Salvation Army Canteen at Currie Barracks in Calgary. Her father and a sister served in the army, her brother in the navy, and another sister in the air force.

In 1947 she married Robert Coulter and had seven children with him. However as a result of his service in the Korean War, Coulter suffered post-traumatic stress syndrome. Thelma said that it altered his character and subsequently led to the break-up of their marriage. She was then a 27 year old single mother with seven children to support.

Thelma was married for a second time to William Chalifoux. Even though she possesses what she calls "a white knight syndrome", believing she can save anybody, she separated from her second husband about one year later. However she did keep his surname. She was again a single woman with a number of children to look after.

Since she had an eye for color, Thelma obtained a position as head color designer and formulator for a paint company in Calgary. Concerned about her children during their teenage years, she moved to Stirling, Alberta for five years.

While there she became extremely ill with pancreatitis, an inflammation of the pancreas. She was hospitalized for one year after which she was advised that she had only three years to live. However with her indomitable spirit and deep need to care for her children, she refused to accept this gloomy diagnosis. She moved with her children to Edmonton where there was at the time a specialist in this field of medicine. This specialist was Dr. Jim McCaffery, a cousin of one of the author's of this book, Terry Goulet.

Thelma had joined the Metis Nation of Alberta (MNA) in 1962 and was an active member. Shortly after moving to Edmonton, she went to the offices of the MNA to change her mailing address for the Metis Newsletter. The MNA immediately hired her.

In 1969 Thelma played an essential role in the formation of the Welfare and Land Departments of the MNA. For several years in the 1970s she was involved with the Company of Young Canadians and the Alberta Native Communications Society.

Her social activism led to participation in many community and aboriginal activities. This eventually led to her receiving recognition and awards too extensive to list in detail but some of which are referred to hereafter.

She moved to Slave Lake in 1979 and was a land claims negotiator there until 1982. While there she became the founder of the local Native Friendship Centre and even used her home on occasion as a safe haven for abused women. She also hosted and produced a weekly radio program titled "Smoke Signals from the Peace", thereby becoming the first aboriginal woman to broadcast on commercial radio.

Thelma was appointed a member of the Alberta Provincial Appeals Panel of Alberta Family and Social Services in the late 1980s. She held this position for nearly a decade.

In 1990 she became a Senator of the MNA for a five year period. As a committed social activist, Thelma was the first Metis woman to chair the National Metis Senate and the National Metis Senate Constitution Committee. She also co-chaired the Alberta Metis Elders Senate which developed the Metis anthem and prayer.

In addition to these commitments, she served on the Senate of the University of Alberta.

Thelma became the distinguished recipient of the National Aboriginal Achievement Award in 1995. She received an Award of Excellence from Catholic Social Services in Edmonton in June 1999 for her work on behalf of low-income communities.

In 1997 Thelma was a community consultant and conducted workshops in schools on Metis culture, history and value systems. In that year she received a momentous telephone call from the then Prime Minister Jean Chretien who offered to appoint her to the Senate of Canada.

When the Prime Minister telephoned her he asked if she spoke French. In Cree, she answered "No". When she asked Chretien "Why me?" , he responded "When I read your story Madame, I knew you were needed in the Senate."

The following extracts from the Senate Debates of December 2, 1997 set forth some of the welcoming remarks on her first appearance in the Senate.

Senator Alasdair Graham, Leader of the Government in the Senate:

> If there is a word that defines the paths that Thelma Chalifoux has taken in her life, it is 'responsibility' .... responsibility for her own people so that they could learn to manage and govern their own affairs better.

He also said that there was now in the Senate:

> .... a proud and special legacy. It is the legacy of the Metis people, a people of brave hearts, a people renowned in our history .... it is a legacy about one woman's commitment to justice and responsibility, a legacy about caring, a legacy about sharing .... It is a legacy of a woman who had a dream .... about respect and dignity .... about communities and societies where people have the right to hope, liberated from hatred and intolerance, a place where children have the right to grow up equal.

The Leader of the Opposition in the Senate, John Lynch-Staunton indicated that Thelma was a person with "exceptional qualifications and experience." He added that her:

> .... long activities on behalf of the Metis community in

> particular and aboriginals in general will allow all of us to have a better appreciation and understanding of a population too often deprived of the status and acceptance it deserves.

Senator Gerry St. Germain stated that her appointment may be ".... an opportunity to recognize some of the great accomplishments of the Metis people" and he referred to the Riels and the Dumonts among others.

Senator Jean Forest stated that when she was Chancellor of the University of Alberta, Thelma served on the University's Senate. She then stated: "She did a wonderful job there, and I know that she will do the same here."

Senator Joyce Fairbairn commented in part:

> Senator Chalifoux's whole life has been one of trying to build bridges, and to bring courage to her own people to stay in the game and in the fight. She has done so with great skill, internal fortitude and enormous sensitivity to those she represents.

Thelma told the authors of this book that:

> In the Senate I made a lot of statements of who our Metis people were. I saw my role as educating the politicians on both sides of the Chamber as to just who we were and how we fit into the Canadian mosaic. I was very vocal.

Senator Chalifoux exhibited her considerable energy in the duties she undertook in the Canadian Senate. There her particular areas of interest and specialization included Aboriginal issues, the environment, human rights, senior citizens and women's issues. She even did a study on discrimination in the public service.

She served on a number of Senate committees including Aboriginal Peoples, Agriculture and Forestry. Her colleagues recognized her talent and commitment with respect to the indigenous peoples of Canada by naming her the Chair of the Senate Standing Committee on Aboriginal Peoples. She was also a member of the Sub-Committee on Aboriginal Economic Development in relation to Northern National Parks.

On December 4, 2001 Senator Chalifoux introduced a

private Bill No. S-35 in the Senate titled "An Act to honour Louis Riel and the Metis People." The Summary published with the Bill stated that it was to honor "Louis Riel as a Metis patriot and Canadian hero."

This Bill would have:

- vacated Riel's conviction for high treason;
- established an annual Louis Riel Day;
- acknowledged the arrowhead sash as the recognized symbol of the Metis;
- directed the Minister of Canadian Heritage to take appropriate action to preserve the memory of Riel and to advance Metis culture and history.

The Bill was favorably debated by several senators on December 12, 2001, February 19, 2002, and March 13, 2002. The authors of this book (who are advocates of the exoneration of Louis Riel) met with Senator Chalifoux early in 2002 to discuss this Bill and their book on Louis Riel and his trial. This Bill, like many similar previous Bills in the House of Commons, died on the Order Paper when Parliament was prorogued.

On February 5, 2004 (the very last day on which she sat in the Senate) Thelma reintroduced a bill honoring Louis Riel and the Metis people as Bill S-9. This Bill also died on the Order Paper.

However these Bills reflect Senator Chalifoux's deep regard for Louis Riel and the Metis people. She served in this manner from her appointment in 1997 to her mandatory retirement in February 2004 when she celebrated her 75th birthday. On her retirement, her colleagues and members of the government recognized her achievements in the Senate and at many dinners held in her honor.

On her last day in Parliament, no less than 10 Senators acknowledged Thelma's notable personality and memorable achievements. In this respect the Speaker of the Senate allotted more than the usual time for these tributes to her. On this occasion the praise heaped on Thelma was even more complimentary than when she first entered the Senate.

One example was Senator Nick Sibbetson who stated in part that Thelma has been a:

> .... tiger, particularly chairing the Aboriginal Peoples Committee and doing a study on aboriginal youth in urban centres.

He added that she had been a bridge between non-native and Aboriginal people and had been involved all her life in Alberta in assisting in the establishment and effectiveness of Aboriginal organizations.

Another expression of esteem came from Senator Lorna Milne who said that in the Senate:

> Thelma has continued to educate us, and to fight for the rights and betterment of her people

Senator Ione Christensen said of Thelma:

> You have touched so many lives in so many positive ways.

Among the many tributes held in her honor on her Senate retirement was a banquet on February 6, 2004 at the Royal Canadian Legion Hall located in Morinville (a community close to Edmonton where she resides in a modest home). One of the principal organizers of the tribute was John Williams, the Conservative Member of Parliament for St. Albert.

Among the distinguished guests in attendance were the Lieutenant-Governor of Alberta, Lois Hole; Senator Dan Hayes, Speaker of the Senate of Canada; Senator Joyce Fairburn; David Kilgour, then Liberal Member of Parliament from Edmonton; Audrey Poitras, President of the Metis Nation of Alberta; Trevor Gladue, Vice-President of the Metis Nation of Alberta; the Mayors of Stoney Plain, Legal and St. Albert; Doc Horner, Member of the Alberta Legislative Assembly; and a representative of the First Nations.

Presentations were made by a number of those in attendance. Lieutenant-Governor Hole remarked that

Thelma "touched hundreds and thousands of lives" and that she never ceased to attend to the interests of other people. She also referred to Senator Chalifoux's incredible will.

Senator Fairburn told of Thelma educating the Senators about her Metis people leading to their respect for the Metis, and spoke of her "tremendous contribution". She also referred to Thelma as a "national treasure".

David Kilgour talked of "the wonderful lady we honour tonight" who had faced so much adversity in her life, a lady who had done so much for the Metis people and who had so many friends and admirers.

Audrey Poitras stated that Senator Chalifoux was a trail-blazer who enhanced the profile of the Metis people though her government role.

At this dinner Senator Chalifoux's daughter Debbie Coulter said that her family called their mother the "energizer bunny" and that she was always active and a wonderful role model.

Although she has retired from the Senate of Canada, Thelma Chalifoux has not retired. She is a registered lobbyist and the fees she earns go into the operation of the Michif Cultural and Resource Institute which she founded. This Institute is located in St. Albert. She plays an active role in the Institute together with her son Robert Coulter and her daughter Sharon Morin.

As a result of Senator Chalifoux's efforts, on November 16, 2004 the Metis infinity flag was raised for the first time at the St. Albert City Hall by the Mayor of St. Albert. The ceremony to honor the Metis people was performed on the 119th anniversary of Louis Riel's execution on November 16, 1885.

The raising of the flag was followed by a reception in the rotunda of the City Hall. At the reception Senator Chalifoux and others (including one of the authors George Goulet) spoke about the Metis people and their history, heritage and culture.

For her contributions to Aboriginals and to Canada, Senator Chalifoux has received recognition and honors from both the Aboriginal and general community as well as from a prestigious university.

The National Aboriginal Women's Association invited her to sit on its board of directors. The Association's President Pam Paul said of her:

> Senator Chalifoux must be one of the most dedicated women I know when it comes to Aboriginal politics and even more so when it involves Aboriginal women. She definitely brings a wealth of knowledge to the table.

There is a transitional house in Calgary named the Senator Thelma Chalifoux House in her honor. This home provides temporary accommodation to Metis and First Nations elders who require transitional assistance.

On June 2, 2004 the University of Toronto conferred an honorary Doctor of Laws degree on Senator Chalifoux. In doing so it, indicated that she had been a tireless advocate of the Metis community and Aboriginal rights for over 35 years.

In 2005 *Alberta Venture* Magazine in conjunction with Shaw TV conducted a vote to determine who, were the 50 greatest Albertans. The results were published in the December 2005 issue, with Senator Thelma Chalifoux being selected in the top ten. The write-up on her 10th place finish lauded her career and stated in part:

> Thelma Chalifoux is known as a driving force in the Canadian Metis community as a senator .... and is a devoted activist who works tirelessly for the underprivileged.

Senator Chalifoux told the authors that she wants to be remembered as a person who worked not only for the Metis and their causes but also for other people; as a person who helped to make the lives of others a little happier; as a person who helped make the lives of others a little better.

She said that when she was young she belonged to an extended family. That continues today. In addition to her six surviving children, she has 30 grandchildren and 28 great-grandchildren.

Her life has been one of continued growth and progress. From being a struggling single mother looking after her family, Senator Chalifoux became an advocate for the disadvantaged and for her Metis people; a social activist on a provincial level; and a meaningful presence on the national stage.

Throughout the many faceted ventures in which she has been involved she has acted with fervor, enthusiasm and affability. Over a number of decades, she proved to be an unceasing champion of her Metis people, their rights and interests, and their history, heritage and culture. Her colleague Senator Joyce Fairbairn said of Thelma's Senate years that:

> ..... she exuded a huge presence representing Metis, First Nations, and indeed all Albertans in a very dignified and respectful manner.

Senator Thelma Chalifoux, this bright woman of determination with the genial personality, this "national treasure", is and will go down in history as a memorable Metis personality

Chapter Reference Sources

- "Board of Directors", National Aboriginal Women's Association web site.
- *Debates of the Senate,* Dec. 2, 1997; February 5, 2004; and February 10; 2004.
- "50 Greatest Albertans, The", editor Ruth Kelly, *Alberta Venture* Magazine, December, 2005.
- "From single mom to senator", by Anh Hoang, *Western Catholic Reporter* Newspaper, June 21, 1999.
- "Metis Museum, A" pamphlet by Michif Cultural and Resource Institute, St. Albert, Alberta.
- "Rare, unconquerable spirit, A", by Chris Purdy, *The Edmonton Journal,* Feb. 1, 2004, p. 6.
- "Read about the 2004 honorary degree recipients", University of Toronto web site, June Convocation, 2004.
- *Royal Commission on Aboriginal Peoples Report,* Vol. 3, Ch. 2, presentation by Senator Chalifoux, April 22, 1992.
- "Speaker after speaker extol virtues of Senator Chalifoux", by Terry Lusty, *Metis Matters* Newsletter, March, 2004, p. 6.

Chapter XXVI

HARRY DANIELS

Metis Crusader

There are only two men in the history of the Metis Nation who were the prime instrumental forces in having the Metis people enshrined in Canada's Constitution - Louis Riel in section 31 of the 1870 *Manitoba Act* and Harry Daniels in section 35 of the 1982 *Constitution Act.*

Harry Daniels epitomized the qualities of the great Metis leaders of the past. He possessed an indomitable spirit in strenuously striving for the interests of his people and of non-status Indians. He was a pre-eminent 20th century crusader for Aboriginal rights.

Harry's personality seemed larger-than-life. He was charismatic, flamboyant, passionate and a marvelous raconteur.

The clothing he wore was invariably tasteful, stylish and refined. On appropriate occasions he wore a beaded buckskin jacket. His trademark black felt hat, with a partially upswept brim circled by a colorful band, gave him his famed nickname of "Harry the Hat".

His zest for life, including his love of jigging, did not detract from his role as a forthright social activist who tenaciously pursued a wide field of causes and activities on behalf of indigenous peoples.

Harry Wilfred Daniels was born in Regina Beach, Saskatchewan on September 16, 1940. His parents, both Metis, were Henry (Harry) Alfred Daniels and Emma McKay. His maternal grandparents were William Henry McKay and Marie St. Anne Bellegarde who, after they were married in Fort Qu'Appelle, Saskatchewan, established their home in Regina Beach.

In 2005 the authors of this book interviewed Harry's sister Laurena Daniels and his widowed partner Cheryl Storkson about his life. Laurena, who still lives in Regina

Beach, told the authors that her grandfather McKay had obtained land scrip. She didn't know the names of their paternal grandparents or their relatives. This was due to their father being orphaned when he was three years old. Harry did trace the family tree and found roots in Wales which he visited before his death.

When Harry was nine years old, his father abandoned the family and Harry soon assumed the role of the man of the house. Laurena remembers that it was Harry who took his younger siblings to their first day at school.

Harry attended school in Regina Beach and when he was 17 years old he joined the Canadian Navy for three years. His pay checks as a sailor were sent home to his mother as he was the only support for the family.

Harry was married in his early twenties but this marriage was short-lived. His second marriage was to Linda Fisher, a Metis woman from Saskatchewan. He fathered two children from this marriage, but it also ended in divorce. On May 23, 1983 he married for a third time to Janet Wightman, and although there were children from their union, it also did not last.

In 1988 Harry met Cheryl Storkson at a Metis meeting in Sault Ste. Marie, Ontario at which Harry was the chairman. Cheryl told the authors that Harry told her that "He just wasn't good at marriage." As a result they never went through a formal ceremony, but their conjugal union that began a year after their meeting lasted until his death.

After leaving the Navy in his early twenties Harry Daniels returned to Saskatchewan. During the following years he worked at a number of jobs including waiter, actor, and dance instructor at an Arthur Murray dance studio. He eventually ended up as a groom for race horses and in that capacity he traveled to tracks in Winnipeg, Toronto, New Jersey, New York and Florida.

In 1967 at the age of 27 he returned to Canada from Hollywood, Florida. He then furthered his education by attending the University of Saskatchewan, where he took a course in Native Law.

Not long afterwards Daniels made a decision to become involved in Aboriginal politics. He became Executive Director of the Saskatchewan Metis Society in 1969.

In 1971 he was elected a Vice-President of the Metis Association of Alberta (which later became the Metis Nation of Alberta). The following year he was appointed as a representative of the Metis people to an environmental conference held by the United Nations in Stockholm, Sweden.

In 1974-75 Harry was a member of the Organizing Committee for the United Nations Habitat Conference held in Vancouver. In 1975-76 he was the Director of Aboriginal Rights of the Metis Association of Alberta. He also became a Vice-President of the Edmonton Native Friendship Centre in 1975.

During these years Harry became actively involved with the Native Council of Canada (NCC), which at the time was the national organization representing Metis and non-status Indians. The NCC had been founded in 1971 with a view to serving and promoting the rights and interests of off-reserve and non-status Indians and Metis in Canada. A number of years later the NCC changed its name to The Congress of Aboriginal Peoples (CAP).

Harry was originally elected Secretary-Treasurer and became President of the NCC in 1975. He served in this presidential capacity for two periods - 1975 to 1981 and 1997 to 2000. During his first term with the NCC he chaired the Canadian Aboriginal Justice Committee.

In the four year period ending in 1981 he acted as a Director of the World Council of Indigenous Peoples. He also served as Western Vice-President of the NCC from 1983 to 1985. In the course of his varied career Harry traveled to many parts of the world including Japan, New Zealand, Australia and Panama.

At an early stage Daniels assumed a leading advocacy role for enshrining the rights of Aboriginals in the

Constitution of Canada. In the early 1980s the government of Prime Minister Pierre Trudeau took the initiative in pursuing patriation of the Canadian Constitution in order to remove from Canada one of the remnants of British colonialism.

To this end the government convened meetings with, among others, representatives of Aboriginal groups with a view to obtaining their support for patriation.

Harry Daniels was front and center in a number of these meetings. He was a constitutional adviser during this period not only for the NCC but also for the Metis associations of Alberta and the North West Territories. At this time the Metis National Council was not yet formed. It did not come into existence until after the patriation of the Constitution.

In the lead-up to the conferences on patriation, Daniels felt that the voice of the Metis people was not being heard or listened to in government circles. He demanded Metis participation in the constitutional talks.

The NCC was allotted two seats at the constitutional meetings. However when he learned that an Indian women's rights group had been denied participation, he backed them with concrete action since he felt that native women should have a voice at the table. He did so by turning over one of the NCC seats to the Indian women's group in order that they would have representation. They selected as their spokesperson Mary Two Axe Early.

In the summer of 1980 the then Minister of Justice Jean Chretien (Chair of the Cabinet Committee on Aboriginal Affairs) with seven other government ministers held a meeting with Daniels (then President of the NCC) and other Metis leaders to discuss, among other matters, Metis constitutional issues. When the bells for the House of Commons question period rang, Chretien and the other government ministers abruptly left the meeting to return to the Commons Chamber.

Since the meeting had not been formally adjourned, Daniels was incensed. He irately told the departing

Chretien that the Metis would hold a sit-in. Led by their resolute leader Harry Daniels, that is exactly what they did. About 25 of them stayed put in the Commons committee room for over seven hours and refused to budge.

These peaceful Metis protestors finally agreed to leave when Sergeant-at-Arms Gus Clouthier advised them that they posed a security risk to the Parliament Buildings. A newspaper photo of the Metis leader with the Sergeant-at-Arms discussing the matter shows a handsome 39 year old Daniels spiffily dressed in a three-piece suit, white shirt and silk tie. He had shoulder length black curly hair, a trimmed moustache, glasses and a serious demeanor. His whole image was that of a man not to be trifled with, an image that perfectly fit his political and statesman-like personality.

In leaving the Building, Daniels said he was doing so because he respected the House and that what he had been trying to do was "to establish a genuine consultative process." The end result demonstrates that this objective was eventually realized through Daniel's determined efforts.

On January 30, 1981 Daniels as President of the NCC was invited to participate in the deliberations of the Parliamentary Committee dealing with the aboriginal aspects of constitutional amendments leading to patriation. In these negotiations Daniels represented not only the Metis but also non-status Indians.

As noted earlier, the federal Minister of Justice Jean Chretien (who became Prime Minister over a decade later) asked Daniels if he would travel to Britain to back patriation. Daniels said that if the Metis were specifically included in the Constitution he would do so. When Chretien refused this proposition, Daniels reacted angrily with clenched fist and said:

> Then I mobilize my people, that's the only thing we'll accept.

After disappearing for awhile, Chretien returned and said that he had contacted Prime Minister Trudeau and that all of Daniels' points would be agreed to.

During a Parliamentary Committee hearing on the Constitution, Senator Duff Roblin of Manitoba asked Daniels "How do we know who is Metis?" Daniels categorically, confidently and emphatically replied:

> We know who we are; we know the generations of discrimination we have endured; we don't need anybody to tell us who we are. If you identify as Ukrainian or Italian, we don't question who you are or try to tell you who you are. We self-identify, just like everybody else in this country.

As a result of Daniels' persistence, s. 35 of the *Constitution Act, 1982* specifically named the Metis as one of the Aboriginal peoples of Canada and recognized and affirmed their existing aboriginal rights. This feat was the acme of the outstanding contributions of Harry Daniels to the Metis people of Canada.

Daniels had a broader view of the meaning of the term "Metis" in s. 35 of the Constitution than that of some Metis organizations. A letter dated February 17, 1994 that Harry Daniels wrote to Kirby Lethbridge (President of the Labrador Metis Association) was published in the Royal Commission on Aboriginal Peoples (RCAP) Report. In this letter Daniels indicated that it was understood at the time of the constitutional negotiations in 1981 that "Metis" in s. 35:

> .... included the member organizations and their constituents who self-identified as a Metis person .... It was also understood that the term Metis was not tied to any particular geographic area ...

In fact the RCAP Report stated:

> It seems clear that the Metis of Labrador are an Aboriginal people within the meaning of s. 35.

Daniels was not only a Metis politician he was a researcher and author. The Treaty and Aboriginal Rights Research Group of the Indian Association of Alberta engaged his services as a researcher in 1973. In 1988 he acted in the same capacity for the Manitoba Aboriginal Justice Inquiry.

Senator Thelma Chalifoux (profiled in another chapter of this book) arranged for Harry and Professor Paul Chartrand of the University of Saskatchewan to research the meaning of "Metis" in Canada. Daniels and Chartrand issued a research paper in October 2001 titled "Unravelling the Riddles of Metis Definition." This paper gives an insightful review of pertinent factors relating to its subject matter.

Daniels wrote a number of other papers and articles over the years concerning the Metis. On March 2, 1978 as President of the NCC he made a presentation to the Task Force on National Unity. An edited version of the presentation was published the following year titled "The Myth of Two Founding Peoples." He made the point that the issue in the Canadian unity debate of the clash between Anglophones and Francophones cited only two "founding" cultures in Canada. This ethnocentric view excluded native peoples - the first citizens of Canada and their descendants.

In 1979 he wrote an introduction to *The Forgotten People - Metis and non-status Indian Land Claims*. He set forth two bases for claims. One was that the Metis as a distinct people had an aboriginal title to land. The other was that of non-status Indians whom he said had been excluded from the provisions of the *Indian Act* and denied benefits under the Act.

In the same year the NCC issued a *Declaration of Metis and Indian Rights*. Harry Daniels wrote the commentary to the Declaration. One item stated:

> That all native peoples must be included in each step of the process leading to changes in the Constitution.

Harry Daniels was a Commissioner of the Metis and Non-Status Indian Constitutional Review Commission which the NCC established in July 1980. The Commission issued a report in April 1981 titled *Native People and the Constitution of Canada*.

In his Letter of Transmittal Daniels stated that a series of regional hearings and conferences had been held across the country. The Commission undertook research into specific constitutional issues of concern to native people and welcomed the views of non-native people. As well they invited a number of prominent academics and political leaders to its hearings.

The 1985 edition of *Canadian Who's Who* indicated that Daniels was then enrolled in a Masters Program for Northern and Native Studies at Carleton University.

His love of dancing was with him all through his life. He was known to kick-up his heels and do a lively Red River jig whenever the mood struck him.

Another facet of Harry's career was that he studied drama with the Manitoba Theater Center in Winnipeg and with Dora Mavor Moore's New Play Society in Toronto. This led to him performing as an actor on stage and in films.

For example he portrayed the part of Gabriel Dumont in the television mini-series *Big Bear*. Another member of the cast was the well-known aboriginal actress Tantoo Cardinal. It has been said that Harry was the person who recommended her for an acting part when she was first starting out in films. Among other roles, Harry portrayed Louis Riel a number of times in a Regina play that is still being performed there every summer.

To celebrate the Province of Manitoba's 125th birthday in 1995, the government provided a contribution of $150,000 for the presentation of a theatrical performance. A play was produced and directed by Harry Daniels together with the noted Canadian actor and musician Tom Jackson. The authors were told that all of the sales proceeds from this production were donated to the Winnipeg Food Bank.

Among his extensive travels during the 1970s, Harry was part of the delegation from Canada that attended the investiture of Pope John Paul II in 1978 in Rome.

There is an interesting anecdote involving Harry Daniels and Pope John Paul II during a papal trip to Canada in

1984. The Pope's itinerary included a planned visit to Fort Simpson in the Northwest Territories. The residents there, primarily aboriginal, looked forward with eager anticipation to the arrival of the Holy Father.

En route the Pope's journey was delayed at the airport in Yellowknife due to thick fog conditions at Fort Simpson. The Pope stood in the cold hoping for flying conditions to improve. He was surrounded by a number of people including Phil Fontaine, then Chief of the Assembly of First Nations, and Harry Daniels.

Harry noticed that the Pope was shivering in the cold open air. Daniels took off his own buckskin jacket and magnanimously wrapped it around the Pope's shoulders. In an article in the *Globe and Mail Newspaper* of April 4, 2005, shortly after the Pope died, Phil Fontaine is quoted as saying:

> It was the most beautiful beaded jacket. And the Pope just stood there wearing it, looking so proud to have it on.

Due to the inclement weather the Pope's trip to Fort Simpson was cancelled, but the Pontiff promised that he would make that trip one day. At the time Fontaine believed that from the moment he saw the Pope proudly wearing Daniels' jacket this promise would be kept. It was fulfilled by the Pope in 1987. As for Daniels' jacket, the authors were told by his widowed partner that the Pope took the jacket back with him to the Vatican and it is there to this day.

Daniels returned as President of the NCC in 1997 and served in that capacity until the year 2000. Martin Dunn of CAP told the authors that at one time he worked under Daniels and wrote speeches for him. He indicated that Daniels was a consummate actor, a flamboyant and wonderful person but also a demanding boss. Dunn expressed the view that Daniels was "the greatest 20th century Metis leader."

Daniels was a frequent guest lecturer on aboriginal matters at various institutions and organizations. In 2002-03 he lectured in Metis history in the Department of Native

Studies at the University of Saskatchewan.

In December 2000 Daniels and CAP filed a Statement of Claim in the Federal Court of Canada against the Minister of Indian Affairs and the Attorney General of Canada. The lawsuit asked for judicial declarations that:

- Metis and non-status Indians are "Indians" within s. 91(24) of the *Constitution Act, 1867*;
- the Queen owes a fiduciary to Metis and Non-Status Indians, as Aboriginal peoples; and
- the Metis and Non-Status Indians of Canada have the right to be negotiated with in good faith by the federal government, on a collective basis through their representatives, respecting their rights, interests and needs as Aboriginal peoples.

This lawsuit was pending at the time of Daniels' death.

Among the awards that Daniels received during his lifetime were:

- the Metis National Council's Order of the Metis Nation in 2004;
- Honorary President for Life of the Native Council of Canada; and
- three months before his death an "Honorary Doctor" degree from the University of Ottawa.

In introducing Harry for this latter honor, the presenter referred to Daniels as:

> .... a man who has championed the rights of his people and, in so doing, has strengthened Canada for the benefit of us all.

Harry Daniels was suffering from cancer when he received this honorary degree in Ottawa in June 2004. The cancer took his life on September 6, 2004 at Regina. He is survived by his partner Cheryl Storkson and six children from his prior marriages.

Many tributes poured in after his death. Andy Scott, the then Indian Affairs Minister and Federal Interlocutor for Metis and Non-Status Indians, issued a statement of condolence that said in part:

> .... his efforts in getting the term Metis into section 35 of the Act makes him one of our true historic Aboriginal icons .... Mr. Daniels will be remembered for his strength of spirit and the passion with which he lead the Metis and Non-Status Indian peoples of Canada.

Tony Belcourt, President of the Metis Nation of Ontario, stated:

> I can't think of anyone else who was more passionate about life and about the cause of the Metis than Harry.

The well-known Metis author Maria Campbell, a long-time friend of Harry, stated:

> .... the Metis community has lost its most able statesman and courageous warrior.

Professor Paul Chartrand, a former RCAP Commissioner, said that:

> He will be remembered for many things: his great contributions to Canada, to the cause of Aboriginal Peoples and to his people, the Metis.

His close friend Murray Hamilton of the SUNTEP Department of the University of Saskatchewan said:

> He will be greatly missed by all he knew and touched.

Exactly 64 years after he was born there, a memorial service and a celebration of Harry's life was held at Regina Beach, Saskatchewan on September 16, 2004. Although he had been brought up as a Roman Catholic, he had requested that his funeral service be more native. As a result an Indian medicine man and a little Scottish minister performed the service.

In his honor a plaque has been erected on the outside wall of the CAP office building in Ottawa. It has a carved image of a younger Harry Daniels followed by an inscription reading:

> Harry W. Daniels (1940-2004)
>
> This building is dedicated to the memory of a great Aboriginal leader, Harry Wilfred Daniels.
>
> A Metis from Regina Beach, Saskatchewan, he rose from

> humble beginnings to the presidency of the Native Council of Canada (1975-1981) and the Congress of Aboriginal Peoples (1997-2000).
>
> He dedicated his life to working on behalf of Aboriginal peoples throughout the world, with a primary focus on 'The Forgotten People', Metis and Non-Status Indians living throughout Canada.
>
> He will be remembered particularly for his leadership in ensuring that the Aboriginal and treaty rights of the Aboriginal peoples of Canada (Indians, Inuit and Metis) became enshrined in the Constitution of Canada, 1982.
>
> He will be deeply missed by his family and friends.
>
> His legacy will last forever.

In April 2005 the Metis National Council (MNC) held its General Assembly in Calgary. A highlight of the Saturday night banquet was the presentation of a film produced by the MNC and by the Metis Nation of Alberta paying tribute to Daniels' remarkable life. It was titled *Harry Daniels, a Metis Voice for the People*. The eyes of many of those in attendance, including his sister Laurena and his partner Cheryl, were filled with tears when the film came to an end.

The many contributions which Daniels made to the advancement of Metis and Non-Status Indians and, in particular, his prodigious efforts in having the aboriginal rights of the Metis recognized and enshrined in the *Constitution of Canada, 1982* will be his everlasting legacy. Harry Daniels, a man who exuded panache and vitality, will indeed be remembered by posterity as a pre-eminent Metis crusader.

Chapter Reference Sources

- "Daniels, Harry Wilfred", *Canadian Who's Who 1985*, Vol. XX, p. 285.
- *Declaration of Metis and Indian Rights,* with commentary by Harry W. Daniels, Native Council of Canada, 1979.
- *Forgotten People Metis and non-status Indian Land Claims, The,* edited and introduction by Harry W. Daniels, Native Council of Canada, 1979.
- "Harry Daniels", (unpublished) Citation for Honorary Degree awarded in 2004 from the University of Ottawa.
- "Harry Daniels 1941-2004", *The Sash* Magazine, Sept/Dec. 2004, p.

28.
- *Harry W. Daniels, a Metis Voice for the People*, Executive Producer Kathy Hodgson Smith, CD-Video Produced by the Metis National Council and the Metis Nation of Alberta, 2005.
- "Harry W. Daniels, Metis Leader", by Cheryl Troupe *New Breed* Magazine, May/June 2004, p. 9-10.
- "In a white vestment made of caribou skin, Pope kept a promise to aboriginals", by Roy MacGregor *Globe and Mail*, April 4, 2005, p. A 2.
- "Metis cease sit-in without concessions", *The Calgary Albertan*, July 3, 1980 p. 9.
- "Metis end Parliamentary sit-in, but bid for moratorium rejected", newspaper clipping of July 3, 1980 from Calgary Public Library, Calgary, "Metis Files".
- "Metis Nation Mourns Passing of Harry W. Daniels", *Metis Messenger* Newsletter, Fall 2004, p. 1.
- "Metis vows to tell world Canada's ruled by racists", newspaper clipping of July 5, 1979, from Calgary Public Library, Calgary, "Metis Files".
- *Native People and the Constitution of Canada*, Commissioner Harry W. Daniels, Native Council of Canada, April, 1981.
- *Royal Commission on Aboriginal Peoples Report* (vol.4, c.5, app.5F) (1996).
- "Unravelling the Riddles of Metis Definition" (unpublished) by Harry W. Daniels and Paul L.A. H. Chartrand.
- *We are the New Nation*, introduction by Harry W. Daniels, Native Council of Canada, 1979.
- *Who are Canada's Aboriginal Peoples*, editor Paul L. A. H. Chartrand, foreword by Harry Daniels, p. 11-14.

Chapter XXVII

TANTOO CARDINAL

Metis Actor Extraordinaire

Tantoo Cardinal has been referred to as Canada's premier Aboriginal actor. Her impressive accomplishments in movies, television and theater reflect a Metis woman with remarkable and versatile talents in her chosen career.

Tantoo was born in Fort McMurray, Alberta on July 20, 1950. At the age of four, because of unfavorable parental circumstances, she moved to Anzac where she was brought up by her grandparents. Anzac is a small community about 50 kilometers south of Fort McMurray. From grades one to nine, she attended a one-room schoolhouse in Anzac.

With the help of her grade nine teacher Ted Walter and the Mennonite community, arrangements were made for Tantoo to take her high school education in Edmonton. In that city, the fifteen year old Tantoo quickly experienced culture shock. She became aware that many in that city considered aboriginals as lazy, drinkers, and not very intelligent. This prejudice and bigotry initially got to her. She lacked confidence and had a very poor image of herself.

However one morning she experienced an epiphany. She felt that the Creator had given everyone a gift. She knew that she had to find out what hers was and had to make changes in her life in order to realize it.

In 1969 she did volunteer work in Edmonton with an Indian association. However that association would not let her take part in the classes that it was offering. The reason given to her was that "I was not treaty, I was Metis."

At that time she did not know what the term "Metis" meant and decided to find out. The following weekend she went to Athabasca in order to attend her first Metis assembly.

At this meeting she witnessed the remarkable Harry Daniels at the microphone proudly expounding on who the Metis people are, on Louis Riel, on Gabriel Dumont, on the Provisional Government, and on other matters. Harry Daniels is profiled elsewhere in this book.

In an interview with the authors Tantoo said of this electrifying speech given by Daniels:

> In one lesson I got the whole background about who we were.

In 1968, shortly after her high school graduation, Tantoo married Fred Martin. They had a son Cheyenne who currently lives in Toronto. Tantoo's marriage to Martin ended in 1976, but today she states that he was a good man.

Tantoo married for a second time in 1988 to John Lawlor. A daughter was born from this union to whom they gave the name Riel after the great Metis hero Louis Riel. Tantoo's marriage to Lawlor also ended in divorce.

Tantoo lived in Vermont for seven years, and her daughter Riel received her education there. In the 1990s while Tantoo was living in Vermont, she starred in the role of Bangor in the movie *Where the Rivers Flow North*.

Tantoo also has a 20 year old son Clifford who lives in Toronto. Clifford is an actor and has worked with his mother in stage productions.

It was through Harry Daniel's that Tantoo, who had no formal training as an actor, received her first acting assignment. She was given a small role in a Canadian Broadcasting Corporation docudrama on Father Lacombe, a Catholic priest who was a missionary in Alberta in the 1800s.

Tantoo soon came to the realization that acting was her gift from the Creator and that this was what she should devote herself to. In this way she could contribute to herself as well as to her people and could tell their stories.

In the late 1960s the Canadian Radio-Television and Telecommunications Commission mandated requirements respecting Canadian content in television schedules. The Canadian Content Rule led to more opportunities in the entertainment field for Canadian artists, including those of Aboriginal descent such as Tantoo.

Tantoo's career, spanning over 35 years, has embraced many aspects of the entertainment industry. She has performed in dramas and documentaries and has also done voice-overs in several productions. She has acted in numerous cinematic and television films, both in leading roles and as a character actor.

She has made many guest appearances on television and has been a director, a producer and an author. This versatile performer has also acted in a number of theatrical performances. In 1982 she appeared at the 25th Street Theatre in Saskatoon in the title role of *Jessica*, the stage production based on the book *Halfbreed.* This story is based on the early life of the Metis author Maria Campbell.

Tantoo received the Elizabeth Sterling Haynes Award in 1990 for Best Actress for her performance at the Catalyst Theatre in Edmonton in the play *All My Relations* written by Floyd Favel.

There are too many motion pictures and television shows in which Tantoo has performed to list in this profile. However, among the more notable feature films in which she appeared on the big screen are *Dances with Wolves*, *Legends of the Fall*, *Black Robe*, *Where the Rivers Flow North*, and *Loyalties*.

Dances with Wolves was a grand motion picture set on the Western prairies. Tantoo Cardinal portrayed an impressive Aboriginal woman in this 1990 movie that was directed by Kevin Costner, and in which he played Dunbar the lead male role.

In this movie, Dunbar is a lieutenant in the Union Army who befriends members of a Sioux Tribe. He goes to live with them, learns their culture and falls in love with a tribe member played by Mary McDonnell.

Tantoo portrayed the part of Black Shawl. In an

interview that the authors had with Tantoo, she told them that she attended a casting call for *Dances with Wolves* at a time when she was living and working in Los Angeles.

When she arrived in the appointed room, she found the chairs in a series of rows. She told the assembled group that the chairs should be placed in a circle as is the custom with many Aboriginal groups.

The casting agent was present when the group followed Tantoo's recommendation concerning the chairs, and she was the first one from the group selected for the film. This agent later told her that it was her initiative in having the chairs rearranged that resulted in her being selected for a role in this movie.

It has also been said that it was Kevin Costner who chose her to play Black Shawl after she translated her script into Cree. Tantoo has a working knowledge of the Cree language and actually spoke it in this film.

In the movie Graham Greene, another outstanding Canadian Aboriginal actor, played the role of Kicking Bird, a Lakota medicine man married to Black Shawl. This film won the 1990 Oscar at the Academy Awards and garnered international recognition for Tantoo.

Legends of the Fall, while depicting tragedies affecting a Montana rancher and his sons, was actually shot in 1994 in Alberta, the Province in which Tantoo Cardinal was born and where she now lives in Calgary. This film received an Oscar for Best Cinematography. It starred Anthony Hopkins and Brad Pitt, two of Hollywood's premier actors. In this film Tantoo played the part of Pet, the mother of Brad Pitt's wife. Another Canadian native actor Gordon Tootoosis was also in this film.

In 1991 Tantoo had a supporting role in the movie *Black Robe*, a Canadian/Australian production. It was directed by Bruce Beresford and it was based on the 1985 novel by Brian Moore who also wrote the screen play. This movie told of the efforts of a Jesuit priest, played by Lothaire Bluteau, to Christianize North American natives. His actions resulted in a greater understanding by him of those he was attempting to proselytize.

Tantoo played the wife of Chomina. Her untimely death from a lethal arrow wound in the neck was a particularly compelling scene highlighting Tantoo's acting artistry.

In the year 1991, the national Canadian magazine *Macleans* recognized Tantoo's acting abilities when they named her "Actress of the Year".

One of Tantoo's most fulfilling roles was that of Bangor in the production of *Where the Rivers Flow North*, written and directed by the independent film maker Jay Craven. This film was a period piece set in Vermont in the 1920s. The spirited but sadly childless Bangor, together with an old logger Noel Lord (played by Rip Torn), oppose construction by a power company of a huge hydro dam which would endanger their way of life. Another Canadian born actor, Michael J. Fox, was also in the cast. Bob Mondello of National Public Radio in the United States called this movie "Breathtakingly beautiful."

The year 1993 was a banner one for Cardinal. At the 18th Annual American Indian Film Festival in San Francisco, she received the "Best Actress Award" for 1993 for her role in *Where the Rivers Flow North*. With respect to this Award, Tantoo stated at the time:

> This is a nice recognition for work and a marker of a tremendous opportunity I've had to play a lead role. She's [Bangor] just a great character. I'm proud of the film, the way it was written, made and presented.

In that year Tantoo was also awarded an Honorary Doctor of Fine Arts degree from the University of Rochester in Rochester, New York. Another highlight in that year was her haunting title role in the movie *Silent Tongue* directed by Sam Shepard. In this film Tantoo portrayed the ghost of a woman who had been raped and murdered.

Also in 1993 Tantoo was given the periodically recurring role of Snow Bird in *Dr. Quinn, Medicine Woman* a fictional drama series televised over several years on the Columbia Broadcasting System. The eminent actress, Jane

Seymour, starred in the title role. Tantoo portrayed the Cheyenne woman who befriended Dr. Quinn, a white female medical practitioner in frontier America.

An earlier Canadian production released in 1986 was *Loyalties* directed by Anne Wheeler. In this feature Tantoo played the leading role of Rosanne Ladouceur. The story line involves an Englishman who emigrated to the Canadian west to distance himself from his previous life.

One reviewer, George Garrett, wrote "I found the film riveting from start to finish". Her moving performance garnered Tantoo a Genie nomination for Best Actress by the Academy of Canadian Cinema and Television.

In addition to her acting roles in more than 50 films on the big screen over three decades, Tantoo has made many appearances on a number of television networks. Besides *Dr. Quinn, Medicine Woman* some of her other televisions appearances include *Gunsmoke, Return to Dodge*; *Lonesome Dove*; *Cold Squad*; *North of 60*; *Street Legal*; and *Moccasin Flats*.

Particularly notable was her role as Running Second in the 1998 mini-series *Big Bear.* Tantoo played the wife of Big Bear, who was portrayed by Gordon Tootoosis. The basis of this series was the historical novel *The Temptations of Big Bear* by the Saskatchewan born Rudy Wiebe. This work of fiction was focused on Big Bear, the Plains Cree Chief who was later imprisoned for his involvement in the North-West Uprising.

Tantoo's talents were recognized by her peers in 1998 when she became the recipient of a National Aboriginal Achievement Award in the category of Film and Television. She was honored for her accomplishments in these fields, but felt the Award was a celebration of the Aboriginal community she is proud to be a part of.

In referring to her Metis background, Tantoo stated that she had come to terms with the fact that she was also part European. She is quoted as saying:

> I want to be more involved in the whole process of getting our

> stories out. We have to strengthen ourselves and look after the young ones coming up.

The Canadian Encyclopedia states of Tantoo that:

> She is known for her strong film presence and the unspoken eloquence and depth of her performances.

In the Gemini Awards of 1996, Tantoo received a Best Actress Performance Award in a Dramatic Series for her guest role in *North of 60*.

Tantoo was featured in the full-length movie *Smoke Signals* which premiered at the Sundance Film Festival in 1998. This motion picture was made by American Aboriginals about their own culture. It won both the Audience Award and the Film Makers Trophy.

The Sundance Film Festival is based in Park City, Utah. It is under the artistic management of the Sundance Institute, in which the well-known actor and director Robert Redford is prominently involved. This Festival is considered to be the premier venue for exhibiting independent films made in North America.

The year after *Dances with Wolves* brought Tantoo widespread recognition, a video titled "Tantoo" was produced in 1991 by Great Plains Production Inc. This was part of the series *My Partners, My People*. It was directed by Gil Cardinal and shot at a time when Tantoo was living in Hollywood with a view to furthering her career. The blurb on the video cover states of Cardinal:

> Her performances have been described as passionate and magnetic, powerful and uncompromising, credible and enchanting.

In this video Tantoo discloses much of her inner self and the struggles she faced in her younger years. She was in debt, hungry, reliant on her friends for clothing and meals, living in a van with no source of income. It was at this time that she felt that she had nothing to offer the world. As mentioned earlier, from seemingly nowhere a voice entered her mind and her heart telling her that the Creator gives a gift to each of us.

As Bernelda Wheeler wrote in Eagle Feather News in February, 2000 "... the voice [was] from no place and every place" and Tantoo had to find what her gift was. Waiting for her scene during her first small acting assignment (obtained with the assistance of Harry Daniels), she fell asleep on the grass. She awoke with a revelation "This [acting] is what I can do". This was the way she could contribute to herself, to her people, to society. She had found her vocation, her way of life.

In her career, Tantoo has disdained the stereotypical image of Aboriginals as irresponsible, shiftless, none-too-bright people who drink too much. When she thinks it appropriate or necessary, she firmly advances her views to the director of a film. She has indicated that she has been fortunate to have directors who listened to her, adding "You have to push them."

In Hollywood where she lived in the early 1990s, Tantoo engaged the services of Darryl Hickman, an acting coach, to assist her in her profession and in communicating with her inner being. In the "Tantoo" video, she talks about one's "river of life" whose waters bring forth matters ".... from the deepest places, the memories, the pain."

Tantoo realizes that in what she does she is a role model for a younger generation of Aboriginal artists. In that respect she has worked with Aboriginal drama groups in such places as Calgary and Edmonton. She provides these young people with advice and the benefits of her experience and talent.

On November 18, 2004, Tantoo was the keynote speaker at the third annual Winnipeg Aboriginal Film and Video Festival. In her address at this Festival, she geared her remarks to Aboriginal youth.

In addition to her other artistic talents, Tantoo is an author. She contributed the short story "There is a Place" to an anthology titled *Our Story, Aboriginal Voices on Canada's Past* that was published in 2004.

In her Contributor's Note to this book, Tantoo wrote that

she chose for this story the period in Metis history from 1915 to 1928 because it was a time of hopelessness. She stated that the proud Metis history of Red River and Batoche was forgotten.

In the Preface to the anthology, Rudyard Griffiths stated that:

> .... each of the Aboriginal authors has chosen an historical event and through the act of storytelling turned it into a work of fiction.

In the Foreword to this book Adrienne Clarkson, the then Governor General of Canada, wrote;

> Metis life in the early 20th century, plagued by despair in the face of a proud history ignored, is seen through the eyes of Francis in Tantoo Cardinal's "There is a Place".

Another accolade came to Tantoo on June 8, 2005, when the University of Calgary invested her with an Honorary Doctor of Laws Degree. In presenting her to the Chancellor of the University, Dr. Adrienne Kertzer of the Department of English stated in part:

> Tantoo Cardinal is an actor, writer, and producer whose work brings together the political and the aesthetic. She became an actor because she realized that the stage and screen offered her the best way to use her talent while maintaining her commitment as a Metis woman to political change.
>
> .... In her work in drama, documentary, and film she has broadened our understanding of the historic and contemporary experience of Aboriginal peoples and helped bring about substantive changes.
>
> .... her career has been truly groundbreaking. To a generation of young women, she is a role model.
>
> .... Tantoo Caroline Rose Cardinal .... demonstrates that the best actors are always first and foremost tellers of truth.

In March 2006, Tantoo Cardinal received the Sun Hill Award for Excellence in Native American Filmmaking from the Harvard Film Archive. This Award is granted annually to "an individual who has made a significant contribution as a director, actor, producer, or writer to the legacy of Native American film."

Harvard Film Archive (HFA) and Cinematheque is part

of the Faculty of Arts and Science of the famed Harvard University in Cambridge, Massachusetts. The HFA's purpose is to further artistic and academic appreciation within Harvard and the New England community of the cinema and the moving image media. It does so by having film makers and artists interact with the audiences.

During its March 2006 exhibition, the HFA screened six of the films in which Tantoo has appeared. Tantoo was present for several of the screenings including *Where the Rivers Flow North*, *Postmark Paradise*, and *Black Robe*. The HFA bestowed on Tantoo its second annual Sun Hill Award in conjunction with exhibiting a number of her films.

From humble beginnings in a small community in Alberta, Tantoo Cardinal has risen to achieve international recognition in the difficult and demanding movie and television industry. Through a combination of her artistry and being in the limelight, she has advanced public awareness of both the past and the present realities of her Aboriginal people.

Her impressive artistic talent enables her to realistically assume the persona of each part that she portrays. In her acting, she strives to communicate a true picture of Aboriginals that is far different than the negative image held by some people.

In her own unique way and through hard work and perseverance, she has overcome many adversities in order to showcase the remarkable gifts that she received from her Creator. As a role model for Metis youth, Tantoo Cardinal has demonstrated that by discovering one's innermost talents and by combining them with determination and dedication, one can achieve success in their chosen career.

Chapter Reference Sources

- "Cardinal, Tantoo", by James DeFelice, *Canadian Encyclopedia*, p. 400.
- "Tantoo", Episode of *My Partners My People*, video (Great Plains Production, 1991).
- "Tantoo Caroline Rose Cardinal", unpublished citation by Dr.

Adrianne Kertzer, on conferring of Honorary Doctor of Laws Degree at the University of Calgary, June 8, 2005.

- "Tantoo Cardinal", by Bernelda Wheeler, *Eagle Feather News*, February, 2000, p. 11 and March, 2000, p.15.
- "Tantoo Cardinal - Best Actress for Bangor in *Where the Rivers Flow North*", *ICE*, Winter, 1994 featuring the 1994 American Indian Motion Picture Awards Show.
- "There is a Place,", by Tantoo Cardinal", *Our Story Aboriginal Voices on Canada's Past*, Rudyard Griffiths, ed., p. 107.
- "Tribute to Tantoo Cardinal" March 3-4, 2006, *Harvard Film Archive* web site.

Chapter XXVIII

THE PHOENIX HAS RISEN

Before his execution in 1885, Louis Riel stated:

> My people will sleep for one hundred years and it will be the artists who awaken them.

Riel was prophetic in this respect in that it took close to one hundred years for his Metis people to be officially recognized in the Constitution of Canada. After his untimely death the Metis were effectively excluded from mainstream society.

Being marginalized politically, socially and economically they receded into the background for generations. Through these dark years a nucleus of their people remained committed to preserving and promoting their history, their heritage, and their culture. They fought to preserve Metis nationalism and their identity as a unique people.

Their efforts eventually resulted in the recognition of the Metis as one of the Aboriginal peoples of Canada in the *Constitution Act, 1982.* In pursuing their objectives they stood on the shoulders of those who had gone before them.

This book profiles a number of their ancestors whose lives evidence the struggles and achievements of the Metis people from earliest times. It also demonstrates that throughout their existence the classic historical Metis of the west have had to fight for their rights and, in some instances, for their existence as a people.

They did so in memorable events chronicled herein such as the Pemmican Proclamation, the Battle of Seven Oaks, the Sayer Trial and Free Trade, and the Battle of the Grand Coteau.

Some of the other notable occurrences included in this Metis history are the Red River Resistance, the North-West Uprising, Constitutional Recognition, Government Recognition, and Supreme Court Recognition.

Unlike other groups asserting their Metis ancestry, the historic western Metis and the events occurring in their traditional homeland were discussed in writings and memoirs by a number of contemporary observers who drew on their firsthand knowledge. These authors (whose works are referred to in the Bibliography) include among others Alexander Greenfield Macdonell, Alexander Ross, Joseph James Hargrave, Alexander Begg, John Flett, Louis Goulet, Francis Dickens, and others.

There are also numerous documents available that were written at the time relating to the Red River Settlement; the historic western Metis; and Metis culture, symbols, way of life, and events in which they were involved. These records embrace books, pamphlets, articles, letters, petitions, proclamations, diaries, and so on.

There are thousands of similar items on the western Metis which have since been written or produced. They include manuscripts, historical collections, biographies, creative fiction, parliamentary speeches, government reports, treatises, theses, television shows, documentaries, movies, archives, videos, CD-Roms, comic strips, and on and on.

There are a number of museums, heritage parks, cultural institutes, historical sites, and resource centers featuring the western Metis and Louis Riel. These facilities are located in such places as St. Boniface, Winnipeg, St. Vital, and St. Norbert in Manitoba; Batoche, Duck Lake, Regina and Saskatoon in Saskatchewan; St. Albert in Alberta; and in other places. In the fall of 2004 the new National Museum of the American Indian of the prestigious Smithsonian Institute in Washington, D.C. showcased an exhibit on St. Laurent, Manitoba as a representative community of Metis culture. It is a continuing display

No other group claiming Metis identity other than the classic Metis Nation of the west has been the subject of such detailed and extensive study, documentation, and interest. The voluminous historical record spans some two centuries. It confirms with incontrovertible evidence that these Metis were a distinctive Aboriginal people with their own customs, symbols, traditions, shared experiences, homeland, culture, heritage, political structures, form of self-government and way of life. These components were the essential traits that constituted their unique identity. They were a nation – a New Nation – the Metis Nation.

They were a people who would not allow their assimilation or annihilation. Throughout their history the Metis used whatever means were necessary or appropriate (whether political, military, legal, economic, or other) to preserve their existence and their identity. They succeeded beyond measure, today enjoying recognition at the highest levels in the Constitution, in the courts and from governments.

The impact on the history of Canada that the Metis have made cannot be understated. This unique indigenous people and their memorable events and memorable personalities have added a colorful dimension to its annals. The mosaic of the Canadian people has truly been enriched by their contributions and achievements.

Members of the Metis Nation today continue to defend, honor, and celebrate the unique traditions, history, heritage and culture handed down to them by their remarkable ancestors. They are proud of who they are - they are “Proud to be Metis”.

They are no longer Canada’s “forgotten people”. Like the phoenix, the Metis have risen.

Appendix A

Significant Dates in Metis History

1670 HUDSON'S BAY COMPANY (HBC) RECEIVES ITS CHARTER FROM THE KING OF ENGLAND.

1684 YORK FACTORY, MANITOBA ESTABLISHED BY THE HBC.

1684-1713 YORK FACTORY & AREA SHIFTS BETWEEN THE FRENCH & THE ENGLISH.

1713 TREATY OF UTRECHT AWARDS CERTAIN POSSESSIONS OF FRANCE TO ENGLAND.

1726 LA VÉRENDRYE ENTERS FUR TRADE - NORTHERN LAKE SUPERIOR.

1730s LA VÉRENDRYE BUILDS FUR TRADE FORTS & STARTS EXPLORATION WEST.

1756-1763 SEVEN YEARS WAR - FIRST GLOBAL WAR

1759 BATTLE OF THE PLAINS OF ABRAHAM & SURRENDER OF QUEBEC TO THE BRITISH.

1763 CANADA GRANTED TO ENGLAND BY THE TREATY OF PARIS.

1775-1783 AMERICAN REVOLUTION

1776 MONTREAL FUR TRADERS FORM THE NORTH WEST COMPANY (NWC).

1780-1821 - NWC WAS A MAJOR FORCE IN THE FUR TRADE.

1779 ALEXANDER MACKENZIE ENTERS NWC SERVICE.

1793 ALEXANDER MACKENZIE TRAVELS OVERLAND TO THE PACIFIC.

1792 SIMON FRASER APPRENTICED TO THE NWC.

1797 DAVID THOMPSON JOINS NWC AFTER SERVICE WITH HBC FROM 1784.

1799 ROCKY MOUNTAIN HOUSE BUILT BY NWC TO DEVELOP FUR TRADE IN THE KOOTENAIS.

1808 SIMON FRASER EXPLORES FOR THE NWC TO THE PACIFIC OCEAN VIA THE FRASER RIVER.

1811 DAVID THOMPSON - OVERLAND TO THE PACIFIC OCEAN VIA THE COLUMBIA RIVER.

1812 ARRIVAL OF FIRST SELKIRK SETTLERS IN RED RIVER.

1812 USA DECLARES WAR ON GREAT BRITAIN

1813 DUNCAN MCDOUGALL SELLS FORT ASTORIA TO NWC & FORT RENAMED FORT GEORGE.

1814 PEMMICAN PROCLAMATION.

1814 TREATY OF GHENT ENDS THE WAR OF 1812.

1816 THE BATTLE OF SEVEN OAKS - FIRST REFERENCE TO METIS AS A "NEW NATION".

1821 NWC AND HBC MERGE UNDER CONTINUING NAME OF HBC.

1840 THE LARGEST BUFFALO HUNT ON THE PRAIRIES IS HELD.

1841 RED RIVER EXPEDITION TO THE OREGON COUNTRY, LED BY JAMES SINCLAIR.

1846 OREGON TREATY ESTABLISHES BOUNDARY WEST OF MOUNTAINS AT 49TH PARALLEL.

1849 THE SAYER TRIAL & FREE TRADE.

1851 THE BATTLE OF THE GRAND COTEAU.

1869-70 THE RED RIVER RESISTANCE.

1870 MANITOBA ENTERS CONFEDERATION AS A PROVINCE OF CANADA ON JULY 15th.

1880 DECLINE IN NUMBER OF BUFFALO RESULTS IN THE DEMISE OF THE BUFFALO HUNT.

1885 THE NORTH-WEST UPRISING.

1885 LOUIS RIEL HANGED FOR HIGH TREASON ON NOVEMBER 16TH

1887 L'UNION NATIONALE METISSE ST. JOSEPH DU MANITOBA IS FORMED.

1905 ALBERTA & SASKATCHEWAN BECOME PROVINCES OF CANADA.

1930s METIS ORGANIZATION FORMED IN ALBERTA.

1960s METIS ORGANIZATIONS FORMED IN MAN., SASK. & BC.

1972 NATIONAL ASSOCIATION OF FRIENDSHIP CENTRES FORMED.

1970s-1983 NATIVE COUNCIL OF CANADA ACTS FOR METIS & NON- STATUS INDIANS.

1982 RECOGNITION OF METIS IN THE *CONSTITUTION ACT OF CANADA, 1982.*

1983 METIS NATIONAL COUNCIL FORMED.

1991 CANADIAN GOVERNMENT ESTABLISHES ROYAL COMMISSION ON ABORIGINAL PEOPLES.

1993 NATIVE COUNCIL OF CANADA BECOMES THE CONGRESS OF ABORIGINAL PEOPLES.

1993 METIS NATION OF ONTARIO FORMED.

1996 REPORT OF THE ROYAL COMMISSION ON ABORIGINAL PEOPLES ISSUED.

1998 STATEMENT OF RECONCILIATION MADE BY CANADA TO ABORIGINAL PEOPLES.

2003 SUPREME COURT OF CANADA DECISION IN THE POWLEY CASE.

2005 METIS NATION FRAMEWORK AGREEMENT WITH FEDERAL GOVERNMENT.

2005 KELOWNA ACCORD - FIRST MINISTERS MEETING ON ABORIGINAL ISSUES.

Appendix B

Metis Organizations

Metis National Council
350 Sparks St., Ste. 201,
Ottawa, ON, K1R 7S8
Tel: (613) 232-3216
1-800-928-6330
www.metisnation.ca

Metis Nation of Ontario
#3-500 Old St. Patrick St.,
Ottawa, ON, K1N 9G4
Tel: (613) 798-1488
1-800-263-4889
www.metisnation.org

Manitoba Metis Federation,
150 Henry Avenue,
Winnipeg, MB, R3B 0J7
Tel: (204) 586-8474
1-800-665-8474
www.mmf.mb.ca

Metis Nation of Alberta,
100-11738 Kingsway Ave.,
Edmonton, AB, T5G 0X5
Tel: (780) 455-2200
1-800-252-7553
www.albertametis.com

Metis Nation of Saskatchewan
219 Robin Crescent, 2nd Fl.
Saskatoon, SK, S7L 6M8
Tel: (306) 343-8285
1-888-343-6667
www.metisnation-sask.com

Metis Nation of British Columbia,
1128-789 West Pender St.,
Vancouver, B.C., V6C 1H2
Tel: (604) 801-5853
1-800-940-1150
http://www.mnbc.ca

Congress of Aboriginal Peoples,
867 St. Laurent Blvd.,
Ottawa, ON, K1K 3B1
Tel: (613) 747-6022
www.abo-peoples.org

National Association of Friendship Centres,
275 MacLaren St.,
Ottawa, ON, K2P 0L9
Tel: (613) 563-4844
www.nafcgen@nafc.ca

Appendix C

Talks on the Metis & Louis Riel by George & Terry Goulet

April, 2000	Kappa Kappa Gamma University Alumni, Calgary, Alberta
Sep. 01,2000	Montana Metis Festival, Lewistown, Montana
Oct. 19,2000	Students of Lindsay Thurber High School, Red Deer, Alberta
Oct. 19,2000	Central Alberta Historical Society, Red Deer, Alberta
Nov. 14,2000	First Nations Longhouse, University of British Columbia, Vancouver, British Columbia
Nov. 14,2000	Secondary School Teachers, School District #35, Langley, British Columbia
Nov. 15,2000	Main Branch, Vancouver Public Library, Vancouver, British Columbia
Nov. 16,2000	Main Branch, Port Moody Public Library, Port Moody, British Columbia
Nov. 21,2000	Main Branch, Greater Victoria Public Library, Victoria, British Columbia
Mar. 05,2002	Debate v. Thomas Flanagan, University of Calgary, Calgary, Alberta
Mar. 26,2002	Metis Nation of Alberta Region 3 Metis Youth Group, Calgary, Alberta
Apr. 24,2002	Students of St. Paul's High School, Winnipeg, Manitoba
Apr. 24,2002	Students of R. B. Russell Vocational School, Winnipeg, Manitoba
Apr. 25,2002	Manitoba Historical Society at the St. Boniface Museum, St. Boniface, Manitoba
Jan. 20,2004	Students of Springbank Middle School, Springbank, Alberta
Nov. 16,2004	Metis Flag Raising Ceremony at City Hall, St. Albert, Alberta
Jan. 12,2005	University of Manitoba, Continuing Education

	Program, Winnipeg, Manitoba.
Jan. 22,2005	Southern Ontario Metis Round Table, Hamilton, Ontario
Jan. 26,2005	Aboriginal Program, York University, Toronto, Ontario
Feb. 02,2005	Four Separate Talks at Brookswood Secondary School, Langley, British Columbia to: (1) Grades 9 and 10 Classes; (2) Grade 8 Class; (3) Grade 10 Class, and (4) Grades 8 and 12 Classes.
Feb. 03,2005	Waceya Metis Council Monthly Meeting, Fort Langley, British Columbia
Feb. 06,2005	Vancouver Island Cowichan Valley Metis Meeting,, Nanaimo, British Columbia
Feb. 23,2005	Grade 10 Students, Collége Louis Riel, St. Boniface, Manitoba
Feb. 23,2005	Class 2 of Grade 10 Students, Collége Louis Riel, St. Boniface, Manitoba
Feb. 23,2005	Students at the Aboriginal Youth Rebuilding Program, Winnipeg, Manitoba
Feb. 23,2005	Book Reading at Dinner in honor of George and Terry Goulet held by the Manitoba Metis Federation, Winnipeg, Manitoba
Feb. 23,2005	Public Meeting held by Students at St. Boniface College, St. Boniface, Manitoba
Feb. 24,2005	Grade 11 Students, Dakota Collegiate, St. Vital, Manitoba
Feb. 24,2005	Grade 11 Students, R. B. Russell School, Winnipeg, Manitoba
Mar. 04,2005	Students and Staff of the Saskatchewan Urban Teachers Education Program, University of Regina, Regina, Saskatchewan
Mar. 16,2005	Musée Héritage Museum, St. Albert, Alberta
July 08, 2005	Red River West Rendezvous, Malahat, Vancouver Island, British Columbia

July 09, 2005	Red River West Rendezvous, Malahat, Vancouver Island, British Columbia
July 10, 2005	Red River West Rendezvous, Malahat, Vancouver Island, British Columbia
July 22, 2005	Back to Batoche, Batoche, Saskatchewan
July 23, 2005	Back to Batoche, Batoche, Saskatchewan
July 29, 2005	Hivernant Metis Festival, Big Valley, Alberta
July 30, 2005	Hivernant Metis Festival, Big Valley, Alberta
Aug. 12, 2005	Annual General Meeting, Metis Nation of Alberta Workshop, Peace River, Alberta
Aug. 13, 2005	Annual General Meeting, Metis Nation of Alberta Workshop, Peace River, Alberta
Sep. 21, 2005	Grade 11 Students of South Peace Secondary School, Dawson Creek, B.C.
Sep. 21, 2005	Grade 9 & 10 Students of South Peace Middle School, Dawson Creek, B.C.
Sep. 22, 2005	Grade 10 & 11 Students of North Peace Secondary School, Fort St. John, B.C.
Sep. 22, 2005	Grade 12 Students of North Peace Secondary School, Fort St. John, B.C.
Sep. 22, 2005	Grade 11 Students of North Peace Secondary School, Fort St. John, B.C.
Sep. 23, 2005	Annual General Meeting, Metis Nation of B. C. Workshop, Fort St. John, B.C.
Oct. 13, 2005	Thunder Bay Metis Council, Thunder Bay, Ontario
Oct. 14, 2005	Aboriginal Students at Lakehead University, Thunder Bay, Ontario
Oct. 14, 2005	Education Students at Lakehead University, Thunder Bay, Ontario
Oct. 19, 2005	Students and Staff of University of Sudbury, Laurentian University, Sudbury, Ontario
Oct. 26, 2005	Law Students of University of New Brunswick,

	Fredericton, New Brunswick
Nov. 01,2005	Students of University of Prince Edward Island, Charlottetown, Prince Edward Island
Nov. 01,2005	Students, Staff and Guests of Mount Allison University, Sackville, New Brunswick
Nov. 02,2005	Students, Staff and Guests of St. Francis Xavier University, Antigonish, Nova Scotia
Nov. 03,2005	Students of St. Mary's University, Halifax, Nova Scotia
Nov. 04,2005	Students of Mount St. Vincent University, Halifax, Nova Scotia
Nov. 07,2005	Students of the University of Ottawa, Ottawa, Ontario
Nov. 26,2005	Dinner and Dance of the Fraser Valley Metis Association, Abbotsford, B. C.
April 12,2006	Bow Valley College Students and Staff, Calgary, Alberta.

BIBLIOGRAPHY

In the preparation of this book numerous materials, both primary and secondary, were reviewed and assessed. The following is a selection of the more pertinent references.

Barbeau, Marius, "Sashes for the Fur Trade", *The Beaver* (June, 1941).

Barkwell, Lawrence J. et al editors, *Metis Legacy* (Pemmican Publications, Winnipeg, 2001).

Beal, Bob and Rod Macleod, *Prairie Fire - The 1885 North-West Rebellion* (Hurtig Publishers, Edmonton, 1984).

Begg, Alexander, (1) *The Creation of Manitoba or a History of the Red River Troubles* (Hunter, Rose & Co., Toronto, 1871).

– (2) *Dot it Down, a Story of Life in the North-West* (Hunter, Rose & Co., Toronto, 1871).

– (3) *Alexander Begg's Red River Journal* (Champlain Society, Toronto, 1956).

Belcourt, G. A., "Buffalo Hunt", *The Beaver* (Dec. 1944).

Betts, William J., "From Red River to the Columbia, the Story of a Migration", *The Beaver* (Spring 1971).

Brown, George W., *Building the Canadian Nation Vol. 1 1492-1849* (MacFadden-Bartell, New York, 1968).

Brown, Jennifer S. H., "Metis" *Canadian Encyclopedia* (McLelland & Stewart, Toronto, 2000 ed.).

Bruce, George, *The Remarkable History of the Hudson's Bay Company,* (Sampson Lowe, Marston, London, 1910).

Bumsted, J. M., (1) *Fur Trade Wars, The Founding of Western Canada* (Great Plains Publications, Winnipeg, 1999).

– (2) *Louis Riel v. Canada, The Making of a Rebel* (Great Plains Publications, Winnipeg, 2001).

– (3) *Trials & Tribulations, The Red River Settlement and the Emergence of Manitoba 1811-1870* (Great Plains Publications, Winnipeg, 2003).

Burger, Albert, "On Building a Birch-bark Canoe", *The Beaver Outfit* 304 (1) (1973).

Burns, Ken, *Lewis & Clark, The Journey of the Corps of Discovery,* a Florentine Film Production Video.

Cameron, William B., *Blood Red The Sun* (Hurtig Publishers, Edmonton, 1977).

Campbell, John V., "The Sinclair Party - an Emigration Overland Along the old Hudson Bay Company Route from Manitoba to the Spokane Country in 1854", *Washington Historical Quarterly*, Vol. VII No. 3 (July, 1916).

Campbell, Marjorie Wilkins, *The North West Company*, (MacMillan Co. of Canada, Toronto, 1973).

Cardinal, Tantoo, "There is a Place", *Our Story - Aboriginal Voices on Canada's Past* (Doubleday Canada, Toronto, 2004).

Carey, Charles H., "British Side of Oregon Question 1846, *Oregon Historical Quarterly* vol. 36 (Mar./Dec. 1935). Including an article reprinted from *The Topic*, London Issue III (April 18, 1846)

Champlain Society, editors, *The Papers of the Palliser Expedition 1857-1860* (The Champlain Society, Toronto).

Charette, Guillaume, translated by Ray Ellenwood *Vanishing Spaces - Memoirs of Louis Goulet* (Editions Bois- Brûlés, Winnipeg, 1976).

Charlebois, Peter, *The Life of Louis Riel* (New Canada Publishers, Toronto, 1975).

Chartrand, Margaret, "Falcon, Pierre" *Canadian Encyclopedia* (McLelland & Stewart, Toronto, 2000 ed.)

Chartrand, Paul L. A. H., editor with foreword by Harry Daniels, *Who Are Canada's Aboriginal Peoples* (Purich Publishing, Saskatoon, 2002).

Cherney, Bruce, (1) "Battle of Seven Oaks - Semple, 20 settlers and one Metis killed" *Winnipeg Real Estate* News (Nov. 28, 2003).

– (2) "North West Fiddle to once again travel down city streets", *Winnipeg Real Estate* News (July 26, 2002).

Complin, Margaret, (1) "Cuthbert Grant, The Warden of the Plains", *The Winnipeg Tribune* (June 19, 1937).

– (2) "Pierre Falcon - The Singer of the Plains", *The Winnipeg Tribune* (July 9, 1938).

Daniels, Harry W. (1) and Paul L. A. H. Chartrand "Unravelling the Riddles of Metis Definition" (unpublished).

– (2) foreword by, *Who Are Canada's Aboriginal Peoples* (Purich Publishing, Saskatoon, 2002).

Davidson, William McCartney, *Louis Riel 1844-1885* (The Albertan Publishing Co., Calgary, 1955).

DeFelice, James "Cardinal, Tantoo", *Canadian Encyclopedia* (McLelland & Stewart, Toronto, 2000, ed.).

Dickens, Francis, *Dickens of the Mounted*, edited by Eric Nicol

(McLelland & Stewart, Toronto, 1989).

Eccles, W. J., *The Canadian Frontier 1534-1760* (Holt, Rinehart and Winston, New York, 1969).

Ens, Gerhard J., *Homeland to Hinterland, The Changing Worlds of the Red River Metis in the Nineteenth Century* (University of Toronto Press, Toronto, 1996).

Flanagan, Thomas, (1) *Louis 'David' Riel - Prophet of the New World* (University of Toronto Press, Toronto, 1979)

– (2) *Riel and the Rebellion 1885 Reconsidered* (University of Toronto Press, Toronto, 2nd ed., 2000).

Flett, John "A sketch of the immigration from Selkirk's Settlement to Puget Sound in 1841", *Tacoma Daily Ledger* (Feb. 18, 1885).

Francis, Daniel, *Battle of the West, Fur Traders and the Birth of Western Canada* (Hurtig Publishers, Edmonton, 1982).

Francis, R. Douglas and Howard Palmer, *The Prairie West, Historical Readings* (Pica Pica Press, Edmonton, 1985).

Fraser, Esther, *The Canadian Rockies, Early Travels and Explorations* (Hurtig Publishers, Edmonton, 1969).

Fresonke, Kris and Mark Spence, editors *Lewis & Clark, Legacies, Memories and New Perspectives* (University of California Press, Berkeley, 2004).

Frideres, James S., *Native People in Canada, Contemporary Conflicts* (Prentice - Hall, Scarborough, 1983).

Friesen, Gerald, *The Canadian Prairies, a History* (University of Toronto Press, Toronto, 1987).

Galbraith, John S., *The Hudson's Bay Company as an Imperial Factor 1821-1869* (University of Toronto Press, Toronto, 1957).

Gibson, James R., *The Lifeline of the Oregon Country - The Fraser-Columbia Brigade System 1811-1847* (UBC Press, Vancouver, 1997).

Giraud, Marcel, translated by George Woodcock, *The Metis in the Canadian West Vol. II* (University of Alberta Press, Edmonton, 1986).

Glover, R. "York Boats", *The Beaver* (March, 1949).

Goulet, George R. D., *The Trial of Louis Riel - Justice and Mercy Denied* (FabJob.com Limited, Calgary, 3rd ed., 2005)

Goulet, Louis see Charette, Guillaume,

Graham, Clara, *Fur and Gold in the Kootenays* (Wrigley Printing, Vancouver, 1945).

Gray, John M., *Lord Selkirk of Red River* (MacMillan Co. of Canada,

Toronto, 1964).

Griffiths, Rudyard, editor, *Our Story - Aboriginal Voices on Canada's Past* (Doubleday Canada, Toronto, 2004).

Hardy, W. G., *From Sea Unto Sea - The Road to Nationhood 1850-1910* (Doubleday & Co., New York, 1960).

Hargrave, Joseph James, (1) editor G. de T. Glazebrook *The Hargrave Correspondence 1821-1843* (Champlain Society, Toronto, 1938)

– (2) *Red River* (Lovell, Montreal, 1871).

Healy, W. J., *Women of Red River* (Women's Canadian Club, Winnipeg, reprint, 1977).

Hill, Douglas, *The Opening of the Canadian West* (Academic Press Canada, Don Mills, 1967).

Hodgson Smith, Kathy, Executive Producer *Harry W. Daniels, a Metis Voice for the People*, C-D Video Produced by the Metis National Council and the Metis Nation of Alberta, 2005.

Howard, Joseph, *Strange Empire, Louis Riel and the Metis People* (James Lewis & Samuel, Toronto, 1952).

Huel, Raymond J. A., *Archbishop A. - A. Taché of St. Boniface - The Good Fight and the Illusive Vision* (University of Alberta Press, Edmonton, 2003).

Hughes, Katherine *Father Lacombe - The Black-Robe Voyageur* (Moffat, Yard & Co., New York, 1911).

Jackson, J. A. "Goulet, Elzear", *Dictionary of Canadian Biography* Vol. IX - 1861-1870 (University of Toronto Press, Toronto).

Kane, Paul, *Wanderings of an Artist among the Indians of North America* (Hurtig Publishers, Edmonton, 1968).

Kelly, Ruth, editor "The 50 Greatest Albertans" *Alberta Venture Magazine*, (Dec. 2005).

Kerr, John Andrew, "Gabriel Dumont: A Personal Memory", *Dalhousie Review* Vol. XV (1935-36).

King, W. Cornwallis as told to Mary Weekes "York Boat Brigade" The Beaver (Dec. 1940).

Lamirande, Todd, "Resistance Activist Elzear Goulet" *Metis Legacy*, Chapter 4 (Pemmican Publications, Winnipeg, 2001).

Larocque, Emma, "Grant, Cuthbert" *Canadian Encyclopedia* (McLelland & Stewart, Toronto, 2000 ed.)

Lent, D. Geneva, *West of the Mountains - James Sinclair and the Hudson's Bay Company* (University of Washington Press, Seattle, 1963).

Long, Morden H., *A History of the Canadian People Vol. I New France* (Ryerson Press, Toronto, 1942).

Luca, Claudio, Executive Producer *Big Bear*, Video.

Lussier, A. S. editor, *Louis Riel and the Metis* (Pemmican Publications, Winnipeg, 1988).

Lussier, Antoine S. and Bruce Sealey editors, *The Other Natives: The Metis Vol. I* (Manitoba Metis Federation Press, Winnipeg, 1978).

Macdonell, Alexander Greenfield, *a narrative of transactions in the Red River country, from the commencement of the operations of the Earl of Selkirk till the summer of the year 1816* (published 1819).

MacGregor, James A., *Father Lacombe* (Hurtig Publishers, Edmonton, 1975).

MacKay, Douglas, *The Honourable Company* (McLelland & Stewart, Toronto, revised 1966).

MacLeod, Margaret A. (1) "Red River New Year", *The Beaver* (Dec. 1953).

– (2) "Bard of the Prairies", *The Beaver* (Spring 1956).

MacLeod, Margaret Arnett and W. L. Morton, *Cuthbert Grant of Grantown, Warden of the Plains of Red River* (McLelland & Stewart, Toronto, 1963).

Macleod, Roderick C. "Dumont, Gabriel", *Dictionary of Canadian Biography* Vol. XIII - 1901-1910 (University of Toronto Press, Toronto).

Manitoba Library Association, editors *Pioneers and Early Citizens of Manitoba* (Peguis Publishers, Winnipeg).

Martin, Joe "Bloodshed at Seven Oaks", *The Beaver Outfit* 297(1966).

McDonald, A. A., "H.B.C. Inland Transport", *The Beaver* (Oct.-Dec. 1923).

McKee, Sandra Lynn editor, *Gabriel Dumont, Jerry Potts - Canadian Plainsmen* (Heritage House Publishing Co., Surrey, B.C., 1982).

McLean, Don, *Home from the Hill - a History of the Metis in Western Canada* (Gabriel Dumont Institute, Regina, 1987).

Merk, Frederick, *Manifest Destiny and Mission in American History* (Vintage Books, New York, 1963).

Mitchell, Elaine Allan, "A Red River Gossip" *The Beaver* (Spring, 1961).

Moberly, Henry J. and W. B. Cameron, *When Fur was King* (J. M. Dent & Sons, Toronto, 1929).

Morton, Arthur S., *A History of the Canadian West to 1870-71*

(University of Toronto Press, Toronto 2nd edition, 1973).

Morton, Desmond, (1) *The Last War Drum* (A. M. Hakkert, Toronto, 1972)

– (2) *The Queen v. Louis Riel* [Trial Transcript] Intro. (University of Toronto Press, Toronto, 1974).

Morton, W. L., *Manitoba: A History* (University of Toronto Press, Toronto, 2nd edition, 1967).

Neumann, Klaus, "Backstage with the PM's Western Hero", *Maclean's Magazine* (Dec. 6, 1958).

Newman, Peter C., *Caesars of the Wilderness* (Viking Penguin, Markham, 1987).

Nicol, Eric , editor see Dickens, Francis.

Nute, Grace Lee, *The Voyageur* (Minnesota Historical Society Press, St. Paul, 1955).

Ord, Lewis Redman, with R. C. Macleod, editor, *Reminiscences of a Bungle by One of the Bunglers* (University of Alberta Press, Edmonton, 1983).

Owram, Doug, *Promise of Eden - The Canadian Expansionist Movement and the Idea of the West 1856-1900* (University of Toronto Press, Toronto, 1980).

Pannekoek, Frits, *A Snug Little Flock - The Social Origins of the Riel Resistance 1867-70* (Watson & Dwyer, Winnipeg, 1991).

Parkin, George R., *Sir John A. Macdonald* (Morang & Co., Toronto, 1909).

Peel, Bruce, (1) *Early Printing in the Red River Settlement 1859-1870 and its effect on the Riel Rebellion* (Peguis Publishers, Winnipeg, 1974).

_ (2) "Falcon, Pierre", *Dictionary of Canadian Biography* Vol. X - 1871-1880 (University of Toronto Press, Toronto).

Peeling, Albert and Paul L. A. H. Chartrand "Sovereignty, Liberty, and the Legal Order of the 'Freemen' (Otipahemsu'uk): Towards a Constitutional Theory of Metis Self-Government" *Saskatchewan Law Review*, Vol. 67 (1) (2004).

Peterson, Jacqueline and Jennifer S. H. Brown, editors, *The New Peoples - Being and Becoming Metis in North America* (University of Manitoba Press, Winnipeg, 1985).

Poitras, Audrey, Foreword *Metis Memories of Residential Schools - A Testament to the Strength of the Metis*, (Metis Nation of Alberta, 2004).

Pope, Joseph, *Correspondence of Sir John Macdonald* (Oxford University

Press, Toronto, 1921).

Prud'hommme, Judge L.A., "La Famille Goulet", *Societe Royale du Canada*, vol. 29 (3rd Series, 1935).

Racette, Calvin, *Flags of the Metis* (Gabriel Dumont Institute, Regina, 1987).

Rich, E. E., *The Fur Trade and the Northwest to 1857* (McLelland & Stewart, Toronto, 1967).

Robinson, H. M., *The Great Fur Land or Sketches of Life in the Hudson's Bay Territory* (G. P. Putman's Sons, New York, 1879).

Ross, Alexander, *The Red River Settlement: Its Rise, Progress and Present State.* (Ross and Haines Inc., Minneapolis, 1957, 2nd ed.).

Royal Commission on Aboriginal Peoples Report Vol.4 Ch. 5 "Metis Perspectives" (Ministry of Supply and Services, Ottawa, 1996).

Sealey, D. Bruce & Antoine S. Lussier, *The Metis, Canada's Forgotten People* (Pemmican Publications, Winnipeg, 1975).

Shore, Fred "Delorme, Pierre", (1) *Dictionary of Canadian Biography* Vol. XIV - 1911-1920 (University of Toronto Press, Toronto).

– (2) "The Emergence of the Metis Nation in Manitoba", *Metis Legacy*, Chapter 3 (Pemmican Publications, Winnipeg, 2001).

Siggins, Maggie, *Riel, A Life of Revolution* (Harper-Collins Publishers, Toronto, 1994).

Silver, Alfred, *Lord of the Plains* (Ballantine Books, New York, 1990).

Simpson, Kieran, editor, *Canadian Who's Who 1985*, Vol. XX, (University of Toronto Press, Toronto, 1985).

Smith, James K., *David Thompson - Fur Trader, Explorer, Geographer* (Oxford University Press, Toronto, 1971).

Southesk, Earl of [James Carnegie Southesk] *Saskatchewan and the Rocky Mountains ....* , (Edmonston & Douglas, Edinburgh, 1875).

Spry, Irene M. (1) "Sinclair, James" *Dictionary of Canadian Biography* Vol. VIII - 1851-1860 (University of Toronto Press, Toronto).

– (2) "Routes Through the Rockies", *The Beaver*, (Winter, 1960).

Steele, Sam B., *Forty Years in Canada* (H. Jenkins, London, 1915).

Stanley, George F. G., (1) "Gabriel Dumont's Account of the Northwest Rebellion, 1885", *Canadian Historical Review*, vol. 30 (3) (1949).

– (2) *Louis Riel* (Ryerson Press, Toronto, 1963).

– (3) *The Birth of Western Canada, a History of the Riel Rebellions* (University of Toronto Press, Toronto, reprint, 1963).

– (4) "Riel, Louis", *Canadian Encyclopedia* (McLelland & Stewart, Toronto, 2000, ed.).

Starowicz, Mark, Executive Producer "Taking the West" Episode 10 of *Canada, A People's History*, Video Produced by the Canadian Broadcasting Corporation, (2001)

Stubbs, Roy St. George, *Four Recorders of Rupert's Land* (Peguis Publishers, Winnipeg, 1967).

Swainson, Donald, editor, *Historical Essays on the Prairie Provinces* (McLelland & Stewart, Toronto, 1970).

Thomas, Lewis G, (1) "Riel, Louis", *Dictionary of Canadian Biography* Vol. XI - 1881-1890 (University of Toronto Press, Toronto).

– (2) general editor, *The Prairie West to 1905* (Oxford University Press, Toronto, 1975).

Thompson, David see Tyrrell, J. B.

Tremaudan, Auguste Henri de, translated by Elizabeth Maguet, *Hold High Your Heads (History of the Metis Nation in Western Canada)* (Pemmican Publications, Winnipeg, 1982).

Tyrrell, J. B. editor, *David Thompson's Narrative of his explorations in Western America 1784-1812* (Greenwood Publications, New York, reprint, 1968).

Van Kirk, Sylvia, *Many Tender Ties, Women in Fur-Trade Society, 1670-1870* (Watson & Dwyer Publishing, Winnipeg, 1980).

– (2) Women and the Fur Trade", *The Beaver Outfit*, 303:3 (Winter, 1972).

Watson, Patrick, Narrator *Gabriel Dumont - Prince of the Prairies*, C-D Video Produced by History Television and the CRB Foundation (1998).

Welsh, Norbert, as told to Mary Weekes, *The Last Buffalo Hunter* (Macmillan Co., Toronto, 1945).

Woodcock, George, (1) "Dumont, Gabriel" *Canadian Encyclopedia* (McLelland & Stewart, Toronto, 2000 ed.).

– (2) "Gabriel Dumont the forgotten hero", *Saturday Night Magazine* (July, 1973)

– (3) *Gabriel Dumont, the Metis Chief and his Lost World* (Hurtig Publishers, Edmonton, 1975).

– (4) "Grant, Cuthbert", *Dictionary of Canadian Biography* Vol. VIII - 1851-1860 (University of Toronto Press, Toronto).

INDEX

OTHER LITERARY WORKS BY THE AUTHORS

GEORGE GOULET,BA.; LL.B; LIM & TERRY GOULET, BSC (H Ec)

The Trial of Louis Riel, Justice and Mercy Denied, by George R. D. Goulet, Principal Research Associate Terry Goulet (Tellwell Publishing, Calgary, Alberta, 1st ed., 1999); (FabJob.com Ltd., Calgary, Alberta,2nd ed., 2001); (FabJob.com Ltd., Calgary, Alberta, 3rd ed. 2005).

On Eagles Wings, by George and Terry Goulet (FabJob.com Ltd., Calgary, Alberta, 2004).

Prostate Cancer -Treatment and Healing, by George and Terry Goulet, (FabJob.com Ltd., Calgary, Alberta, 2004).

"**The Role of Grandparents**", *Birth Issues,* by Terry and George Goulet (ASAC & CAPSAC, Calgary, Alberta, Spring 1997).

Public Share Offerings and Stock Exchange Listings in Canada, by George R. D. Goulet, Principal Research Associate Terry Goulet, (CCH Canadian Ltd., Toronto, Ontario 1994).

A Comparative Analysis of Constitutional Aspects of Securities Regulations in Canada and Australia, by George R. D. Goulet (Thesis for Master of Laws Degree, University of Toronto, 1990).

"**Overview of Canadian Securities Laws with Respect to Oil and Gas Financing**", by George R. D. Goulet, *Canadian-American Law Journal,* Vol. One (Gonzaga University School of Law, Spokane, Washington, Spring, 1982).

Forthcoming:

Louis Hebert and Marie Rollet - The Remarkable First Permanent Colonial Settlers of Canada, by George & Terry Goulet.

Dominus Vobiscum